A Spiritual History Of Planet Earth

Jacob's Ladders on Lotus Ponds

Om Raja Mani

Copyright © 2015

Om Raja Mani

All rights reserved.

Placed at the Feet of the One,

The Inner and Outer Teacher

Heart and Heaven Dweller

Who is in Love with Planet Earth

And so Descends from time to time

CONTENTS

1. In a Murky Lake Avatars and Masters Bloom — 7
2. Love is Fully Present on Earth — 31
3. Cosmic Parents and Divine Sources — 45
4. Sage Kapila: Feet on Ground, Head in Sky — 69
5. Lord Dattatreya: The Ancient & Eternal One — 80
6. The Dawn of Tantra — 95
7. Rama---The Eternal Hero-Avatar — 112
8. Hermes: King of the Egyptian Mysteries — 123
9. Rishabha & Dipankara.... — 136
10. Zoroaster---Clarion Call for the One God — 145
11. Lord Krishna---Heart Master... — 149
12. The Integral Practice of Patanjali Yoga — 160
13. The Master of the Ancient Middle East — 168
14. Mind over Everything---Buddha & Mahavira — 177
15. The Great Brotherhood of Sanat Kumara — 187
16. Lao Tzu: The Tao & Its Many Manifestations — 200

17. Yeshua the Christ, Beloved of the World	207
18. Gnosticism and Personal Spirituality	217
19. Avatar Babaji: Eternal Spirit of Himalayas	222
20. Adi Shankara---Father of Modern Hinduism	230
21. The Great Jesus Ambassadors	237
22. A Revelation called Islam	245
23. Sufism and the Bliss of Divine Love	250
24. The Count and Master, Saint Germain	258
25. A New Age of Avatars Begins	266
26. The Love & Surrender of the Modern Era	276
27. Sikhism: God-Centeredness with Spirituality	285
28. The Prophets of the Baha'is	289
29. A Multiplicity of Avatars in the Modern Age	292
30. The Spirituality of the last 200 years	296
31. From Vedanta with Love	309
32. A Futurology of Spirit	317
Reading List	329
APPENDIX 1	330
APPENDIX 2	331

A **Note to the Reader**:

In this book, only even-numbered pages have been given page numbers. Any inconvenience is regretted.

Chapter One

In a Murky Lake Avatars and Masters Bloom

My religion consists of a humble admiration of the illimitable superior spirit who reveals Himself in the slight details we are able to perceive with our frail and feeble minds...The cosmic religious feeling is the strongest & noblest motive for scientific research--- *Albert Einstein*

Welcome to this spiritual history of mankind. I worked on this book over a period of more than two years, and with a sense of awe and conviction. Even as the world grows smaller and life becomes more complex, our spiritual undercurrents are actually growing against all odds, and the time is not far when these undercurrents will gush forth with vigor...I say this with a fair measure of confidence because of indicators such as the unfoldment of human consciousness and potential in diverse ways, even in the midst of seemingly unbridled materialism and capitalism... Besides, the reassuring words of Avatars have played an even more significant role in making this writer optimistic.

This work is about such Great Souls that we call Avatars and Masters, and in that context *Jacob's Ladder* is a somewhat well-known allegory from the Old Testament...In brief, Avatars are Conscious Descents onto the earthly plane, while Masters are said to ascend after successfully traversing the Hallways of Life...and both these processes have been going on for millennia as we're going to see. We humans have commonalities with both Avatars and Masters, and so we too "descend and ascend the ladder" even if in a more mundane vein...

In a world where we humans display and utilize various kinds of literacy, there is also a need for a baseline spiritual literacy, in the opinion of a growing number of "consciousness workers" and spiritually-oriented people, even if such a literacy can take more than one form, and yes, even if some forms are thought to be controversial...This book is a humble attempt to look at our collective Spiritual Inheritance and potential.

As Saint Germain put it: *The grandest resource of any nation is its consciousness.* What is true of a nation is also true of the individual...While spiritual exposure of the kind offered by this book is of course not to be equated with direct perception and personal experience, it isn't difficult to see that a broad-canvas spiritual exposure can indeed lead to a greater sensitivity, and to a more all-embracing consciousness...

In many parts of the world, it has become common to use masculine gender pronouns while making references to Divinity. In this work too, I mostly use masculine pronouns (unless I'm speaking about the Goddess Principle and Her Avatars), and for this I seek your pardon in advance.

While this is a spiritually-oriented work, it does not wish to disparage religions, whether organized or informal... This in spite of the fact that religions are receiving a lot of flak in many parts of the world as being a divisive rather than integrative force...However, if the mayhem of the last 115 years has taught us anything it is this: Both religions and secularism can equally wreak havoc... The rise of Totalitarianism or Communism in the 20th century is one example of a secular doctrine creating major turbulence in the world... Also, many despots and dictators have been atheists rather than believers. And of course, there have been many examples of religion-based conflict, in both ancient and modern times.

If a visitor to my home were to enter the living room, he or she would not see too much furniture. Instead one would see an altar filling one side of the room and containing icons from various world faiths and paths... Many metaphysical events have occurred at this altar, including some in the presence of visitors. These have included manifestations of the grace of the most recent Avatar in my home. He has also visited other homes and public gatherings of His devotees all over the world, and more than a few times responded very quickly to SOS calls made to Him, giving us thereby indications of His Omnipresence. Both Shirdi Sai Baba and Sathya Sai Baba have delighted and inspired people all over the world with Their Love and Grace, causing several of us to have spiritual and uplifting experiences, even after They left their physical bodies. Avatars like these have graced humanity through the Ages. We shall be looking at several of them.

Some spiritually sensitive people known as Lightworkers are also creating new spiritual perspectives for humanity by obtaining direct revelations and teachings from spiritual sources, i.e. by channeling specific Beings, including Avatars, Masters, Archangels and even Deities. They have opened up a fascinating world for students of spirituality and for seekers. Serious communications are being received by us earthlings, and if one wears a mature hat while examining such communications, one can sift the grain from the chaff so to speak...and learn invaluable lessons.

At the outset, let me make an appeal to readers that the material in this book springs from "distant sources" (so to speak, and for many of us)...Rather than seeking agreement on all points from my readers, if this book inspires curiosity and a personal search, it has already been a success. Ultimately the Life Spiritual (or the Life Divine) is indeed a uniquely personal journey for each of us...and so I request the reader to read this book almost like one would read a biography...As Emmanuel Swedenborg once declared, *"I am well aware that many will say that no one can possibly interact with spirits and angels so long as he lives in the body; and many others will say that it is all fancy..."*

Nor is this book an information-doling primer on "other-worldly stuff". Rather, it is a *sensitization* to the great Potency, Love, and Promise of some of the significant appearances of the Universal Spirit on earth, in various forms or beings that one may call "God Quantums". The One Lord or the One Spirit is inextricably bound with us and loves errant humanity. This work is an attempt to relate the workings of the One Spirit in all His diversity and grandeur.

And yes, I'm aware that in this age of science, immense challenges, stark realities, and human skepticism, I have my task cut out for me...I wish to make an important point here: that in matters concerning the great Avatars and spiritual Masters, I'm not speaking from "blind awe" but rather from over 35 years of spiritual search and various spiritual experiences, and after receiving both grace and tough life-lessons, and also being endowed with a certain spiritual intuition, which is a faculty present in all humans, but stultified in many of us because of over-stimulation of the mind by our environment...

As the saying goes, a Gnostic "simply knows"... The Hindus call this faculty Pramaana (a process of direct knowing from the core of one's being). And it is considered a superior faculty, beyond the intellect...The above attributes, as well as sincerity, are present in many others who are just as spiritually and intellectually endowed, and even more so than I am. I have also been inspired by their experiences and exhortations. And of course, the teachings and sayings of Divine Avatars and Masters have been given a great deal of importance.

Let me also say this is not an attempt to produce an academic or scholarly work (even though it may read like one in places!), since this writer is not a theologian or a historian... and so for example, there are no footnotes in this book. Rather, there is a reading list at the end. Having said that, all statements in this book have been made after due consideration, even though by the very nature of the terrain, some rather sensational points may suddenly appear in the narrative...

While this writer has been more than exposed to scientific and rational thinking (a la 20th century) especially while being a PhD student at a University in the United States, something within me kept prodding (and cajoling) into finally accepting it was not my secular education that was going to be the defining period of my life. I dropped out of my PhD studies after a couple of years...and looking back that has been a blessing, given my background in this life and beyond...

The prodding from within continued into my work life for many years, causing upheavals in the body and mind, and finally led to my becoming predominantly a Student of Life... More importantly, I came under the wing of an Avatar who had revealed Himself in dramatic fashion to me in the nineties but who had always been with me throughout this life as became increasingly clear. I realized one day why I've always felt protected, as have many others...

This weak-minded student however had to be saved many times from straying off into the grey... and so I've also received hard lessons and of course later realized them to be most appropriate...

I had actually started off being more attracted to non-theistic doctrines, and was immersed in their intellectual aura for many years, until the paranormal streamed in, followed by Masters, Avatars, and their Love and Light...Like many people who have delved into spirituality, I went through a "Parapsychology Phase" somewhat early in my life, and was more than intrigued by it...

I would now like to take a few moments to set a foundation for this book...Here's a conversation between a Parapsychologist-turned-Spiritualist (PTS) and a Scientist (S). They've both known each other for a long time and so the conversation is somewhat informal...

PTS: So...do you believe in reincarnation?

S: Of course not. Why should I believe in it?

PTS: Do you accept that reincarnation *might* just be true?

S: How can I accept something as nebulous as that?

PTS: OK, so how much time have you spent looking at evidence *for or against* reincarnation?

S: Why should I spend time on something like that?

PTS: I'll answer that in a bit...Did you know parapsychologists have compiled a lot of data on reincarnation?

S: I have a problem with Parapsychology.

PTS: Of course you do! (Smiles) And that is..?

S: They don't use control groups.

PTS: Control Groups?! What if the research is based on a spontaneous recording of data which is qualitative and not quantitative, and requires nothing to be administered (i.e., no treatment group)...besides, as we know most people don't remember their past lives at a conscious level to be subjected to simple questioning. Are you now saying we shouldn't be studying reincarnation at all?

S: (Shrugs) How do you mean? (*for this scientist, research has mostly meant data gathering and number crunching to accept or reject hypotheses*).

PTS: I mean people who are able to remember their past lives are asked to relate in detail what they remember, and this is cross-checked against neutral sources to ensure its validity and only then accepted as a valid case of reincarnation or past life recollection.

S: Why do I get the sneaky feeling that parapsychologists are over-anxious to prove their already biased notions about reincarnation?

PTS: Hey, you know what, that is hardly scientific criticism. Many parapsychologists are as wedded to their profession as other scientists are. They want to be rigorous and genuine. Anyway, think of it this way....even if *one* of these several hundred case studies on rebirth is true and correct, the case for reincarnation is won...you see, the numbers are on *our* side...this is true for all metaphysical phenomena by the way. If a hundred people throughout history have claimed that Mother Mary visited them, even one of them being true is enough to prove Her immortality.

S: Nevertheless, why should I accept reincarnation?

PTS: For me, the *opportunity cost* of not accepting something as vital as this is very huge indeed... And so also is it with other spiritual truths. Reincarnation is a good starting point and leads us to greater sensitivity to truths like karma and beyond...By the way, did you know that Jesus, Buddha, and Krishna all spoke either directly or indirectly about reincarnation? And so did the Gnostics and theologians like Origen?

S: So...?

PTS: Well, I'd rather believe them than some scientist for whom if something can't be measured, it might as well not even exist...and doesn't merit any investigation whatsoever. You scientists are also a divided lot...there are so many theories as to how the Universe began and what the Universe is made of....We have the Quarks and Gluons theory, String theory, M Theory, Dark Matter Theory, etc. Modern Physics has become so abstract it's starting to look more like an art than a science. And as for the soft sciences, or social sciences, we all know they could never match the hard sciences and yet, we still call them sciences!

S: How come we don't remember our past lives?

PTS: Deep down we do remember...Under hypnosis, people recall details of past lives...this again has been studied. People have recalled events from past lives that have been cross-checked and been found to be accurate. We don't remember our past lives so easily because we are bombarded by stimuli in this life right from birth, and our brains get busy adapting to this life...A whisper can easily be drowned out by continuous loud noise don't you think...Deep silence however, the kind that is gotten through intense and prolonged meditation, has also made some people remember their past lives...And some spiritually sensitive souls have déjà vu experiences, and also people who've experienced a sudden and traumatic death...Anyway, got to leave now...let's continue another time. (and so the conversation ends)

In 1927, a major conference was held where legends of the scientific world including Einstein, Bohr, Heisenberg, and Planck met to discuss the various pressing issues in physics and science. However, one of the core features of this conference was that they found themselves in quite a metaphysical debate...This was caused by the statements of Heisenberg and Bohr that *the consciousness of the observer influenced what was being observed in sub-atomic events*...in other words, Consciousness affects Matter. More than a few writers and thinkers have more recently resurrected the Consciousness Movement after it was systematically suppressed by the scientific establishment following 1927... One attempt is the "Science and Non-Duality" Conferences that are held in Northern California... More than a few speakers there are openly embracing the idea of Universal Spirit having created the Big Bang. Thus Matter Comes from Mind and not Mind from Matter. Mind is simply too subtle to come from Matter. The Institute of Noetic Sciences is another movement interested in Consciousness Studies.

In the 20th century and since then, there have been attempts, often by physicists, to move into unexplored realms, which may include even "metaphysical stuff". It's almost as if there is a hidden urge within scholars to move to the cutting edge of their fields, even if it means straying into a twilight zone... In the first half of the 20th century the psychologist Carl Jung had spoken about the Collective Unconscious. By that he meant of course that as a species we humans share an unconscious mind with various archetypes and instincts embedded in it. But later attention began to shift to the *Collective Conscious* because after all, many human limitations also appear to spring from the Collective Conscious, such as the gross and wanton exploitation of the environment, the widespread prevalence of unhealthy political systems, education systems bereft of values-education, widespread corruption in many parts of the world, etc.

Some preliminary work began in the second half of the 20th century when physicists like David Bohm (who studied under Einstein) looked into some of the mysteries of the brain and of thought....Bohn ended up looking at Human Thought as an Interconnected System where all humans are part of a network of thoughts that connect us all, or in other words, we are all part of a collective mind-set. There are scientists today who believe that groups of people can share their attitudes and behaviors seemingly telepathically...Animals have also been shown in studies to be able to do this and this has led some to postulate a "Species Mind". I'm reminded of the 100th Monkey Effect...and thus for example, human conditioning takes place readily, and we become largely "creatures of imitation". Even a strict and minimalist teacher like Krishnamurti began to speak of the collective nature of thought processes.

Bohm also teamed up with a neuropsychologist, Karl Pribram, and their investigations resulted in putting forward the idea of "Brain as a Hologram", since it was found if some part of a human brain was damaged, other parts of the brain stepped in and performed those functions... A hologram is any entity wherein part of the entity contains all the information of the entire entity, in this case the brain. For example, recent studies have shown that memory is distributed throughout the brain and not in localized spots...The brain is -therefore a very complex organ indeed and "has a mind of its own". Bohm also commented on how matter displays a rudimentary mind-like behavior.

Physicist Paul Davies made waves in the 1980s with his book *God and the New Physics.* Davies is of the same mind as Einstein when he says that God is needed to create the complex mathematics that created and now sustains the Universe...In fact he feels that Sustenance requires even more of a Super-mind than Creation. As an aside, a Hindu might well say: Yes, we knew this all along... Vishnu the Sustainer is more significant to us than Brahma the Creator!

In another book entitled *The Mind of God*, Davies again concludes, *"The Universe is not a by-product of mindless and purposeless forces. We are meant to be here."*

Some great paradigms in Physics appear destined to take us closer to Universal Spirit... Among them are Zero Point Energy and Quantum Entanglement. It's somewhat beyond the scope of this book to discuss these in detail and I'm only providing a brief account here. Interested readers may wish to look for more details on the Internet.

The concept of Zero Point Energy was born when it was discovered that even a vacuum has energy in it or in other words, has a base energy level. Thus, nowhere in the Universe is there a place of "zero energy". An all-pervading presence of energy closely tallies with an Omnipresent Universal Spirit...David Bohm is one of those that made the connection, adding, "The

Reality is Fullness, not Emptiness", an idea that is as old as the early Hindu scriptures and teachings. Later, some non-theistic religions preferred to speak of Emptiness, a concept Bohm disagrees with.

Regarding Quantum Entanglement, Einstein had said that if two sub-atomic particles became entangled, they would communicate with each other *no matter how far apart they are placed*...later this was found to be true in studies. Pairs of particles separated even by hundreds of miles are able to "communicate" with each other...so that a change in one immediately produces a corresponding change in the other...Science has so far been unable to adequately explain why this is happening...An interesting question here would be, how is this even possible without an intervening medium to facilitate the "communication"? Either the Universe behaves like a hologram, or the medium is super-intelligent and so anything is possible! Is the medium the message in this case, as Marshall McLuhan famously said? Much still needs to be understood of course, but few can deny mankind has made a significant beginning in exploring the unknown.

Interestingly enough, both modern science and ancient Hindu wisdom say: All is One. The implications of the 1927 Conference are vast of course...If Consciousness of a human can influence Matter, humans are actually repositories of immense potential...and at the macro level the Universe becomes a place of infinite possibilities. This author is one of those growing number of seekers who wish to open doors rather than continue to keep them closed...

Let me conclude this sub-section by saying that besides "mainstream Parapsychology" which studies paranormal phenomena such as telepathy, clairvoyance, etc., there is also a "Spiritual Parapsychology" that is somewhat less-known. For example, there are some beings that have displayed an ability to read the Akashic Records (CW Leadbeater and Anne Catherine Emmerich come to mind). More recently, an Indian spiritual teacher, Nithyananda, with followers in many parts of the world, also claimed to be able to read the Akashic Records going back to the time when ancient Indian scriptures called the Upanishads were first written down...

The Akashic Records are said to comprise the entire detailed accounts of all events that have occurred on earth since the beginning of humanity... Anne Catherine Emmerich could recall even minute details of the life of Jesus starting from when He was a child in the arms of Mother Mary. Emmerich was also a stigmatic and often displayed the wounds of the Crucifixion on her palms. The charismatic C. W. Leadbeater could recall the details of the past lives of several people, including J. Krishnamurti, the darling of the early Theosophists. The details of Krishnamurti's previous lives were published in a book called "The Lives of Alcyone". To Leadbeater and his co-author Annie Besant, the Akashic Records tied in nicely with the laws of karma... Universal Spirit is omnipresent and records forever all the minute details of our past lives, and our current karmic ledger is derived directly from this colossal and eternal memory bank...a memory bank that can't be matched by even an army of supercomputers. Some humans are able to tap into this memory bank because we are not only residing in the field of the One Spirit but we also have a Spirit Quantum residing within us as the Avatars have taught. This Spirit Quantum is said to reside in the spinal cord, as stated by more than one teacher in the recent past...

Also, we have the Nadis of India (such as the Bhrigu Nadi and the Shuka Nadi), which are ancient leaflets about modern personalities...and more than a few books and articles have been written about these Nadis. Many people have been able to find accurate details of their lives in these ancient manuscripts which have been described as an *overwhelming miracle* by those who have personally experienced a reading...The Nadis are considered to have been written down by ancient clairvoyant sages who could read the future like a book. They even knew who exactly would consult the Nadis in the future, and have tailor-made these leaflets for such people. The beloved and ancient Deity Ganesha (yes, the one whose statues were drinking milk in different parts of the world) is also said to have assisted the sages in the making of these manuscripts...

The pineal gland, which is located in the center of the human brain, is said to be the link between the physical and the spiritual worlds...Apparently this allows some clairvoyant people (like Nostradamus) to make both accurate and some controversial predictions of future events... Psychics have even been used by law enforcement agencies in tracking down criminals and solving the apparently unsolvable...

Finally, Vedic Astrology and other schools of Astrology that explore the complex interactions between humans and planets/star clusters could be looked upon as another example of Spiritual Parapsychology...Many people who have studied astrology swear by it. In particular personality differences show distinct patterns when examined from the zodiacal perspective...There are many Vedic astrologers spread throughout the globe and this writer has run into both Vedic Astrologers as well as a Vedic *numerologist* who made some accurate predictions...

In this book, Reincarnation and its sister concept Karma, are treated as givens...and so is human evolution through lifetimes, even though not all humans may appear to evolve in a spiritual direction over lifetimes...in other words, spiritual evolution is a much slower process than intellectual (or civilizational) evolution...

Studying the research of the parapsychologists of course made me ask "Where is all this energy coming from"...and spoke to me of the *co-existence of physical and non-physical energy and phenomena in the universe.* These two spheres are intertwined and not separate...just like our ethereal and gross bodies are intertwined... For example, auras around people can be seen by some clairvoyants, and auras have also been photographed using Kirlian photography...

There are forms of energy that our senses cannot detect, but our inner faculties such as intuition can indeed sense... We think of someone and a few moments later we get a call from that person...this has happened so many times in my life, it no longer surprises me. Speaking of thoughts, they are truly powerful in more ways than one. Thoughts and visualizations can even alter our future.

The well-known biologist-turned-parapsychologist Rupert Sheldrake, during a recent talk, mentioned how studies have shown that people can tell when they are being stared at by others, even if the person staring is directly behind that person…The powers of both sensory and mental perception and intuition can easily be under-estimated… I have personally experienced it many times. On an impulse, I have often turned around and looked randomly at a clock, and noticed that it shows an auspicious time such as 10:08 or 1:08 or sometimes 9:09. These numbers are considered auspicious in Hindu numerology. This phenomenon has happened so many times as to no longer astonish me. Others have reported the same happening to them. A swami in India recently declared: *I can see behind me. I have 360 degree vision.*

As the title of this book suggests, one has cast a fairly wide net…But then what we are dealing with is an ocean, and an ocean of many dimensions.

We live in a world of change and challenges, where there actually isn't much difference between theists and atheists… We all have a conditioned and reactive mind, an intellect, some intuition, a higher consciousness, and yes, a lower self or ego, though of course there are differences among individuals in the relative manifestation of all these… However, almost everyone is caught in the web of life to some extent or the other, and by that I mean is held in a matrix of secular/social/rational mindsets and lifestyles… Modern man appears to have lost his sensitivity to anything other than what he sees, hears, feels, and experiences around him on a regular basis…His spiritual antennas have atrophied and are increasingly being overwhelmed…And this writer therefore views with sympathy the work of all sincere Spiritual Gurus that are movers and shakers, regardless of their persuasion…and also views with sympathy all seekers after the Beyond. As has been said by Hillel the Elder, "If not now, when? If not you, who?"

The following verse from the Gospel of Philip sums it up quite nicely:

Light and darkness, life and death, right and left — are brothers of one another; they are inseparable (in earthly people). Because of this, among them — the good are not good, the bad are not bad, and their life is not life, and their death is not death...
...Those who have detached themselves from the earthly become whole, eternal...

However, we do not need to look at the world as a foe. Rather, looked at in broad terms, it too is a necessity, and a way of "buying time and space," to give humanity an arena to play itself out and *evolve*...through many incarnations.

Given the times we live in however, recent Avatars like the two Sai Babas are calling us to seek liberation. In 1924, the Ascended Master El Morya said to His devotees, "The world is in turmoil...strive for liberation." This is not considered an age conducive to repeated reincarnation, because many unhealthy influences and pulls exist in most parts of the world... And spiritualists know from experience that the various forms of worldliness do distract us away from the Universe of Divinity and its concomitant, Spiritual and Inner Evolution, thus making progress a slow and vulnerable process indeed...and so the question may arise in some: How can we get closer to this Spiritual Universe and perhaps permanently so...

As the most recent Avatar Sathya Sai Baba has mentioned, this is compounded by the fact that our worldliness, at its most basic, is a form of imitation, and imitation has a weakening effect on the mind/ego complex... We see signs of that weakness all around us, in the form of biases, prejudices, addictions, phobias (with xenophobia being one of the most common according to Carl Sagan), inertia (or resistance to change), morals based more on convenience than anything else, exploitation of nature to satisfy our material desires, and irrational behaviors, etc.

And, most people would agree, this firmly entrenched worldliness can't be wished away... Our senses, our bodies, and our minds are all immersed in it...But how we use the world is up to us... According to the Avatars, our mind can be a powerful friend or a great adversary.

Many people in the world today are atheists and one of the characteristics of atheists is to point to the "chaos, uncertainty, injustice", etc., that appear to have become rampant. Well, the Avatars have taught us that life is not meant to be a bed of roses but rather a crucible so that human evolution, when it does happen, is robust and irreversible. As Jesus says in the Gospel of Thomas, *"Perhaps people think that I have come to cast peace upon the world. They do not know that I have come to cast conflicts upon the earth: fire, sword, war."* (!) And sure enough, within a few years of His passing, the Romans invaded Jerusalem and burned and pillaged it with great loss of life...And let's not forget that when Jesus was an infant, King Herod unleashed his cruelty on all first born infants...

The Buddha lived in a time of turbulence and warfare between neighboring kingdoms. There were attempts on His life all of which however, failed. During the time of Krishna too there were great wars (not just the final war of the Mahabharata), wherein untold thousands lost their lives. During the physical tenure of Shirdi Sai Baba, we had the First World War and many conflicts in India against foreign occupation. And during the life of Sathya Sai Baba, we had the Second World War and many other wars...

Nor are such events only restricted to the time of the Avatars. Rather they have occurred throughout history, thus leading many humans to develop somewhat biased views about life on earth, the role of Avatars, etc. However, if life is both tenuous and impermanent, and our Higher Consciousness experiences this life after life, what is likely to happen sooner or later? Hopefully, the desire to transcend...and the desire to know more about how the Divine Universe works...

But let us pause and look at what has happened on the positive side: Not only did the Avatars serve humanity when in their physical bodies, but wonder of wonders, they still serve humanity and we are immensely richer spiritually as a result...Their teachings are with us and Their Love is with us. Now, I don't mean that metaphorically, but quite literally: All the above-mentioned Beings are being experienced to this day by devotees... As for the ultimate grand meaning of the wars and upheavals, only the Avatars know the full ramifications, and perhaps just as well...Similarly only the Avatars know precisely why spiritual aspirants often find themselves "between a rock and a hard place"... and why trials and tribulations increase for seekers though one can perhaps hazard hypotheses (such as acceleration of one's karma by the Master)...

To grow spiritually *while maintaining our integrity* seems to be a formidable challenge, given our fragmented psyches... But many Avatars, including Jesus, have taught us that deep down, we have the needed resources to pull this off... Christ famously said, "...Anyone who believes in me will do the same works I have done, and even greater works..." (John 14:12) And besides, we can and should seek help, and this help is more easily available than one may think...i.e., the steps have been laid down by the Avatars and Masters. One of the theses of this work is that the Ascended Masters, some of whom later descended to serve humanity.

Lord Vishnu has said in a recent teaching to humanity (as described by Cindy Riggs in her book *Vishnu Speaks*), that the truth has already been programmed into all of us and now it is really our choice, whether to make that essence grow within us, or to allow the world to completely overwhelm that essence yet again... For example, we all possess a *Bliss Sheath* deep within us. Surrounding this is the *Wisdom Sheath* (or the Higher Consciousness Sheath). This has been called the "High C" by writers such as Phyllis Krystal. These two Sheaths contain all the knowledge and wisdom of previous lives, which is a proxy for the wisdom of mankind itself... It's truly a case of so near and yet so far! And man uses his free will to often turn away from it all, while God in His Supreme Patience looks on as a father looks upon a child. One of the many ways Divine Love manifests itself in this world is to give us free will and choices...

One of the pillars of spiritual growth is: we have to watch ourselves continually. Awareness is key, as has been said by many teachers. And a broad spiritual literacy can help in making us more sensitive to the various dimensions of life, including promoting awareness and mindfulness, and that is another raison d'etre of this book. The next step, in the humble opinion of this writer, would be to expose oneself to the teachings of the Avatars and the Masters and immerse oneself in their Love and Light.

To spiritualists, spirituality is not at all removed from reality. Rather it is a Super-Reality. The world of Spirit coexists with the world of Mind and Matter, Energy, Space, and Time. To see these as separate is unfortunate, because they are intertwined. And as the yogi Paramahamsa Yogananda liked to say, *Mind is more powerful than Matter and Spirit more powerful than Mind.* However, this is not about power. Yogananda was rather driving home some other points with this statement, such as: our true origin, the chronological order of phenomena in the Universe (i.e., the cause and effect chain), and our limited existence resulting from being rooted to the material plane.

And ultimately this separation of Mind and Spirit is an even more serious fragmentation... The fragmentation of the psyche pales in comparison. To say that man is a "layered creature" with access limited to only some of the layers, would be a gross understatement. How many of us are anywhere near being in touch with our innermost "layer", called the Bliss Sheath?

In the Hindu scriptures called the Upanishads, the 5 Sheaths (or layers) that we all are comprised of are described and they are (starting from the innermost and moving from the subtle to the grosser): the Bliss Sheath, the Higher Consciousness (or Wisdom) Sheath, the Mind-Stuff Sheath, the Energy (or Prana) Sheath and the Physical Sheath or gross body. For more about these Sheaths please see Appendix 2. Some people like to visualize them as the layers of an onion, but these Sheaths are not quite as separate and discrete as that...The Sheath framework resonates with the work of people such as Rupert Sheldrake who has insisted for years that the mind extends beyond the brain...

Looking at a human in the above manner flies in the face of Freudian Psychology which in the humble opinion of this writer has done little to enlighten the world... In Freudian Psychology, the so called innermost layers are the dark side of man...In the Sheath Model however, the innermost layers are the purest and also the strongest: the Bliss layer is untouched and untainted by the environment and also by the limitations of the grosser Sheaths. It dwells in a state called Sat-Chit-Ananda (Truth, Supreme Consciousness, and Bliss). The High-C Sheath comes next and it too is relatively pure. A slightly grosser sub-layer of the High-C is the Intellect, but after that the "mess" begins: The Mind Stuff Sheath where the mind-ego nexus reside has been likened to a drunken monkey by some Avatars and teachers. In this model, the so-called subconscious and unconscious are part of this Mind Sheath and so are *not* the deepest layers of a human. Bottom line: The deeper you go, the more pristine it gets...

This writer came into contact with his Bliss Sheath (and this had nothing whatsoever to do with any hallucinogens), but only once in his life (but as they say, once is enough) ...and I've come into contact several times with my higher consciousness and intuition. And, of course, innumerable times with my lower consciousness or ego-mind. The best I can say for myself is that through all these decades, the mindfulness has survived, the faith and gratitude have grown greatly, and the rewards have been invaluable...I have also been fortunate to receive experiences that have convinced me there is now little need to doubt...The spirituality of the future is however the certainty of Jacob's Ladder in a world where spiritual channels are going to become clearer and more explicit...And the Avatars have promised this.

My first teacher was actually the spiritual antithesis of Avatars....a very rationalistic and minimalistic teacher called J. Krishnamurti, who by then had a worldwide following... This was during the late 70s and early 80s. K, as he was called by some, was a stern master, who aimed for the inner transformation of the individual, without however the individual seeking the assistance of any guru or role model and also without asking for any kind of assistance from any Being, however exalted... And that, perhaps predictably, has led to a petering out of his influence...Many of us K students found ourselves out on a limb... And I had to be rescued yet again by the most recent Avatar...but more about that later.

After reading about K's early life, I moved briefly to Theosophy, then to various forms of Buddhism (taking the cue from the Theosophists who adore the Buddha), including Zen, and concurrently Taoism, followed by Vedanta. Then followed a foray into Esoteric Studies (including the Arcane School and briefly the Church Triumphant), and later I moved into the more spiritual aspects of Christianity and Gnosticism. The word ESOTERIC is sometimes seen as confusing by some. In a sense, the word esoteric became common only in the 19th century writings of Theosophists and similar schools. It usually meant, "Unorthodox and Secretive Teachings for Experienced Seekers" but later merely came to signify something more to do with the Ascended Masters than anything else...

Thereafter I returned briefly to Theosophy and attended several meetings of the Theosophists in the East Coast, including at the Harvard School of Divinity, followed by a growing interest in the ancient Avatars and scriptures of India, and other perspectives such as the teachings of ISKCON (or Krishna Consciousness), Ramana Maharishi the self-knowledge guru, and at long last, the two Sai Babas. I'm sure I've skipped a few while making this list...

There was a gradual but noticeable movement from non-theistic to theistic doctrines...Ultimately they were all Guided Experiences orchestrated by the One Teacher who manifests in a myriad ways, leading inevitably into a flowering of dormant theism from previous lives...for our connection to God is an intrinsic part of the individual soul and has been with us since the very beginning of the Universe...

This writer has always felt this world is far too spiritually rich and diverse to lock ourselves into a state of saying no to anything that doesn't "fit in" or is unfamiliar... Fortunately, my agnosticism later melted away under Divine Guidance. Some people are so entrenched in their agnosticism that even when they have paranormal or Divine experiences, they just shrug their shoulders and go on with their lives…this has become particularly common in modern times. Much could happen if we merely became intensely curious, like spiritual children that we are…

And almost as if it were inevitable, today I belong to a spiritual community that is very open to all religions and paths…and in a spiritual sense rather than an "organized-religion sense"…for spirituality aims at absolute truths and not just relative truths as Ken Wilber pointed out.

A basic axiom in this work is: *The <u>beginning</u> of every religion (that has stood the test of time), <u>is sacred</u>, even if its earthly progression over time may not be so sacred, and in fact may get seriously bogged down by human limitations…*

By that I don't mean to imply even for a moment that Avatars came down to start religions. Humans organize religions and again often in good faith at least initially. What I mean instead is that the *initial impetus* provided by the Avatar is what allows the religion to survive for centuries upon centuries. The Originator(s), especially of "worldwide" religions, are almost invariably Divinely blessed and inspired. I put worldwide in quotes to denote "widespread and known at least in a rudimentary manner all over the world". And their original teachings are Divine. All Avatars and Masters who were prime movers are to be revered for their immense love, divine power, and their willingness to impart spiritual wisdom and teach a path to salvation. We can learn something from all of them…

Some of them have been forgotten because of their antiquity or perhaps relative obscurity…this book is a humble attempt at resurrecting some of these spiritual giants. Mysterious Beings have walked among us and some of them by their very nature, were more introverted than others…

And it's equally true that while the beginning of a particular path may have been very spiritual, its current persona may reek of orthodoxy, and even fundamentalism, as well as strictures and rules of various kinds, and the path may go on to espouse stultifying rather than elevating doctrines over a period of time... What started off as a wonderful, open-ended spiritual adventure, can become somewhat hemmed in and closed-ended over time... However the good news is there are indeed some exceptions to that and they will be highlighted later.

Given human nature therefore, faiths that have stood the test of time would not have been able to do so without some assistance from above and/or an extremely potent initial impetus. This is a verity regardless of what that religion or path looks like today...Just as Divinity has placed both worldly and spiritual humans on the same stage, so too will various creeds in various degrees of evolution need to share the same stage... However, it is also true that in our spiritual history, some cults and paths have indeed been allowed to fall by the wayside...Another point I wish to make here is that both theistic and non-theistic religions have a role to play in the spiritual evolution of humanity. You and I have bounced between the two over several lifetimes. However, towards the end of the road, the Avatars will prevail and spiritually sensitive souls will invariably be attracted by one or more Avatars. This simply means that unless one obtains liberation following a non-theistic path, evolved souls will be adopted by an Avatar sooner or later.

I'm grateful to my first teacher for sensitizing me to certain things such as being careful of the various by-lanes one might come across while on the Eclectic Path, but paradoxically he was also responsible for my eclecticism itself...

It is only after more than 20 years of spiritual seeking that I finally crystallized around an astounding Avatar (or so I thought, until I realized He had been with me all along) and who I shall speak of in the latter half of the book. But wait, He is beyond time...and has appeared in many guises...and so He is in some ways Omnipresent in this book!

I embarked on this project quite conscious of the fact that we live in a diverse milieu, and all kinds of people may well pick up this book out of curiosity if nothing else. This book therefore needs a "Chapter 0" and that is one of the functions of this chapter...

We need to remind ourselves of an important fact: Even in ancient times there were non-believers or atheists. Both the Bible and the Koran refer to such non-believers. In ancient India, even during Vedic times, there was a group called <u>Chaarvaakas</u> who were distinctly anti-religious....It's interesting that long before Darwinism and Modern Physics there were such people. This might well indicate that atheism is not the result of a rational process within the human mind. It is on the other hand quite a psychological response, an emotional response to the human situation...but quite capable of clothing itself in rationality. Humans often make decisions for emotional reasons but later use logic to justify their decision...consumers who buy products are a good example of that.

Also, if we for a moment consider all living creatures (including mammals, especially vertebrates) that have some level of consciousness, we are living in a largely atheistic earth, where rebirth is the norm... However, the period between lives may well be lived in what can be loosely termed as "lower heavens". Sai Baba was once asked, "Can an atheist go to heaven?" and Baba replied, "Yes, it happens all the time."

No matter to what persuasion you may belong dear reader, please reserve your judgment of this book until the end...For there are people who feel that the more ancient the scripture the more it belongs to the realm of mythology (an example may be the Puranas, which are really ancient narrative scriptures that speak of pre-Ice Age events both on earth and ethereal realms) and yet Sai Baba once declared that most of what is mentioned in the Puranas is true...The Puranas therefore can be regarded as also belonging to the category of Revelations to the sages of ancient India.

A world-wide history of spirituality is not as unwieldy a project as it may sound, provided one doesn't insist on being 100% exhaustive... In a world of so many cultures and of long history, it would be impossible to be exhaustive...

But while it's true there have been an innumerable number of saints, sages, as also Archangels and Divine Messengers in various parts of the world, the number of truly influential and pioneering spiritual giants is relatively small… We shall be looking at most of them here. In this context, I do sympathize with my readers…It's only natural to feel a little distant from the unfamiliar, but to repeat, this book is not trying to do anything other than cast a wide net. And yes, spirituality can be glorious, confusing, frustrating and exciting all at the same time.

To live an exemplary life of great courage, love, divine power, *and sacrifice*, and then to wield enormous influence on human beings for hundreds and thousands of years is not something that is within the purview of earthlings, but rather of the Super-Avatars. They are the real heroes of humanity. I began this project one day as I was contemplating these heroes…Is it not time we had a "History of God" but in a spiritual sense, and not merely in the academic/theological sense of the term…

Along with the Avatars, I have also sought to speak of great Masters that have left their mark on humanity, and many of these Masters are also called Ascended Masters, which is a very appropriate term for them indeed, since they have evolved over lifetimes to where they are, and are now great role models for the rest of us…"If they can do it, so can we"…They form another important category in this book.

And as for the difference between these two groups, Avatars and Masters, the Avatars are the true Cosmic Giants of our planet's history, who are within hand-shaking distance of, and represent, Universal Spirit, and have descended, not to lord over us, but rather to serve humanity, and, this is important: *They continue to serve humanity*.

The Avatars are like "owners of spiritual capital which they use to guide and uplift Planet Earth". Their touch is so light they are in essence invisible to most of us…They have displayed great powers such as Omnipresence (examples are Lord Krishna and Sai Baba) and/or a remarkable ability and willingness to bestow Grace, even if they were not equally available to all of us…

The Masters on the other hand, are more like hugely endowed and evolved spiritual teachers and ambassadors who have been promoted to great positions over the Ages. They too display a great level of control over the world of Matter, and they too have wielded (and continue to wield) tremendous influence on planet Earth with their presence and with their teachings, but they typically don't display the same level of Divine Power such as Omnipresence, and don't quite offer the direct connection with Godhead that the Super-Avatars do...Some examples of Ascended Masters are the Master Saint Germain, the Master Kuthumi, the Master El Morya, and the Master Lanto.

When an Ascended Master finally descends for His last physical incarnation on earth, He too is an Avatar ....Examples of this would be the Buddha and Jesus Christ, both of whom have been called the Masters of all Masters.

More will soon be said about the origin of the Super Avatars, those whose *very first descent* was both potent and sublime. I began this project about two years ago to humbly salute these already-sublime Avatars for, do we not owe them our deepest gratitude...And as has been pointed out by many, this gratitude in itself is transforming...And beyond gratitude are devotion, surrender, and love. And then one has already attained.

How about awareness, mindfulness, detachment, transcendental consciousness, etc. ? The non-theistic religions generally take care of that... Your and my spiritual history is more complex than meets the eye...The very fact that you are reading this book is an indication of that.

This writer has gone from theistic foundations to non-theistic paths and back to theism (in other words oscillated between these) over several lifetimes. And so have probably all of us.

Chapter Two

LOVE IS FULLY PRESENT ON EARTH

We are not human beings having a spiritual experience. We are spiritual beings having a human experience---***Pierre Teilhard de Chardin.***

And what a descent it has been for us...far flung from home are we. We are beings in the mists of ego-mind, who have forgotten our origins, say the Avatars. However, a spiritual Mega-Trend is under way:

I would like to state something that sounds more like an audacious proclamation, but for me is a very pleasant announcement to make: *All over the world, for hundreds of people, God is moving from the realm of mere hearsay to the realm of personal experience, and I am one of them.* The One Lord is not my unverified belief, but an awe-inspiring and moving set of experiences, that are also ultimately challenging to us because of the limitations of the mind. The mind would rather continue its worldly and corporeal ways, even if presented with overwhelming evidence of the supernatural...But increasingly, people are reporting success in communicating directly with celestial Beings. And the Human Potential movement is noticeably taking flight.

Yes, in this perilous and turbulent age, the love and light of God are making a startling and awe-inspiring "comeback" as a Living Omnipresence, as is further elucidated in this book. A Golden Age has been promised by the most recent Avatar, and such an Age is apparently not far away…However, it would be presumptuous to think such an Age would become a permanent phenomenon. Rather, it is an opportunity for "gods, angels and humans to walk together on this earth" as has been stated by Sai Baba. That in itself would not be a completely new phenomenon...angels and "lesser" avatars have indeed taken birth quite frequently and then have faced an indifferent sea of humanity... I'm reminded of a line from one of Neale Donald Walsch's books: *(God said) I have sent you nothing but angels.*

The hundreds of people that I referred to above are the relatively small percentage of spiritual seekers in the world. And this includes not only devotees of some Divine Avatar or Spiritual Path, but people from all walks of life, even scientists and academic philosophers. Ultimately the experiences of all these people can't be ignored...There is every indication that the collective experience of this minority will ultimately win over the inherent skepticism of the majority...

This will happen, and is happening, because the Super Avatars are becoming more and more available to us. The extent to which they can be experienced by particular individuals is however, entirely Their will (as it should be), and not something that even approaches human demands for instant grace and gratification. But as the most recent Super Avatar has promised, "Take one step towards me, and I will take ten steps towards you."

Avatars are the very opposite of Impressionist paintings. An Impressionist painting becomes murky as you approach and get close to it...On the other hand an Avatar is murky from afar but becomes increasingly vivid as we move closer. Too many of us have judged these Avatars from afar...

Just as the Avatars are eternal, we (and our connection with Godhead) are both also eternal. This connection may firm itself quite late in life, or even "skip" lives... We are all spirit quantums who have descended onto planet Earth...and in that sense we are all avatars, even if fragile and vulnerable. However, when a *gigantic* Spirit Quantum like a Super Avatar descends to earth, His very presence sets up a Field, and the result is a certain resonance with the smaller spirit quantums (namely us) and over a very large area... Certain parts of the world echo with this field to this day...and then influence succeeding generations in subtle ways. Thus, even in bygone ages of relatively poor inter-regional communications, the influence of Avatars kept growing and sustaining itself.

Let's begin this narrative with the *great antiquity* of our spiritual history down to the present day... Given that Homo Sapiens has been around for at least 100,000 years, it is not an exaggeration to say that the rudimentary beginnings of civilization are at least half that old...and so we are looking at least 50,000 years of civilization and not 5000 to 10,000 as some conventional thinkers would have us believe...As a point of interest, according to one theory propounded by Theosophist Madame Blavatsky, the first sub-race of the current 5th *Root Race* (described in Appendix 1) were the Hindus, who migrated south from the steppes of Central Asia to India about 60,000 years ago and later set up the Vedic Civilization there. Today we prefer to use the term "ethnic groups" rather than race.

According to Lord Sai Baba, the Super Avatars have descended beginning from about 20,000 years ago, which of course is long before recorded history, and just knowing about some of the ancient Avatars is very uplifting and also crucial, as we're going to see. The earliest Avatars lived before the most recent Ice Age ended (the most recent Ice Age is said to have ended about 12000 years ago, and begun about 100,000 years ago). In this book, I am only considering Avatars that appeared in human form, and not the even more primordial animal forms of the Avatars of Lord Vishnu as mentioned in the Puranas, the ancient scriptures of India.

One important feature of the Ice Age was, while most of the world experienced incredibly cold conditions, large parts of India and neighboring areas were spared, since they were protected from the cold northern winds by the Himalayas. Thus, many tribes of various races moved into these areas as far back as 60,000 or more years ago. Some of them came from the area we call the Gobi Desert and among these, at least a few were already budding spiritual adepts...Various kinds of people from all directions converged in the Plain of the 3 Rivers, namely the Ganges, the Yamuna, and the Saraswati (the Saraswati has since dried up)...Thus India is actually a *very old melting pot* of tribes and races.

Deluges and a very long Ice Age did another thing...they got rid of many artifacts and man-made structures in most parts of the world. And partly because of a lack of artifacts, archaeologists and anthropologists have led us to believe that civilization is only a few thousand years old...

It may appear I have given the lion's share of this book to the spirituality of India. It might even appear this book has a Hindu overlay. This has nothing to do with any bias however (in fact in the opinion of this writer, there are many shortcomings in the way Hinduism is practiced by and large)...Rather it is the result of India's being a relatively highly populated area even 20,000 years ago...Also, since this writer was born in India, he does have the advantage of an "insider's view"...However he is more comfortable with English than any other language, and yes even attended a Catholic school and grew up as familiar with Western culture as Indian.

Vedic civilization, which flowered early, has a certain resilience and has bounced back more than once, because of the immense grace of Deities and Avatars which continues to this day. I refer to the somewhat dormant period from 1000 AD to the middle of the 20th century, when India had to bear the burden of successive waves of invasions and occupations by alien forces...

I will bring out the difference between Deities and Avatars more clearly in the next chapter when we consider the origins of the Avatars as proclaimed by the Avatars themselves.

Also, because of the collective prayers and supplications of many advanced sages (or Rishis), devotees, and spiritual seekers, *an immense spiritual vortex was created in India in ancient times, especially during the period from 18,000 BC until about 3000 BC when Lord Krishna left His physical body.*

According to Avatar Sai Baba, Lord Rama, one of the most well-known Avatars in Hinduism, lived about 20,000 years ago. And let me at this point include Lord Dattatreya, a slightly earlier and truly formidable Avatar, whose legacy continues to this day...

Thereafter the vortex began to diminish somewhat with the arrival of Kali Yuga (the Age of Darkness) as described in Hindu literature...but was revived somewhat by the arrival of various Masters and other Beings in India, beginning with the Buddha and Mahavira around 500 BC. Things again plateaued after that, but later, because of the Divine life of Adi Shankara in the 8th century, and still later the grand Descents of various Avatars, the vortex began to grow once again...It is this vortex that has sustained the Indian ethos through 900 years of foreign domination which lasted until 1947.

Avatars, as has been mentioned before, have a profound effect on many people and this effect goes down the generations as time has shown. 2000 years after the appearance of Christ, the religion we call Christianity, while it has seen shocks and splits, still has the highest number of adherents world-wide. Avatars have a remarkable ability of being able to push our energy from the outer Sheaths towards the inner Sheaths... This process while gradual, is both vital and fraught with (inner) conflict. This inner conflict caused by becoming devoted to an Avatar needs to be carefully watched, but is certainly not a reason to give up one's devotion. It is part of a natural process and will begin to dissipate with time if one is patient...

There is little doubt that the great increase in the frequency of Avatars and Ascended Masters during the last 1000 years had a purpose...the preservation as well as the annealing of the entire ethos of humanity, an ethos that was in danger of being seriously damaged due to the horrors of war, human exploitation, stark inequalities, scarce resources, and unprecedented population growth that has led to urban pollution and overcrowding, etc....For example, even while India experienced extreme trials on the physical plane, the country quietly flourished on the spiritual plane...Similarly all over the world, there has actually been a decline in violence as people like Steven Pinker have noted. Pinker calls it a surprising decline in violence, but for this writer it isn't surprising at all...The combined influence of both Eastern and Western Masters cannot be overestimated. Even nations behind Iron and Bamboo Curtains benefit from the sustained presence of Avatars...

In the 13th century AD, India entered the Age of Lord Dattatreya (as described in detail later in this book), and this has led to great spiritual benefits for millions, which continue to this day...And thus we have the apparent emphasis on Indian spirituality in this book. It is a result of two things: a long and checkered spiritual history and a distinct prime-mover advantage...an advantage that is more robust and long-lived than one may suspect.

While we are on the topic of summarizing the last 1000 years let's not forget the Renaissance. The Renaissance in Europe brought together different streams of thought and activity that ultimately resulted in a great synthesis that has benefited humanity, even though the methods employed by colonial powers have also generated a severe karmic debt for them... Some aspects of the Renaissance, especially the art, sculpture, and also the beginnings of the new science were born out of a new consciousness, a higher consciousness than before. The Renaissance made people move away from superstition and tribalism to nation-building (for example the Huns, the Goths, and the Vikings gave way to nations). Besides Christianity, which has always churned out saints by the score, the presence of the Ascended Masters was also responsible for the generation of subtle forces that led to the Renaissance...Saint Germain in particular has played an important role in this.

After 3000 BC, the spiritual vortex began migrating to other parts of the world, such as the Middle East where the 3 Abrahamic religions were born, and the world wide spiritual evolution of mankind began in earnest so to speak...In modern times, the spiritual vortex has also moved to the United States and other parts of the world, even while India continues to be a spiritual oasis, churning out both great Avatars and spiritual teachers or gurus on a fairly large scale. Some very old souls reside in India alongside "young" souls, leading to a complex diversity indeed...

The New World has become the new world in spiritual and evolutionary terms also...while still struggling in the throes of unbridled capitalism, greed, and the socio-biological demands of the human mind...The crucible of life with all its contradictions can be seen as both a grand trial and a blessing...because the crucible also burns karma...We humans have survived over thousands of years and have steadily moved energy into our inner Sheaths, especially the Intellect and Higher Consciousness Sheaths...This planet, with all its problems, is a darling of the Avatars. So much so, they have made a major commitment to this planet and are ever eager to take students and nurture them...

I am privileged and honored to compile a world-wide history of the Universal Spirit's visits to earth, and His continued inhabitation of this planet, in various captivating forms and formats...An Avatar is Divinity attracted to earth by sheer compassion and love for humanity and evolution, but not necessarily because of a desire to better the human condition, as mentioned earlier. Poor people will not suddenly become more prosperous...nor will the world become a paradise or even a more just place...

So then, why did we mention Pinker's view a couple of pages ago? The long term trend is what we glean the most from Pinker, and this lessening of violence can be regarded as the result of evolution due to the slow but steady inner transformation of the human mind as well as the immense Divine Power being unleashed on earth, and one of the purposes of this book is to reveal some of the details of these...Nothing happens without the concurrence of the Lord. As will also be covered in the chapter on Tantra, one characteristic of evolution is the movement of energy up the spine, from the lower chakras to the upper...

The Avatar, whose very frame of reference is spiritual, is here to elevate us spiritually, viz., to bring us closer to our own souls and Higher Consciousness. But not all of us will be equally involved with the Avatar's life when He is present in His physical body....we should have earned that grace by our deeds in previous lives...i.e., disciples and apostles are chosen even if many others will get to see Him and hear His message... Sathya Sai Baba has said that people who are in His proximity have earned that privilege over several lifetimes.

The Avatar would have no reservations about creating a sense of detachment from the world among His chosen ones, and even a serious discontent with the way the world conducts itself. I have personally experienced upheaval caused by discontent and most of it in the prime of my life, at a time when most people would be busy planning their future …and understandably so.

The Avatar's life becomes His teaching as much as His words. He represents a perfect integration of thought, word, and deed. He sacrifices and cajoles, but never seeks to control. In fact, He is the ultimate "anti-boss", never interfering with our free will. Nor is He here to start a new religion, even though His devotees might well end up doing just that…when that happens, in some ways, the decay has already begun. But the spiritual boost that the Avatar has given humanity never dies out completely and in fact, may resurrect itself at any time… The way Lord Krishna's name has been resurrected in different parts of the world in the 20th century by movements such as the ISKCON is one example…

Avatars are here to remind us of the one Absolute Godhead, or the one pure Source, from which all has emerged. Having said this, all Avatars are not uniform proponents of paradigms like God or Godhead. In fact, there are Avatars who have started religions without making God the central paradigm of their teachings, or perhaps making only passing references to God…a typical example is the Buddha. This does not however, make them non-Divine. Great non-dualistic teachings often choose to not mention the existence of a personal God…but they are nevertheless useful and important in their own right…given the inherent diversity of the world, and also given the formlessness of the God Within. Not everyone is ready for a Divine Presence to take over their lives. For example, how intensely can a person born and raised in a Communist country receive the idea of an all-powerful and loving Avatar who was in His physical body from 1926 to 2011? Just when you thought that was a rhetorical question, there are always exceptions in this diverse world… Sathya Sai Baba centers are found even in China, even if only a small number of them exist today.

An Avatar only sometimes appears at random… Rather, He is more like an invited guest, who is both responsive and marvelously detached, and who maintains a respectful distance… If we keep praying He should visit earth, He eventually responds…However, a neighbor also may visit you because He has come to know of a crisis in your house, in order to perhaps help or fill the need of the hour. Such a visit is often task oriented (or multi-task oriented). Thus there have also been "cameo appearances" of short duration with some these Avatars…

Humanity doesn't have, in general, a very good record of playing host to the Divine guests we call Avatars. There were attempts on the Buddha's life as well as Krishna's life during their tenure on earth. And Jesus Christ was crucified. Or, we have just ignored some Avatars to the best of our ability. Avatars like Dattatreya, Sri Vallabha, and others were ignored by many, either because they were not sensitive enough to detect a great Avatar, or because the Avatar Himself wished to not attract too much attention, because the resistance offered by humans is often directly proportional to the visibility of the Avatar…

Paradoxically, we have always harbored great expectations of the Avatars to somehow deliver us, or even to create a heaven on earth. And if we are disappointed in that respect, or in other respects, humans are quite capable of openly confronting an Avatar and even persecuting Him.

Most Avatars descend on earth with enormous powers over matter and mind…However, the way this power is used (or not used) is subject to a lot of variation between Avatars. This book seeks to bring out these variations in a more explicit manner than is usually found in existing literature…

There are indeed some stereotypes regarding Avatars, that they will uniformly provide salvation to anyone who approaches or appeals to them, that they are lighthouses of truth and want to share everything they know… that they will do anything to keep a devotee happy and contented, etc. It is little wonder therefore, that in our impatience, some of us drop out of the field of an Avatar. We need to appreciate that all Avatars are working towards the long-term evolution of mankind and for the salvation of as many souls as deemed to have reached a certain threshold...

Nor is an Avatar anxious to reveal everything to humanity....instead there is a *strong and silent* approach to it all...For one thing, our karma accumulated from past lifetimes can act as a fairly formidable factor in our salvation. But the most recent Avatar has declared, "there is nothing that is impossible for an Avatar and nothing outside His purview" and that includes helping the sincere devotee overcome his or her karma. In fact, many devotees of an Avatar find themselves in a hard place as they are made to discharge their karmic obligations...their earthly lives become very challenging indeed. The good news is that the Lord often tests you and then invariably helps you pass the test.

The whole concept of Divine Grace also needs to be understood at a deeper level. There is no blessing that is not also a burden...and there is no burden that is not also a blessing...given that robust Evolution, within the context of karma, is the goal, not quick promotion to Higher Realms...More than one Avatar has said He is not here to make life a bed or roses, but rather to spread His love in a way that strengthens us, and gives us a Cosmic role model, even if not all of us are ready for Him...Also, He is not, prima facie, equally available to all.

For the record, let me differentiate between spiritual paths and religions for the purposes of this book. Buddhism is a religion, while Vajrayana Buddhism is a path. Christianity is a religion, while Gnosticism is a spiritual path. Hinduism is a religion, while Vedanta is a path. Islam is a religion while Sufism is a spiritual path. A path, almost by definition, has fewer adherents...and is less well known.

How about major rifts within religions...do the fragments continue to be called religions? For the most part, yes, the major criterion here being, is that fragment adopted by a significant number of people. A second factor is: Has that fragment stood the test of time? For example, Catholicism is a religion (in fact the religion with the highest number of adherents). Both

Mahayana and Theravada Buddhism are religions. And similarly both Vaishnavism and Shaivism are religions.

And what about Esoteric Doctrines (doctrines such as Theosophy that were not expected to be adopted by the masses at large), especially as exemplified by the Ascended Masters, who after all also provide us glorious examples of human evolution? In this book I am taking a Student of Life (**SOL**) perspective more than an esoteric perspective. This is an important distinction. The esoteric perspective usually focusses on spiritual evolution a la "Masters and the Seven Rays" the House of Sanat Kumara, Hermeticism, the Occult, etc... Such a perspective has been taken by some Theosophist writers, as well as those from the Arcane School, and other esoteric writers. And so there is already much literature about the Ascended Masters and their service to humanity…

However, in the SOL perspective, Avatars and Deities are, generally speaking, given more attention and salience…In other words, Conscious Descents and Cosmic Parentage are given importance. It is more about souls coming under the influence of Beings that descended, to pull us "together and up" out of sheer compassion and love for humanity. This writer considers the teachings of Avatars and Deities as being more fundamental, as well as the most robust spirituality there is…In my humble opinion, there is, considering the spiritual events of the last 750 years, a need to bring a balance into our perspective…and not rely solely on paths such as esotericism or New Age spirituality. In short, Conscious Descents trump everything. Their influence is more everlasting and will keep resurfacing through the Ages.

And as I've said before, unless one comes close, one cannot appreciate an Avatar. They don't seem coherent unless we come to know their teachings, their incredible presence, and their love and grace. It is a complete package if you will. One downside to that is that most organized sects and faiths are born to age and wither with time…unless periodically regenerated in some manner. Splitting up into denominations doesn't help, to say the least. And every major religion, with no exceptions, has split up into denominations. The Buddha once predicted that His order would not last forever...Hinduism, if not for Avatars, would have petered out long ago...

Having said that, there have also been some very humble and retiring Avatars who have shunned the limelight and been content with radiating their energy far and wide, even while occupying a humble station. It is really quite remarkable, how the very presence of an Avatar can influence world events even among people who haven't heard of the Avatar. That is because of their immense powers that include the following:

- An Omnipresence that only needs will power from the Avatar to manifest itself. Both Krishna and Sai Baba showed this omnipresence in good measure. Both have demonstrated an ability and willingness to respond very quickly to the supplications of devotees, no matter where they are located on the planet.
- An ability to appear to every devotee as if the Avatar was dedicated to the devotee almost exclusively. This includes an ability to even micro-manage and sculpt the devotee in a way that hastens his or her evolution, burns up karma faster, etc.
- Also, a true Avatar will never solicit funds from the public for any reason. And yet, all His earthly objectives come true and the money, if needed, appears without effort.
- An ability to bring back people from the dead and to heal even cases that were considered hopeless and untreatable.
- Pure teachings that almost any human, however humble, can comprehend.

We are living in an age of Avatars more than we are living in an age of Masters. As the density of Avataric activity has increased recently in the history of mankind, there is a slight receding of Ascended Master activity, almost in a very gracious act of deference and respect towards the Avatars ?

This is not to decry in any manner the importance of the Ascended Masters. I do discuss them since they too are divine and have fully evolved into a life of great service unto humanity...and so they too inspire us immensely. I speak of the Great Brotherhood of Sanat Kumara, which is of course an important perspective in the esoteric tradition. I have had the privilege of having been exposed to Theosophy, and to a lesser extent, the Arcane School, and the works of Rudolf Steiner.

The Anthroposophy of Rudolf Steiner is something that, along with the science of Parapsychology, can serve as a gateway into the world of spirituality for a beginner, given they are both fairly contemporary in the world and both capable of waking up our spiritual intuition...I agree with Steiner when he says the spiritual world is *not* an inaccessible one, and that it can be understood as an objective reality just like the physical world. It is a matter of being initiated in that direction by a guru or teacher, becoming a sincere seeker, leading a controlled life (spirituality is not a free ride) and using one's intuition and insight also, in addition to one's intelligence and maturity. There is no need to merely be "intrigued from a distance." Sathya Sai Baba has written: To know your reality, you need the mirrors of Self-confidence (Faith in your soul) and Divine Grace. Let us seek both of these. One can begin by "contemplating the spirit" (called Atma Vichaar by the Hindus). And then one can find a Divine Avatar or Master, and even choose a Deity. Faith in the soul takes us into our innermost Sheaths, which is what we all need to do. Mere chanting of the sentence, *"I am not the body, I am not the conditioned mind, I am an eternal soul and a limb of the Lord"* has taken even beginners very far...

Of course there is a delicate balance between outright rejection of the unfamiliar on the one hand, and blind acceptance on the other. Neither of these extremes is warranted or even healthy. This writer wishes to recognize the greats and to spark the reader's curiosity and to make this a work of "comparative spirituality".

The world has seen many attempts to reach out into the spiritual unknown. The Vedic Sages, the Ancient Greeks, the Gnostics, the Tantrics, the Kabbalists, the Sufis all attained respectable states...even if things seemed to plateau after a while.

And this is where the Avatars are again our refuge, because they have often reiterated their willingness to offer salvation.

Separating Spirit from Mind/Matter is needed to both understand the Universe as well as make inroads. The problem of theodicy for example, is more easily understood from the aspect of mind, which is far from perfect. Theodicy is the seeking of an explanation as to why a good God allows the manifestation of evil in the world…The granting of free will to a mind that is still developing alone can do it, regardless of all other factors and circumstances…

People have sought the truth since time immemorial and have sought the transcendent energies of the Universe also with the same zeal. However, the path has not always been easy, and entire movements have petered out. The spiritual history of mankind is strewn with some failed attempts.

Finally, it is with a sense of awe that we need to be delving into things…this is to be done without a sense of ownership but rather with the mind of a budding student.

I wish to end this section by saying that in this work I am sticking to the spirit and letter of the title: A Spiritual History of Planet Earth. I feel obligated to say this is only one version of a colossal topic that can be examined from so many angles. The Spiritual History of Planet Earth intersects with Galactic and even Inter-Galactic Spirituality. As of now, I am restricting myself to Planet Earth in a suitably concrete manner as I see fit. Those who are into esoteric spirituality that seeks to go beyond, such as the world of Archangels, Galactic Commanders, Demi-Gods, and the like may find this book somewhat tangential to their interests…This book is only a beginning towards a broad-based spiritual literacy. This may be the first word but it's certainly not the last…

Chapter Three

COSMIC PARENTS AND DIVINE SOURCES

God takes a human form from time to time to show humanity how human lives can be divinized. Also, human beings find it difficult to worship or revere the Formless Absolute and so Avatars descend to enable humanity to experience the Formless in a form that is accessible and helpful---*Sai Baba*

Sathya Sai Baba and others have made several comments on the very nature of Divine Descents that we call Avatars. When the Divine comes down to the level of the human, no blemish attaches to the Divine as a result of this descent. And there is no diminution in His might or power. However, and this is important, the Avatar may not actually end up using all His power and instead even take great pains to live as ordinary a life as befits the situation... And then suddenly, due to circumstances, He acts in a way that astounds onlookers...

While there have been countless avatars, there have been relatively few Super-Avatars. In this book I will be using Avatars (with the upper-case A) as denoting Super-Avatars. The good news is that these Avatars will never stop descending. Also, Avatars have the grace and power to provide salvation from rebirth, if that is what one wants.

How did the Avatars spring from the One Source? Is there a "missing link" between the impersonal Godhead and the personages of our beloved Avatars? In the Puranas or Ancient Indian Scriptures, some light has been cast on this matter. There are parent Deities in Hinduism, among whom both Lord Vishnu and Lord Shiva are very much with us, aiding in the evolution of humanity, sometimes appearing to their admirers and devotees. They in turn are said to have a symbolic source and that is the Divine Mother-Spirit, who "gave birth to the Deities". She therefore symbolizes both the Ability to Generate Super Spirit Quantums such as Lords Vishnu and Shiva, as well as the ability to eternally sustain them...There is no death or end of any kind for these Deities. At the end of this Universe, They will go on to the next...

The One Universal Spirit is the symbolic Father...and the Mother Goddess too came from the same Source, Universal Spirit...This Goddess Principle (called Barbelo by the Gnostics, and Sophia by others) still remains much of a mystery to mankind. Called Adi Parashakti by the Hindus, this ultimate Goddess appears well beyond human comprehension. Melchizedek, the illustrious priest from the Old Testament, and said to be one of the previous incarnations of Jesus Christ, says in a prayer to the Goddess Barbelo: "Holy are you, mother of the eons, forever and ever".

Rather than descend to earth as an Avatar, the Goddess appears to have mostly split up into Celestial Forms or sub-deities. Among them are Lakshmi and Parvati (or Shakti), who are the eternal partners of Lord Vishnu and Lord Shiva respectively. The Ancient Scriptures speak at length about the transactions and interactions of these three female deities, without being actually clear as to their origins...

The credibility for Cosmic Parentage comes from the Avatars themselves. Some Avatars have openly declared their connection with particular Deities. For example, in the Uddhava Gita, Krishna says He is Lord Vishnu. Sai Baba for a long time was known as the Avatar of Shiva-Shakti (Lord Shiva and His consort Shakti) by His devotees, but later Baba also revealed His connection with Lord Vishnu (also called Lord Narayana). The "mist" finally cleared when it was realized that, like Shirdi Baba, He could no longer be thought of as only Shiva or only Vishnu...rather both the Sai Babas are manifestations of Dattatreya, the Being who is a Cosmic Partnership between Shiva and Vishnu and who Himself was an ancient Avatar, as we are going to see.

When Lord Shirdi Baba sometimes exclaimed "Dattatreya Malik!" (or *Dattatreya is the Ultimate Lord*), He was tacitly stating this world owes much to the partnership between Lords Shiva and Vishnu... As for Sathya Sai Baba, His Avatar is so in

One with all the Deities, including the Goddess Principle (Shakti), that He is today regarded as nudging Universal Spirit Itself...Yogananda Paramahamsa, Sri Aurobindo, and Swami Nithyananda have all said words to that effect regarding Sathya Sai Baba.

What do we mean by Deity? A Deity is a truly primordial Quantum of the Universal Spirit that has existed for so long that the Deity is a virtual parent of our planet. And that of course includes the material and energy spheres as well as mental and ethereal spheres...

For some of us, the names Shiva and Vishnu may seem as remote as Zeus and Apollo. But for others, these extremely ancient Hindu deities are still very much with us. And they have been channeled in the 21st century by mediums such as Cindy Riggs and Julie Miller, which means their new teachings are also available to humanity. Some of these channelings have been carried out even in public places....

Spiritual writers Gene Matlock and Gregory Alexander, in separate works, have written extensively on *the sameness of Jehovah and Shiva*. In fact, as you are reading this, many theologians and others are researching Lord Shiva. Both Abraham and Jesus Christ have been connected to Lord Shiva, by mostly Western writers. Lord Shiva is one of the first major Deities to be worshipped by earthlings. Another was Lord Vishnu. Shiva worship spread to other parts of the world even in ancient times...Shiva temples and lingams (more about lingams or pillars later) have been found in Europe and various parts of Asia...

Abraham's grandson Jacob is described as worshipping a pillar and pouring oil on it, and this is how Shiva Lingams have been worshipped since time immemorial...Abraham named one son Isaac (Ishaak) and his other son Ishmael. The prefix "Ish" has long been associated with Lord Shiva who has been called Ishwara, a word that is both a name for Him and a description of Him as Supreme Soul.

Ishmael in turn named his first son Nebajoth (derived from the Sanskrit Navjot) and his second son Kedar. One of the names of Lord Shiva is Kedarnath (or Lord of Kedar). Kedarnath is a revered pilgrimage town in the Himalayas and has long been associated with Lord Shiva.

The uncle of the Prophet Muhammad was a devotee of Lord Shiva and wrote a devotional hymn to Him that has come down to us…According to some, the Kaaba in Mecca, the holy shrine of the Islamic religion was once a Shiva temple...

Matlock and Alexander have gone through great pains to sift the evidence and slowly piece their arguments together. In the oldest religion in the world, Hinduism, there are 3 Parent Deities, Brahma, Vishnu, and Shiva. In the traditional view, Brahma is the Creator, Vishnu the Preserver or Sustainer, and Shiva the Transformer and the Ultimate Destroyer of the Great Experiment we call the Universe.

Thus, we can't restrict our discussion to only Avatars in a work of this kind. Let's also keep in mind that they represent (or are here under the auspices of) Deities, whether Vishnu or Shiva or **Shakti** (the Divine complement of Shiva) or indeed, some combination of all of the above. An example of a combination is of course Lord Dattatreya.

We say therefore that Avatars fall under some categories, depending on their affiliations. The two main categories are the Vishnu Principle and the Shiva Principle. The Vishnu Principle signifies *Protection, Stabilization and Continuity.* Inherent in these however, is physical evolution and the mobilization of constructive human energy. But here we do not mean only the "long haul evolution" which is a species-wide and a biological phenomenon. That is only the most rudimentary kind of evolution and is always taking place in the background...

The sort of evolution implied in the Vishnu Principle is more subtle, and is brought about by things such as Curiosity-led Knowledge Acquisition, Growth of the Intellect and of Powers of Discrimination, Increasing Control over the Environment and the growing ability to Invest Energies in a Focused Manner, all leading to higher efficiencies, but is more an *individual phenomenon* and less of a species-wide phenomenon. Many millions of human beings have evolved over many lifetimes to become highly adaptive and able to select from a variety of options. But not all of us are equally adept at doing that and this is partly because not all of us have the same level of Life Experiences. Thus reincarnation is an inherent part of the plan of Planetary Evolution under the Vishnu Principle. Lord Vishnu helps this evolution along by bringing in the principles of Right Living into the equation. For example, Krishna has been called the Great Teacher of Dharma (Righteous Living).

The Shiva Principle on the other hand, is the ability to undergo Inner Transformation, Progressively Reduce Resistance to Change, Grow in Consciousness and Tolerance, Gain New Perspectives, Become Increasingly Mindful of our own emotions for example. It is also the ability to undergo trials and tribulations by transcending them internally and thus retaining one's sanity. In short, the Shiva Energy allows the growth and expansion of Consciousness Itself. It enhances our Higher Intelligence and makes us spiritually more sensitive. Lord Shiva has been called the First Yogi and First Tantric. He is the originator of all the various Yogas, including Hatha Yoga which has become popular all over the world.

The psychological growth of a person who meditates, who begins to contemplate the deeper truths of life and who patiently accepts change (and is not rigid) are all examples of the Shiva Principle in action. Such a person can make sacrifices for the benefit of humanity, and also has the ability to detach from the past and even from the world (i.e., the principle of transcendence). The Shiva Principle therefore helps one break new ground and bring about spiritual evolution in the world. However, this too is not intended to be a fast process.

The Sophia (or Goddess) Principle has to do with nurturing and overt love combined with a strong nesting instinct and a quiet wisdom that values peace and harmony (as symbolized by Mother Mary for example), while the Shakti Principle (another aspect of the Goddess Principle) has to do with the primordial energy that produced the Universe in all its diversity... At the individual level it is the power to given birth to offspring, and the ability to mobilize inner reserves while performing one's obligations (or fulfilling one's goals for that matter). For some, the Shakti Principle also encompasses altruistic attributes such as selfless service (Amrit-anandamayi Ma, the hugging saint, is an example) and developing relationships.

Finally, there is another *ultimate category* of the most potent Avatars, and they are the Dattatreya Avatars who represent the combination (or integration) of *both the Shiva and Vishnu Principles*. When a Dattatreya (or Datta) Avatar looks upon an individual, He immediately knows the past lives of the individual. In other words, a Datta Avatar can look very deep within a person...Sai Baba has said that in a few seconds of looking at a person, He knows both her Past and her Future. Also, Datta Avatars very commonly display Omnipresence, and examples of such Avatars are Shirdi Sai Baba and Sathya Sai Baba.

The Datta Avatars have played a supreme role in the spiritual history of the planet. They, almost invariably, encourage us to adopt or at least accept "simple living and high thinking" (as Thoreau would say), and to also include the Goddess Principles (such as love and service) in our spiritual evolution, and thus attain liberation from the repeated cycle of birth and death. They encourage detachment towards the world but attachment to God...and the use of such practices as chanting the names of the Lord and singing hymns that glorify God, and a lot of service activities, as well as non-dualistic thinking (One Source, One God, and Oneness of All). For their advanced disciples and chelas they may even encourage some forms of asceticism...

The format of a Vishnu Principle Avatar can be quite different from that of a Shiva Principle Avatar...the Vishnu Principle is fully immersed in the conduct of life on the planet, and such Avatars can even be highly visible figures....an example would be Krishna. Shiva Avatars however, are often more reclusive and quite detached from worldly affairs. Their work is often done quietly and only a small portion of what they actually do for humanity is visible to the lay population. The rest of their work is on the spiritual plane. Many Shiva Avatars have gone unnoticed as such by the rest of us, thus it is beyond the scope of this book to list them all...Adi Shankara and Avatar Babaji are two examples.

Many Datta Avatars have graced the planet. And they each have their own format as was pointed out by Sai Baba Himself. We will be looking at a large number of Datta Avatars in a future chapter.

As I'm hoping to show later in this book, the very nature of salvation has changed in modern times...The "Nirvana" of old, which was the purview of the gifted few, has given way to a more inclusive bliss of collective service to humanity and the Universe, based on love, fellowship, and devotion...Sai Baba once said God wishes to be a *friend* of human beings more than anything else... and Lord Sanat Kumara, the son of Shiva and one of the custodians of humanity, also recently described Himself as a friend of humanity in a channeling session...

Besides Avatars, we have other Divine Instruments as well as Divine Messengers (such as Archangels, with Archangel Gabriel being perhaps the best-known) who have sometimes interacted with humans. And then we have the other gods and demi-gods that have played mostly indirect roles in our spiritual history.

The Ascended Masters come next, with their vast evolutionary experience that has made them rise to almost the level of Avatars. And finally, we have divinely inspired sages like St. Francis of Assisi and Ramakrishna Paramahamsa and many prehistoric sages and prophets of both East and West.

All Avatars originate from Cosmic Sources who are with us to this day, as experienced by various advanced devotees such as sages, teachers, and hermits in places such as the Himalayas, and also in a lesser way experienced by us due to Divine communications received from Them through spirit mediums and trance channels.

In the Hindu tradition, Brahma is sometimes described as the Creator, but with a caveat as mentioned below. Lord Vishnu is called the Preserver, though this needs to be seen in a newer light following His recent communications with humanity, and Lord Shiva is the so-called Lord of Destruction, but "destruction" when examined in a spiritual vein is a nebulous concept that needs to be seen in both the short and long terms...In the short term, it is transformation, and the long term is so incredibly long that we would not be remiss in putting that in a back-burner...

In the short term, Destruction means the "destruction of the old, the impermanent, and the outworn" and the taking on of new forms and attributes. Thus Lord Shiva is the lord of all change and yes, evolution itself...and He also represents the *awareness* of the constant changes that are going on, and thus is also Supreme Consciousness... He "destroys" both thesis and antithesis by going beyond them...in other words *Lord Shiva contains all opposites within Him.* And, yes in the long term, Destruction means the ending of the Universe itself, because while the entire Universe is an exercise in Love, it is not meant to be a permanent exercise...one day the manifest love will take on an un-manifest nature... Thus the term Shiva has multiple meanings and implications...

Some writers have noted the similarity between the names Brahma/Saraswati on the one hand and Abraham/Sarah on the other. Saraswati is the consort (wife) of Brahma while Sarah was Abraham's wife. Both Brahma and Abraham are considered to be "Fathers" of a kind. Abraham is considered the Father by the Abrahamic religions (Judaism, Christianity, and Islam), while Brahma is considered the Father in Hinduism (even though He is not worshipped to any appreciable extent by Hindus, and in fact, later the whole aspect of being a progenitor was more commonly attributed to Lord Vishnu, of whom Brahma is now considered an offshoot, or protégé or even Cosmic Assistant).

The very word Shiva appears in Jewish culture in more than one form...There is little doubt that Abraham was influenced by the religious ethos of India, the land east of the Indus River, which was a trading partner of the Middle East. Over millennia the spiritual reputation of India grew to such an extent that India came to be seen as a spiritual oasis. Later, the Middle East and

China followed suit and became spiritual vortices too, and it is not surprising therefore that nearly all the major religions of the world have been born in these three areas…

Also, ever since the life of Krishna, i.e., since 3000 BC, legends about Him undoubtedly traveled to the Middle East, and implanted His name in the consciousness of the people as one of the names of God, so that the term Christos (or Christ) later came into being as a derivative of Krishna…

Abraham's interactions with God make him a supremely interesting figure in the spiritual history of mankind. He is known for His surrender to the Lord and His ever-willingness to carry out instructions. After He proved His worth so to speak, it is said that He was rewarded in two ways: His name was changed from Abram to Abraham, and also, He and Sarah conceived a child even though Sarah was almost 90 years old at the time… The name Abraham has an honorific significance, since it is a derivative of Brahma the Father…

Later in the Middle East there arose a Jewish clan known as the Essenes… The word Essene is said to be a derivative of Eeshani (or devotee of Lord Shiva). The Shaivism (a way of saying *Shiva-ism*) of India appears to have influenced the Essenes, and in particular, Kashmir Shaivism probably had the biggest influence, since it was near the trade routes. They lived ascetic lives and many of them were vegetarians. And the most famous Essene was of course, Jesus Christ. An indirect or direct connection with Lord Shiva is present in nearly all Avatars as we are going to see…

In the Dasa Granth, one of the holy books of the Sikhs, it is said that Brahma, who sometimes committed transgressions, had to pay for those by taking birth several times on earth, and He almost invariably became a wise sage in each of those births rather than a full blown Avatar…Since these descents of Brahma to the earthly plane are more in the nature of "penance", His avatars are not given much importance in the Hindu religion and in fact, rarely referred to.

However the scenario is very different with Lord Shiva and Lord Vishnu. They are considered the guardians of the world and their Avatars or Descents, are given extreme adoration and credibility by the Hindus and by spiritualists, who are now spread throughout the world. The whole concept of Avatar is also slowly becoming more widespread... however their sources are often uninvestigated.

Here is a caveat before we continue: It is all too easy to label beings as Avatars since we would all love to come into contact with such an exalted being...While Avatars have indeed become more frequent, one needs to exercise some caution here. A true Avatar will exhibit *extraordinary* powers and abilities as mentioned before, as well as lead a life of Divine Service while being a beacon of Love. His teachings will be unabashedly spiritual. In fact, the very frame of reference of a true Avatar is spiritual, i.e., everything is seen from the vantage point of Spirit. An Avatar also displays the ability to teach in complete silence if He so wishes...In all my years of chela-hood under an Avatar, He spoke directly to me only a few times...the rest of the time He was a silent Divine Sculptor who taught me in various ways, both gentle and not-so-gentle, what life was all about and its pitfalls...

The words and at times, actions, of the Avatars reveal their origins to us. At times the origins are stated explicitly, and sometimes they have to be inferred by us. Krishna in the Uddhava Gita states His origins quite explicitly while the Rama Avatar barely said anything regarding His origins...

Avatars are truly the greatest link between heaven and earth. They are so potent that they often bring with them a cluster of advanced beings who take birth at around the same time to support the Avatar in His mission...these may be angels, demi-gods or even devotees from previous lives...but more of that later.

Mankind has had to make sacrifices just to receive the benediction of the Avatars, and for the sake of human evolution, we need to wake up and benefit from their glorious lives. For, as I more than suggest in this book, any evolution that is not God-centered is not only meaningless, but also somewhat wishful thinking...any evolution that is not God-centered can be lost or perverted very quickly, because of its weak core. By "weak core" I mean that the obvious diversity of humanity will ensure that the energy gain of any other kind of evolution will be dissipated very easily by its detractors and also other passive people who are just not ready to receive the new knowledge and consciousness...Thus even Science appears in various forms, with the propagators of each form thinking it is "more fundamental" than the others, and it all ultimately becomes very fragmented...And so also do Art, Culture, and Lifestyles appear in myriad forms. *More importantly, all of these divide humanity rather than unify it.* Spirituality (not organized religion) is however fundamentally unifying and expansive, even if it is the purview of a relative minority to begin with...

We share this world with all kinds of humans, from those who have lived many lifetimes to those who may have been residing in animal bodies until this life...This huge Cosmic Diversity is something to keep in mind and it makes life that much more stark and challenging...One of the great features of an Avatar is He or She will interact with, and attract, devotees from all walks of life. However, quite predictably given the circumstances, He is not available to all, as Lord Sathya Sai Baba has said.

One obvious question a seeker may ask is: Why did the Avatars come down to earth at all? What is the essence of their mission? Many seekers will then usually end up answering their own question by saying, "The main aim of the Avatars is to bring us straying sheep back to Godhead", and of course that is a statement that can't be disputed...However, is there something more to it than that? Why did ancient Avatars come down every few thousand years or so? Why has the frequency of Avatars increased over the last 1000 years? What weaknesses in man are the Avatars trying to help overcome?

Man in some ways is an energy transformer. He receives the vertical and pure energy of the Divine and invests this energy in the material or worldly plane for personal gain, even if within a societal framework... The pull of bodily needs and comforts also occupy much of his life, closely followed by societal conditioning and obligations, and the like. He has become a socio-biological creature. Now, this is not to be seen as inherently evil. However he is forever trying to consolidate his position in the material plane, and in so doing commits two "errors": He forgets that life is impermanent (or tries to push that truth away by claiming to be trying to create a "better world for successive generations"), and secondly, he easily forgets his Source and over a period of time even becomes alienated from the Divine. As my friend Swami Mukundananda once said quite simply: The mind has turned away from God.

Man has forgotten that he is a "top-down" creature (meaning that he has descended from above...it couldn't be otherwise because Universal Spirit preceded Matter) and instead feels he is a "bottom-up" creature that has created civilization from nothing...thus feeling entitled to the fruits of the earth and the conveniences of a life-supporting earth that is however beginning to seriously fray and wilt...Needless to say, we need to also take a "top-down" view of the spiritual history of mankind...

Even when he seems to accomplish things effortlessly, man is unable and/or unwilling to connect his effortlessness to his Source...The result of all this is an increasing immersion in the earthly plane. A student of tantra might say: A lot of energy is lost in the lower chakras...

Over a period of time, almost all our energy is invested on relatively short term gains, leading to increased stress on the human being and the biosphere. This almost invisible stress leads to a loss of bliss, or real happiness. The amount of street smartness, competition and manipulative behavior increase in the world, and even after centuries of so called development, show no signs of abating...

The scene is set for the Avatar. Through His exemplary life He seeks to raise human consciousness to the level that makes man more mindful of his narrow existence. Through His Love, the Avatar shows us an alternate path or worldview. The Avatar is in no way opposed to the earthly energy investments that man is making. He however is there to warn us of the dangers inherent in losing ourselves in this world...in other words He is there to try and save us from "gaining the world while losing our souls".

Let us note here that sustenance and preservation are also Divine goals, and that needs humans to make earthly investments also. And so, worldly and mundane existences are also manifestations of Divine Energy as was reiterated recently by Lord Vishnu. The concept of "maya" (or illusion) in Hinduism is to serve as a reminder rather than a stricture...Of course, those interested in a transcendental spiritual evolution will do well to heed it. For them, the world is indeed an illusion...and something to be escaped from.

In any case, an Avatar is more interested in our inner space than our environment. Sai Baba has said, "Do not worry about the world." He is not out to make the world a better place for our children. Instead, He is here to empower us from within, and bring us closer to our source, all in one fell swoop. If the world seems to overwhelm us anyway, it is entirely because of the way the human ego and the reactive mind work. If the mind is too immersed in the mundane, the Inner Lord will merely become a Witness. If on the other hand, we take even one step towards the Lord, He will take many steps towards us (one of Sathya Sai Baba's sayings).

The witnesses of Avatars and the recipients of revelations regarding the Avatars were so grateful and elated by the actions and teachings of an Avatar that they made it a point to preserve the name and ethos of the Avatar through the later generations using anecdotes and eye witness accounts. Now, in India there was an unwritten rule that no student should ever try to alter the words of His preceptor or teacher...doing so was considered an ultimate act of disrespect towards one's teacher, and could lead to severe social ostracization, and so there was a strong tendency for legends to retain their original veracity for even thousands of years...

And last but not least, Avatars have been known to reappear and reiterate details about their former appearances to their favorite devotees. The word "reappear" has more than one meaning here. Either the Avatar that had left His physical body came back to His devotees, centuries after having disappeared, such as Lord Krishna appearing to Meera long after He left His physical frame....or an Avatar (like Lord Dattatreya for example) reappeared in another form (i.e., in other bodies), such as Sai Baba of Shirdi in Western India, and Sathya Sai Baba of Puttaparthi in South India.

In the depths of rigorous and devoted meditation, telepathic communication with an Avatar or even a Deity became quite possible. Many people, not just parapsychologists working in labs, have experience with telepathic communication...for example, one thinks of an individual and that individual suddenly calls on the phone or appears on the scene.

As mentioned before, there is another important reason so many Avatars have appeared in India. They have descended because in the Hindu tradition, sages and high priests would pray ardently for the advent of God in their midst. The power of these collective petitions and prayers to the Divine should not be under-estimated...just like the power of prayers to heal and cure illnesses should not be under-estimated. In any case, these Avatars belong to all of humanity and are best viewed as global entities even if they spent their physical lives in a relatively small portion of the earth...

It may be apropos to point out that it hasn't exactly been a bed of roses for India. She has had to pay a fairly high karmic price, so to speak, for this lion's share of Avatars. The tumultuous history of India during the last 1000 years is one testimony to that. Indian and Vedic culture have been stifled and oppressed greatly by foreign invasions and occupations during the last ten centuries, and the old Vedic Culture is only recently making a return... And yes, the comeback is noticeable and as Avatars have declared, divinely inspired.

Also, there is nothing particularly redeeming about the mindset of the rest of the Indian population (I mean other than sages and adepts) that there have been many Avatars in India. It is happening entirely because of the will and grace of the Avatars, old and new. For example, the herculean efforts of Adi Shankara in the 8th century greatly helped to preserve the Indian ethos from the later invasions by alien powers in India... The network of monasteries and temples that Shankara established all over India, as well as His writings and exhortations, became one of the key pillars for Hindu sustenance. Later, the lives of Matsyendranath and Gorakhnath also helped to cement things... And then we had the setting in of the Age of Dattatreya, and that further protected this religion and culture... we will see more about the Age of Dattatreya in subsequent chapters...

Later, the lives of God-intoxicated souls such as Kabir, and other greats such as Chaitanya Mahaprabhu and Meera provided an important boost to pre-modern and modern era India. In the present age, the advent of Shirdi Sai Baba, Ramakrishna Paramahamsa, and Sathya Sai Baba, among others, will ensure the sustained revival of India's ancient ethos, an ethos that emphasizes virtuous living and self-control encased in faith and patient service. Perhaps due to the rank materialism of the age, this spiritual rebirth of sorts that did its work in the background is largely taken for granted by people both in India and outside.

Also as stated before, both Lord Vishnu and Lord Shiva, who I call the parents of the Avatars, have graced us with their presence from time to time, down to the present day and age... For example, in her delightful book *Vishnu Speaks*, Cindy Riggs describes in detail her channelings of Lord Vishnu, and the teachings of this Creator Lord are sublime, to say the least. Ms. Riggs has also channeled Lord Vishnu in public gatherings witnessed by many.

Swami Sivananda, the renowned sage of Rishikesh, has described one of Lord Shiva's appearances (called Darshans) in a small town called Farukkabad in North India in 1934. As recently as a few years ago, Lord Shiva appeared at a Yogini's home in the Cleveland, Ohio area, and awakened her Kundalini and left...she was in bliss for a long time after that... Recently Julie Miller has received (or channeled) discourses by Lord Shiva. Other deities like Ganesha and Durga have also been channeled, as have also Avatars such as Rama and Hanuman. I have myself had the fortune of seeing deities like Lord Shiva, Ganesha, and Lord Narayana (Vishnu) in dreams. It is their will alone that leads to such isolated and short dreams or visions, lasting for just a few seconds...They take place rarely and are never repeated...

Among the "Hare Krishnas" (of the ISKCON movement), narratives of interaction of devotees with Lord Krishna (i.e., Lord Vishnu) abound.

Lord Shiva became a very hallowed Deity indeed and He was lavished attention and importance by the Avatars themselves. More details I will provide later in this book, but Lord Krishna openly declared His love and adoration for Lord Shiva and even asked His disciple Arjuna to do a great Penance to Lord Shiva.

As mentioned earlier, Lord Shiva is the Lord of all Yoga and Tantra and has been called the First Yogi. Generally speaking, both yoga and tantra target the body/mind complex but yoga is more lay-person-oriented while Tantra mostly targets the mind and the psychic chakras of more advanced seekers... The Vedas also refer to Lord Shiva as the Great Healer. His teachings are found in Tantric texts and in the Shiva Sutras. The devotees of Lord Shiva are called Shaivites, and the religion, Shaivism.

There have been attempts to isolate the Shaivism of South India (also called Dravidian Shaivism) with the Shaivism of North India (also called Kashmiri Shaivism). Such distinctions are superfluous when one considers that according to ancient scriptural texts, Lord Shiva Himself visited various places all over India (say the Puranas) and blessed certain spots which later saw Shiva temples springing up. There are 12 especially sacred sites in India (called the 12 Jyotirlingas) and they are scattered all over India. It is completely unnecessary therefore to separate South Indian from North Indian Shaivism. They have both been inspired by the same Source, as It descended equally in all parts of India.

Lord Shiva is said to reside in Mount Kailash in the heart of the Himalayas in present day Tibet...Anne Catherine Emmerich indirectly paid homage to Him in her visionary dictations. Further south in the Gangetic Plain of North India, Banaras (or Varanasi), called the Capital of the World by the writer Jack Kerouac, houses one of the most revered temples of Lord Shiva. However there are also sacred spots in the south that rival Mount Kailash and Varanasi, and they are Arunachala Hill and Rameshwaram in the deep-south, which is the place where Avatar Lord Rama worshipped Lord Shiva before embarking on His mission in Sri Lanka.

Lord Shiva, say the Puranas, first appeared as an incredibly long "pillar of fire and light" that stretched through Space. This was long before civilization began on earth. This pillar is still celebrated in the form of the "Shiva Lingam" by Hindus. However it has been grossly over-simplified to be a phallic symbol by some.

This appearance of Lord Shiva as a pillar of light was apparently in response to an argument between Lord Brahma and Lord Vishnu as to which of these two was more important to the Universe. Lord Shiva then appeared to them as an infinitely long pillar of fire and light. He asked them to find the end of this pillar. Vishnu flew in one direction and Brahma in the other, but neither could find the end of this pillar (or lingam) of light particles. Finally, they came back to where the Lord was and realized what the Lord was all about...

For this and other writers, this pillar of light represents the closest link to the Ultimate Godhead that humans have knowledge of. It has a metaphorical connotation as well as a literal meaning. Were these so-called particles of light billions upon billions of atmic (or soul) particles that were with Lord Shiva? Are these atmic particles now in living creatures? To stretch the analogy, were you and I in that pillar? And now living in bodies that are made up of stardust...We are all Avatars, descended to have earthly experiences, and if we don't wake up, we will merely be spinning our wheels, life after life.

This pillar is the closest one comes to Universal Spirit in the scriptures, and it represents the formless God, who is everything and everyone. As we will see later, it is also mentioned in Exodus in the Old Testament.

An individual soul quantum can inhabit a plant, animal, or human, and in the larger sense, it matters little which creature the soul inhabits, for after all, its stay is impermanent. Sooner or later, physical death will bring an end to that particular descent...

In India there has long been a division between the devotees of Vishnu (Vaishnavites) and the devotees of Shiva (Shaivites). The Smartha sect begun by Adi Shankara in the 9th century AD, tried to bring these two sides closer to each other by taking a middle ground, much like the Unitarian Universalists have done in the West, notably in the USA. Both the Smarthas and the Unitarians are liberal minded, with the Unitarians being even more so.

Both the Vaishnava tradition and the Shaiva tradition go back thousands of years. Krishna and Rama were Avatars of Vishnu or Lord Narayan, the Divine Protector and Sustainer of the Universe. Rishabha, Hanuman and Adi Shankara were emanations of Lord Shiva, the Lord of Human Evolution, who stands guard over the earth and provides for and serves the cause of humanity.

ONE + ONE = THREE

He that will believe only what he can fully comprehend must have a long head or a very short creed--- Pierre Teilhard de Chardin

But as mentioned before we also have the Integrated Avatars. Lord Dattatreya, Shirdi Sai Baba and others mentioned later belong to this category of Integrated Avatars. In fact Lord Dattatreya was the first truly great Avatar and was born even before Rama who is recognized by the Vaishnavites as the "first great one." He occupies a special position in that He is both an

Avatar and a Deity who has appeared several times in the spiritual history of the planet...

As we progressed into the 20th century, a "Super-Integrated" Avatar descended, with Shakti (the Divine Mother) also joining in. Thus Sathya Sai Baba is a Complete (or Super) Integration of Narayan, Shiva, and Shakti (or in other words Dattatreya and Shakti), thus leading to a colossal presence on earth and a vast array of powers, all manifesting in an energy field of service and love towards humanity. While He left His physical body in 2011, He continues to make His presence felt... In response to the query "What is the meaning behind the Your Avatar?" Sai Baba declared: *I am the servitor of humanity.*

Avatars and Masters can also be divided into two broad categories: God-affirming (Theistic) and Non-Affirming (Non-Theistic). As we know there are both theistic and non-theistic religions in the world. They both serve important functions. However, in the future it is expected that non-theistic religions will begin to wane, if they haven't already done so, because people all over the world will begin to experience metaphysical and Divine events in their lives, or hear about such experiences from near and dear ones, and this will slowly bring about humanity into a more theistic platform, followed later by increased devotion...and that in turn will be intensified by the theistic Avatars who began appearing about 700 years ago and will continue to appear amongst us.

Some Avatars and Masters have openly declared themselves as being of Divine origin. Examples would be Jesus and Sai Baba. Others hesitated to do so, such as Buddha, and mostly sought to build their missions on a non-theistic foundation... but as we are going to see later in the chapter on Lord Buddha, He is as much a metaphysical and spiritual being as other Avatars...All Avatars have emerged from the same Godhead, Brahman, and so any comparisons and stratifications between them become a somewhat superficial exercise. We can learn from all of them.

The most recent Avatar, Sathya Sai Baba a few years ago said to a large audience, "You have all come from Brahman

(Source), and I have too." There can be only one Source and therefore only one Guru or Teacher. And yet, for the sake of appreciating our beloved Avatars better, let us look at them as either: Consolidators or Reformers,

or again as: Protectors and/or Motivators towards Evolution,

And from: "Long-term teachers" to "Divine Sculptors".

The first category in each of the three pairs above embodies what can be called the Vishnu Principle, and the second category can be called the Shiva Principle. However, as is mentioned in the book *Vishnu Speaks* by Cindy Riggs, Lord Vishnu is now intimately concerned with the evolution of humanity. Lord Vishnu is now emphasizing the Dattatreya Principle of Cosmic Integration in His teachings…and as we are going to see, that's a very natural consequence of the current age...

The Vishnu Principle usually works by promoting Right Living and the Shiva Principle works on Personal and Societal Transformation. An Avatar that embraces the Vishnu Principle lives out of love and service, and teaches life-supporting and life-sustaining principles. A classic Avatar in this category is Krishna and a typical spiritual teaching of His is the Uddhava Gita, which is a more spiritual work than the better-known Bhagavad Gita.

In the Shiva Principle Avatars, there will be a tendency to work towards a psycho/spiritual transformation of the individual devotee as well as larger groups of people, and even entire nations. In the process a new religion might be formed (such as the Jainism of Lord Rishabha) or perhaps a new sect (such as the Smartha sect of Adi Shankara)…As I have mentioned before, a classic Shiva Avatar is Shankara who lived around 800 AD, and transformed India by travelling all over the country and establishing some important monasteries (or ashrams) and houses of worship that are there to this day.

Trailinga (or Trailanga) Swami, who had an extraordinarily long life and lived for about 300 years beginning from 1610 or so, is another classic Shiva Avatar, who in Benares in India did the most amazing things such as meditating while sitting cross-legged on the Ganges river and reviving the dead. He remained naked almost throughout His life. His nakedness earned Him the ire of the British and of law officials...Every time they imprisoned Him however, He was found walking outside the prison or on the roof within about 5 minutes after having been carefully locked inside.

However, devotion is also a part of the teachings of these Shiva Avatars. Hanuman was immensely devoted to Rama and Rishabha was devoted to Lord Shiva Himself. Adi Shankara, besides being an embodiment of the highest non-dualistic teachings, also emphasized worship and utterance of the Divine names of 5 Deities as modes of transformation. These 5 Deities are Vishnu, Shiva, Shakti, Ganesha, and Surya (the Sun God).

In the Integral (Dattatreya) category, the Avatars emphasize strong bonds of faith to be created between the aspirant and a chosen Guru and Deity. Sai Baba advised His devotees to have both a Guru and a Deity.

The Datta Avatars speak of a multi-dimensional relationship between humans and divinity (who is Mother, Father, Guru, God, and Ally). They also emphasize the seeking of liberation from the cycle of birth and death or Moksha. However, there is also an emphasis on patience as a supreme virtue, because not everyone qualifies to come into contact with an Avatar. These Datta Avatars became increasingly needed because of the gravity of the times or the "Age of Spiritual Waning" called Kali Yuga by the Hindus. There have been several Datta Avatars in the last 200 years, according to Shirdi Sai Baba.

As this book later describes, we're living in the Age of Dattatreya, and this Age also welcomes other category Avatars and Masters. In other words, the world of great beings has opened up tremendously, resulting in spiritually uplifting times. Spiritual vibrations are being felt throughout the planet, with more people participating in spiritual activities, New Age retreats, Meditation Groups, etc., than ever before. Channelings which were done in small groups before are being done in public places in front of many people.

Another hallowed parent is *Lord Sanat Kumara* who has nurtured many an Ascended Master. He is one of four Kumaras but more involved with earth's evolution than the other three. We will see more about the Four Kumaras soon. Another name for Sanat Kumara is Lord Subramanya or Kartikeya. While He has also descended to earth in various forms (such as Dipankara Buddha in India and Quetzlcoatl in Latin America), He has mentored many Ascended Masters such as the Buddha. He was Ahura Mazda of the Zoroastrians and is worshipped in India as Subramanya (the son of Shiva). Thus He is a conglomerate of both Deity and Avatar. He is said to have descended from the planet Venus to Earth many millennia ago. This Lord, who now describes Himself as a friend of humanity, has also been channeled several times... He likes to go by the name Raj and speaks often about the Divine Mother...almost as if He would like to prepare humanity to receive the Goddess Principle once again, a Principle that has been languishing on earth due to the overwhelming presence of patriarchal religions.

As an aside, thanks to the Internet, we can listen to the sublime teachings of Beings such as Sanat Kumara. If science and technology are used wisely, we can all ascend that much faster...however, if they are misused or in other words are used only for material conveniences and pleasures, our ascent will be seriously delayed and fraught with risk...

All the Ascended Masters of the Great Brotherhood are His former chelas, many of whom are now well advanced on the Path and self-sufficient in their own right, and filled with the spirit of service to humanity. Sanat Kumara, the Beloved of the Theosophists and other Esoteric Movements, being the son of Lord Shiva, naturally reflects His father's glory and so belongs to the Shiva Category of Multi-Dimensional Evolution. He, whose vehicle is said to be a peacock, has appeared in different parts of the world and has left a subtle imprint on humanity...

He works with the Maha Chohan (or Great Lord), a highly Ascended Master who is one with Sanat Kumara and does the latter's work. The Maha Chohan in turn oversees a "Cosmic Team" of the Lords of the 7 Rays who form another Divine layer to step-down a little closer to the levels of human beings the subtle energy of the Four Kumaras. The Sanskrit word Chohan (or Chauhan), approximates with the concept of an Archangel or Divine Agent who is deeply committed to the Upkeep of Humanity.

I would be remiss if I ended this chapter without a mention of the Divine Mother or Shakti who has over the millennia branched off into different female forms. The Divine Mother symbolizes Mother Nature herself and especially the nurturing aspect of Mother Nature as reflected in an incredibly life-supporting Earth. As I will also state in one of the concluding chapters, *A Futurology of Spirit*, Goddess Worship is going to come back on a significant scale, and the next Avatar will promote it.

Mother Mary, Anandmayi Ma, and other female Avatars have come from the bosom of the Divine Mother. It is also significant that these various manifestations of Shakti (the Goddess Principle or Sophia) have always aligned with their Male counterparts and sought to serve humanity. Thus, Durga is aligned with Shiva, Lakshmi with Vishnu, and Saraswati with Brahma. All these Goddesses ultimately represent the Principle of Sustenance, whether by acquisition of knowledge (Saraswati), or abundance (Lakshmi) or spiritual/inner strength (Durga).

Their Lordships, often working together, are gently piloting the planet's spiritual life. They are not felt strongly by us because they will not interfere with our free will. Their love for us is so immense that they give us much rope. A lot of rope. Their Lordships sit in human hearts and "watch the world go by".

Lord Vishnu says in the Bhagavad Gita: *I am the supreme goal of all living beings, and I am also their sustainer, master, witness, abode, shelter, and friend.*

There is an important axiom implied here: While Masters, demi-gods, and angels are numerous, the same cannot be said of the Parent Deities. They are, almost by definition, a much smaller number. It is a Cosmic Pyramid, with less room at the "top" and more room at the "bottom"…

The most ancient deities to be worshipped on earth were Lord Shiva, Lord Vishnu, Lord Ganesha, and Lord Surya, as well as the Goddess in various forms. They regularly appeared before blessed sages and sometimes before other devotees. However, until this point in time, no Deity has walked side by side with humans. That has been done only by Avatars. Lord Vishnu recently declared that Deities would henceforth communicate with humanity through mediums, rather than descend as an Avatar repeatedly.

Sathya Sai Baba has said that a Golden Age will be upon us in the not-too-distant future, and a time will come when Gods, Angels, and Humans will walk side by side on this earth! He has also said He has recently turned off Kali Yuga, even though it will take some time for this Yuga to fully subside... Sai Baba likened it to a spinning fan. Even after the switch is turned off, the fan continues to spin for a while...

Right now, as far as humans are concerned, Avatars are more accessible to us than Deities. In fact, that is one of the raisons-d'etre of Avatars. In many parts of India, the worship of Avatars like Shirdi Sai Baba has become as common as the direct worship of Deities...

I'd like to end this section with a quote from Corinthians:

There are different kinds of gifts, but the same Spirit distributes them. There are different kinds of service, but the same Lord. There are different kinds of working, but in all of them and in everyone it is the same God at work...
...To one there is given through the Spirit a message of wisdom, to another a message of knowledge..., to another faith by the same Spirit, to another gifts of healing..., to another miraculous powers, to another prophecy, to another distinguishing between spirits, to another speaking in different kinds of tongues, and to still another the interpretation of tongues. All these are the work of one and the same Spirit...

However, Avatars sometimes carry <u>all</u> these gifts with them.

Chapter Four

Sage Kapila: Feet on Ground, Head in Sky

"States of consciousness" are only products of Prakriti (Nature) and can have no kind of relation with Spirit, the latter, by its very essence, being above all experience. However in Kapila's Samkhya Philosophy, the most subtle and transparent part of mental life, that is, Intelligence, in its mode of pure luminosity, has a specific quality, that of reflecting Spirit or Purusha---***Mircea Eliade***

To start at the beginning, and with a great ambassador of spiritual philosophy, is to begin with Sage Kapila, considered to be one of the world's first great Gurus, or spiritual teachers, whose insights have come down to us through the ages. He lived before any of the other Super Avatars that are mentioned in this book. And yet His influence has permeated down to recent times...

Many thousands of years later, He would be acknowledged by Lord Krishna as one of Krishna's own faces...and so Kapila can indeed be regarded as an elevated being, who apparently was born to lead a life of inner contemplation and disciplined meditation, to obtain insights into the nature of life, the Universe, and the energies present on this planet. He then readily shared His insights and experiences with His students. He's also known as Rishi Kapila, Rishi being a Sanskrit word for "advanced sage".

People who are into Yoga have Kapila to thank. His Samkhya philosophy influenced Patanjali, one of the Fathers of Yoga. Kapila, after being exposed to the Yoga teachings of Lord Shiva the First Yogi, taught the principles of Yoga to His devotees and students, and this knowledge ended up influencing Patanjali and his philosophy of Yoga. Samkhya also influenced Tantra and other spiritual practices.

One point about Kapila that might make Him more palatable to Western sensibilities is that He did not speak at all about Maya or Illusion. For Kapila, "Everything is Real". While the mundane world is real, the individual soul is "super-real" and thus spiritual growth is a worthy goal...

It is said that Virtue, Knowledge, Non-attachment, and spiritual Power were all "born with Kapila". His powers and insights came from his intense meditation. Kapila effortlessly embraced the life of a hermit, and launched himself into years of intense spiritual practices that made Him realize the "vertical" nature of Consciousness as opposed to the "horizontal" nature of the Mass/Energy Universe we live in, and that they were "distinct"...That led Him to develop the twin concepts of Purusha (Consciousness) and Prakriti (Nature) as elaborated below.

In the Mahabharata it is said, "Have no doubt that Samkhya is the highest knowledge." Much later, Avatar Babaji would quote from Samkhya principles when He taught His chelas (or spiritual students) such as Swami Satyananda Maharaj who lived from 1896 to 1971.

The Bhagavad Gita (perhaps the most well-known Hindu scripture in the West) refers to Kapila as a Yogi hermit, who was endowed with spiritual powers called Siddhis. Both Kapila and Krishna espoused the Samkhya philosophy, though Krishna did go much beyond that. Krishna declared at one point that He had come to elucidate and complete the work of Kapila. The word Samkhya is pronounced Saankhya (with a nasal n).

What is the Samkhya philosophy? It is perhaps the first to proclaim the presence of Consciousness on Earth, and Kapila called conscious entities "Purushas". The only other great reality according to him is manifest Nature, or Prakriti. An important point in this context is that Nature encapsulates grey matter (the brain), the mind, as well as the ego (or the sense of separation). Thus Kapila was implying that brain, mind, and ego are not always in sync with Purusha which manifests as pure consciousness or awareness (also called the Higher Consciousness or High-C by some writers like Phyllis Krystal), while Prakriti manifests itself in the workings of the body and its interactions with the environment...

These two great phenomena are to be seen as orthogonal (or perpendicular) to each other and not in conflict with each other in any way...

At the macro level, Purusha is like an infinite waterfall, constantly "falling" on Prakriti (as births take place all over the world), and m*ind/ego is the mist that is formed as a result*...We are Ethereal Gorillas in the Mind Mist...and over the millennia, the mist is getting thick...It's a non-local phenomenon we all share.

Mind is under the illusion that it has emerged only from the body, and views its energy source as the body, and so mind is deeply wedded to the interests and welfare of the body...However due to both gregariousness and competition for scarce resources, mind has also extended its involvement to "other bodies" and so has become a socio-biological entity...and constantly in a state of flux (i.e., thoughts come and go). Receiving mixed signals from the environment and growth of the ego lead to an emotional cauldron in the mind and that in turn has led to a body/mind/ego complex that is the root of many challenges...Truly it is said: The mind cannot comprehend God nor can the tongue describe Him.

David Bohm hints at the illusory nature of the mind when he says: *Thought is constantly creating problems... and then trying to solve them. But as it tries to solve them it makes it worse because it doesn't notice that it's creating them, and the more it thinks, the more problems it creates.*

However, Purusha is present in all of us, just like Prakriti is. When we are mindful (or *attentive*, as Krishnamurti would say) we are using the perpendicular (or "vertical") energy of Purusha. To keep this energy pure and untainted, Krishnamurti urged us to "observe without words". He would caution his audiences to avoid using words to interpret or expand on what was being observed so that no past conditioning (mind) would come in and taint the process...And as Mircea Eliade points out in the opening quote, Purusha is also manifest when the brain is operating in a state of insight or pure luminosity or pure light. Effortless creativity is another manifestation of Purusha...Many humans are very talented in one thing or the other and this well-spring of talent is again the divine Purusha at work.

One of the great teachers who exhorted humanity to unite our limited minds with this vertical energy of Purusha was the Buddha. Mindfulness was an important part of His teaching. The Buddha has been esoterically linked with Kapila by some people... But the connection is not through Lord Vishnu but rather Lord Sanat Kumara...Also, it is more than likely that the early teachers of the Buddha, before He achieved Nirvana, had made Him familiar with the teachings of Kapila.

Lao Tzu was another "vertical teacher" and a sharp contrast to Confucius who was mostly "horizontal" (i.e., concerned about the maintenance of a harmonious society, about the correct rites and practices, etc.)...This is why these two never saw eye to eye. It is said they did meet each other but soon parted company, unable to arrive at anything even remotely resembling a consensus...

Since the Buddha and Lao Tzu there have been many such vertical teachers such as Bodhidharma, Adi Shankara, and Gorakhnath. Krishnamurti, who took his energy from the Buddha (and was a direct student of the Buddha in a previous life according to C. W. Leadbeater), not surprisingly also anchored his teaching almost exclusively on attention or mindfulness.

Prakriti, or Nature, is "open-ended", and has the tendency to fan out in different directions and that has led to countless life forms and also various forms of matter. For example, the intense heat and pressure inside stars led to the synthesis of many elements heavier than hydrogen and helium...

Some philosophers have been somewhat hasty in referring to Samkhya as "atheistic philosophy" or an "agnostic philosophy". This has happened because apparently Kapila did not extend the idea of an individual soul to a Universal Spirit or Godhead....(Incidentally, it was Dattatreya who did that quite unequivocally a little later...In other words Lord Datta filled in the gaps left by Kapila).

But Kapila was far from being an atheist. He was a devotee of Lord Shiva and the Lord is said to have gifted Kapila with the Chintamani, a jewel whose possessor was immediately endowed with power over the world of matter. This is described in a Purana called the Mudgal Purana. If Krishna spoke of Kapila in such superlatives, there appears to be little doubt that the first Sage Kapila was not someone who would even downplay the role of God (or even the demi gods) in the spiritual life of the earth...let alone seek to promote an atheistic doctrine or even an agnostic doctrine. It is not surprising therefore, that to this day, there are temples in India dedicated to Kapila, where He is worshipped.

Another indication that He was a devotee of Shiva is that He led the life of a renunciate... In those times, Lord Shiva was regarded as the patron deity of hermits and sages in the Hindu religion. For many thousands of years, only Shiva worshippers tended to be ascetics and hermits. It is only in the last 1000 years or so that followers of Lord Vishnu have also embraced the life of renunciation... Kapila is also said to have possessed a very powerful Third Eye, which in those days was considered a Gift from Lord Shiva...

Do Purusha and Prakriti interact with each other? The answer of course is yes, and there is no better place on earth for the interaction of Purusha and Prakriti than in humans...In fact one of the aims of Yoga is indeed to bring Purusha and Prakriti together, and that is also an aim of Tantra...

Kapila said: *The Purusha is the entity that adds the element of reason to the human that is absent in animal life. But there is one delusion that even the soul is not immune to, and that is: the delusion of individuality...that it is a separate being in its own right...* In other words, the soul gets into a feeling of separation and "doer satisfaction" that is the beginning of immersion into the material world and material activities and thought processes. Implied in that sentence is also Kapila's view that the soul inside humans is *more evolved* than the soul inside animals...but in both humans and animals it is the Purusha that provides the ultimate ingredient for s*entience* to occur.

Also, it's not in the nature of the soul to fight any fundamental urge in the body-mind-ego complex....Nor will the soul oppose the individual's attraction towards the world...it simply witnesses and apparently "goes along." However, it does make its presence felt if a threshold is crossed, and if the individual is sensitive and evolved, the voice of Purusha becomes even more strident... The voice of conscience does speak up sooner or later in most us does it not?

So how does an individual evolve? We have to begin with the mind....Over a period of time, when the mind begins to sense the presence of Purusha and is willing to become silent (a process that can take lifetimes), the intellect responds and finally, after customary periods of inner conflict and turbulence, the individual becomes a "realized soul". Kapila insisted that liberation (or Kaivalya) can be obtained by the individual who realizes he is not the physical body, he is not merely mundane matter...However, what is also needed is to have the situation evolve to where the Purusha in that individual realizes the ultimate superficiality of this temporary or impermanent experiment we call life. So in that sense it is a two-way street... Later, the Jains also used the word Kaivalya as an alternative to the Buddhist word Nirvana...Kaivalya can be translated as "aloofness".

An elevated Being like Kapila is for the sake of simplicity, an extremely large Spirit Quantum, "Experienced and Spiritually Sensitive", that descends to feed the spiritually hungry, and even grant meaning to life...Some very large Spirit Quantums however, never descend to earth but remain as demi gods in other planes...An Archangel can be seen as a large spirit quantum that is closely associated with a Deity or Avatar and wishes to serve the Master in His mission, but not necessarily on the visible plane...

Kapila was also a person deeply concerned about various ways of knowing...He was the first to outline different ways of arriving at the truth...such as by direct observation, by seeking expert and reliable opinion, or by objective inference. Later, other means of knowing would be accepted, but Kapila was more parsimonious and accepted only these three.

One of the criticisms leveled against Samkhya is that it is a dualistic philosophy that considers the ultimate truth to be twofold: Consciousness and the Phenomenal World. Later in our spiritual history, non-dualists like Adi Shankara spoke out against it. However, it must be said in Kapila's defense that His version of duality is quite elevated and transcendental in its own right, and certainly does not automatically lead to more mundane notions of duality, such as the unbridled exploitation of Nature, or the notion that humans are different from God. On the other hand, Kapila insisted that "God resides in Man". And so, the notion of "Devotion to the God Within" was born.

In this context, it must be said that there has been more than one Kapila in the spiritual history of India, and there were one or two Kapilas who promoted a more atheistic Samkhya... There was even one Kapila who tried to explain all phenomena in terms of primordial mathematics. For such a teacher, there is, in a sense, only Prakriti and hardly any Purusha to speak of. I therefore sympathize with those who have called such teachers "Impostor Kapilas".

The first Kapila even describes atheism as a tamasic quality in his Tattva Samasa...The word tamasic means, in a sense, "dulled by ignorance" (it also refers to intransigence and inertia) and comes from Tamas, one of the three Fundamental Modes of Existence (or Gunas) as given below. The three Gunas as enumerated by Kapila are: Sattva, Rajas, and Tamas.

- People who are Sattvic possess qualities such as inner poise, serenity, tolerance, optimism, positive and holistic outlook, not easily prone to temptations, easily satisfied, non-violent, interested in intellectual and/or spiritual growth, etc.
- Rajasic people on the other hand often display a high degree of proactivity, ambition, high energy, goal-orientation, competitiveness, etc.
- Tamasic people are somewhat inert and even slothful, prone to vices, temptations, fond of soothing themselves through habits and addictions, prone to

thinking the same thoughts repeatedly, highly resistant to change etc.

While it is generally true that all of us have some level of each of these Gunas within us, it isn't difficult to see that human personality types usually display a predominance of one of the above 3 Gunas, although in some of us there may be 2 Gunas predominating or even all three Gunas somewhat equally balanced. For example many years of intellectual activity can make a Rajasic person more Sattvic and if he then decides to rest on his laurels he might well invite the Tamasic Guna too into his life...

Kapila went on to apply Gunas to Nature Herself. He claimed we can find the Gunas in the animal kingdom, in inanimate things and processes, and in the plant kingdom...

The path of devotion to God was later echoed by Krishna and the later sages of the Bhakti movement in India, who were basically saying that Faith, Devotion, and Surrender to the Lord are what will ultimately save man, because the Lord can and will personally grace such a devotee with liberation, if that is what the devotee wants and if the time is karmically appropriate. This path called Bhakti has taken a lot of beating in India and other parts of the world, but is now making a comeback, with the two most recent Avatars, the two Sai Babas, teaching us that in this Dark Age of Corruption and Waywardness, this path of Bhakti is an easier alternative than the Path of Knowledge or the Path of Right Action, both of which are also considered pathways to liberation...

Kapila was one of the first to openly declare the principles of reincarnation. He came to the realization that living creatures are born again and again into this crucible of life we call the earth, and he was filled with the urge to help humans gain liberation from this cycle of birth and death. His great teaching saw a revival in the 16th century, and is given in a work from that period entitled the Samkhya Pravachana Sutra.

When did Kapila live? Kapila was the teacher of His younger sister Anasuya who in turn was the mother of Dattatreya, the great Avatar who we will meet in the next chapter. This makes Him a little more than 20,000 years ago according to the framework provided by Sai Baba which we will reexamine shortly.

Kapila, Dattatreya, and Rama were not separated by too many years. For our purposes, they were almost contemporaries, who all lived around 18000 BC…We know this because Rama is said to have visited the abode of Anasuya, the sister of Kapila and the mother of Lord Datta. Also another exalted being, Parasurama, who was a student of both Lord Shiva and Lord Datta, at one point meets Rama and surrenders to Him…These four form the <u>first great Cluster of Descents</u> along with a couple <u>of other sages, Vasishta and Vishwamitra (who we will also meet soon)</u>. Sage Agastya can also be said to belong to this great Cluster. As we are going to see later, other such clusters have occurred throughout our spiritual history…

Some people wonder why the Samkhya is silent about the Vedas…this is because <u>Samkhya in all likelihood, predates the Vedas</u>. Besides from all indications, Kapila was a fiercely independent soul who preferred to depend on His own inquiry.

Now, as mentioned before, civilization is far older than what conventional historians and archaeologists are willing to accept…As authors like Graham Hancock have shown, recent underwater explorations have revealed entire cities buried under the ocean…for example, a large land mass called Kumari Kandam now lies under the Indian Ocean. It is said to have gone under about 16000 years ago. The civilization that existed in Kumari Kandam is of course much older than that…at least 30,000 years old. This is not at all a big number, considering that Homo sapiens or modern man has been on earth for at least 100,000 years. India's Vedic Civilization, even by some relatively conservative estimates, is at least 30,000 to 40,000 years old. Earlier, I've mentioned an even higher estimate…

Both these spiritual giants, Kapila and Lord Dattatreya have been preserved through Hinduism's meticulous oral tradition which was passed from generation to generation through the priestly class. While in the modern age the oral tradition is not given too much credibility, in India it was taken very seriously. Moreover, these two figures, Kapila and Dattatreya, have resurfaced many times in Divine literature.

Kapila was a manifestation of the Vishnu Principle, which seeks to provide mankind with spiritual and emotional support and seeks to consolidate the forces of preservation of mankind as also the self-preservation of the individual. Even though only a handful of temples dedicated to Kapila still exist in India, He is considered in many quarters as a truly gigantic force in the spiritual history of Hinduism, the oldest religion that is still practiced today…His only shortcoming perhaps is that He did not "extrapolate enough" from individuals to the Universe. But Lord Dattatreya took care of that...

It is said in esoteric circles that Kapila's service to Planet Earth was held to be so significant, He was raised into the hallowed circles of the Four Kumaras, the flag-bearers of Earth's Spiritual Evolution, with Sanat Kumar being the most well-known and significant Kumara in the spiritual history of the earth. The 4 Kumaras are considered to be Omniscient and completely liberated from the mundane world, and yet committed to the spiritual evolution of humanity. They were so attracted to the Samkhya philosophy they became students of it, and mastered it.

The Kumaras surface now and then in Indian mythology. One of them appears in the Mahabharata to deliver a teaching. In the Ramayana, it is recounted that the 4 Kumaras, being extremely keen on seeing Lord Rama, ended up meeting Him. Even heaven is filled with gratitude towards Avatars, who take the risk of descending into the mundane...

Some people include <u>Sage Ribhu</u> in this hallowed group of Kumaras… Sage Ribhu is also a very ancient sage, who attained the Ultimate Liberation and who had been personally mentored by Lord Shiva. This sage is known for a teaching called the Ribhu Gita, which was a favorite of the 20th century sage, Ramana Maharishi, introduced to the West by Paul Brunton.

And as mentioned, the Buddha has also been linked with Sage Kapila…and there are commonalities between Buddhism and Kapila's Samkhya Philosophy.

When Prakriti is realized as the impermanent hardware of Nature and that it is Purusha that is pure and permanent, a transcendence of sorts has already taken place…By restricting himself to only these two categories, Kapila was actually paving the way for the Vedanta (or non-dualistic) philosophy to take root… (i.e., "From Many to Two to *One*"). In Vedanta everything is one whole, and in other words, Manifest Nature is a creation of Spirit or Consciousness.

Life is the result of Divine Will and the subsequent interaction of Energy and Matter. Yes, Life does evolve, but over a base of intelligent design and so we find many fascinating things in living creatures, including instantaneous change (the 100the monkey Effect) and Irreducible Complexity.

What is irreducible complexity? For example, for our eye to function we need many different processes to take place at the same time, or vision cannot take place…one view says there are 13 processes required for vision to take place. All these processes cannot develop one after the other or step by step, because until that last step occurs, all the earlier steps are of no use… According to Darwin's theory of evolution, genetic variations occur without specific design or intent. If that's the case, how did something as complex as the eye possibly develop by accident…Also, the brain is able to convert all kinds of inputs from the various senses into electro-magnetic signals…this could be only brought about by a Higher Consciousness.

Purely Darwinian processes take place over millennia, but the "downward" force of spirit on matter can bring about change very quickly, thus leading to irreducible complexity in life systems today. Sensory organs come into being fairly rapidly, and not little by little…The Theory of Evolution by Charles Darwin with all its innate grey areas and discontinuities, has however, indeed raised our consciousness. Things do not need to always be a case of "either or".

Chapter Five

Lord Dattatreya: The Ancient & Eternal One

Myself, Tajuddin Baba, Dhuniwale Dada, Narasing Maharaj, Swami Samartha, and Gajanan Maharaj, *we are all incarnations of Dattatreya---Shirdi Sai Baba*

To use an analogy given to us by Meister Eckhart, we have above a direct reference to the fecundity of Lord Dattatreya. Out of an abundance of love, humanity is gifted with many avatars. All the Avatars mentioned in the above quote were on earth during the 19th and early part of the 20th century. There are many anecdotes relating Shirdi Sai Baba with Dattatreya so let's first take a look at this ancient Avatar.

Lord Datta was the first great Divine Descent (or Avatar) on earth at least as far as the extent of our knowledge goes. Many spiritual seekers are very grateful for the teachings handed down from Him through the oral tradition of Ancient India. These teachings have such an authentic ring to them that we end up feeling Lord Datta was indeed a Guru of Gurus.

So, is Lord Datta a Deity or an Avatar? There might be understandably, some confusion about this. Even though Lord Dattatreya was an Avatar (or rather a Combination Avatar), this Avatar is so filled with Cosmic Potency that He became a Source of Avatars Himself, and so for all practical purposes He is indeed a Deity...While older Avatars of Datta are unknown to us at this point, we have a much better idea of His Avatars in the last 800 years.

When God Quantums split up into fragments, each fragment is an Avatar of almost equal magnitude. Thus it is said, *a part of Him is all of Him.* By extrapolation, each of us is a part of Him and so each of us is Him...

While Rama and Krishna both studied under gurus in their youth, Lord Datta was His own guiding light...though He once did claim that Nature was His teacher. He was the first great soul to assert "Nature is a great teacher", a view echoed by William Wordsworth and Sai Baba. There is a reference to Nature being His teacher that has been reproduced recently by the Canadian Journal of Environmental Education. The article touches upon the 24 teachers of Dattatreya....all of which were forces of Nature or natural processes.

Here was an Avatar who seems far ahead of His time with a teaching that left no stone unturned for the serious seeker. He was an integrated Avatar espousing both the principle of Consolidation (or the Vishnu Principle) and the principle of Transcendence and Evolution (or the Shiva Principle). This is in keeping with the legend, with various parties saying He was mostly a manifestation of Shiva and others claiming He was mostly a manifestation of Vishnu. His birth can be regarded as a glorious case of the Vishnu Principle, the Shiva Principle, and the Brahma Principle (or Creative Principle) working together. For either the Vaishnavites or the Shaivites to claim Him for their own is a short-sighted act, for He belongs to us all...

About one thousand years ago, there lived a great Hindu adept called Gorakhnath. He was blessed with many yogic powers, and became one of the torch bearers of an ancient tradition of super-yogis, called the Nath Tradition. Gorakhnath insisted his tradition had sprung up from Dattatreya, the Supreme Yogi and Tantric Master. In the Nath tradition, Dattatreya is mostly a manifestation of Lord Shiva. His very nature of asceticism and sacrifice, His Yogic and Tantric powers and teachings, are all more reminiscent of Lord Shiva than Lord Vishnu...

The credence for Dattatreya comes from the mention of Him in various Hindu epics and scriptures. Also, there are various temples dedicated to Him that have existed for millennia... In more recent times the great poet-saint Dasopant Digambara who lived in West India from about 1550 to 1615 had more than one direct encounter (or darshan) of Lord Dattatreya after contemplating on the Lord for many years. So did another famous poet-saint called Eknath who was a contemporary of

Dasopant Digambara. Saint Eknath's teacher was also a devotee of Dattatreya.

It is commonly believed that Hinduism has "no single founder". While it's true that Hinduism is a very ancient religion, it is more than possible that a hitherto unknown Founder (such as Lord Vishnu) gave Hinduism its initial impetus…However, such a founder has been lost in the mists of time…In the Puranas, the ancient folklore of India, it is said that Lord Vishnu authored the Vedas and then transferred them to humanity through the assistance of sages…thus in a sense founding Hinduism.

When one reads about the amazing life of Lord Dattatreya though, one is tempted to call Him the "father of Hinduism". His Avadhuta Gita contains the highest teachings of Hinduism, and sounds like a precursor to everything that Hinduism, and especially Vedanta, later stood for. He was the guru of Lord Parashurama who is himself considered an Avatar by many, and also was the guru of several other spiritual (and worldly) luminaries. A brief note on Parashurama follows.

Parashurama---The Grim Reaper

Parashurama was born into a very spiritual family. His father was a renowned sage and His mother an extremely devout wife who doted on her family. He grew up in an ashram and was tutored in all the scriptures. He later propitiated Lord Shiva and is said to have visited Mount Kailas, the abode of Shiva, more than once. He is indeed a mysterious Avatar, using His energy to cleanse the world of the warrior clan, who He felt were an anti-spiritual violently driven mob of scoundrels.

This kind of cleansing is also spoken of in books of other faiths, such as Islam. In the Koran, the Lord sends messages to Muhammad where He speaks of having cleansed entire cities. This tells us something about the nature of life on earth and its relationship to Divinity so to speak. Apparently, "weeds" are sometimes removed to make way for the larger good…

This somewhat sobering account of a "Grim Reaper Avatar" should be tempered by mentioning that Parashurama did do much to bring about pleasant outcomes for human beings. He is said to have helped in the setting up of many villages and ashrams. He also constructed many temples.

Lord Datta's disciple Parashurama wielded enormous power and made His influence felt for a very long time. This was because Parashurama was granted earthly immortality until the end of this cycle of the Universe. For example, Parashurama was the teacher of Bheeshma, who appeared on earth some 15,000 years after the birth of Parashurama. Perhaps for this virtual immortality, Parashurama is also considered an Avatar. He was an Avatar of the Vishnu Principle.

It is said that Lord Datta taught Parashurama...It is somewhat incongruous that one Vishnu Avatar would end up teaching another Vishnu Avatar, which makes it all the more likely that Lord Datta was predominantly a Shiva Avatar. However, He is usually shown with 3 heads as a symbolic gesture to show that He was a perfect collaboration of Brahma, Vishnu, and Shiva.

The relationship between Parashurama and Dattatreya brings us to an important point: Avatars often occur in pairs, with one Avatar being much more potent than His counterpart. One can speak of them as Solar/Lunar pairs. Sometimes, more than one minor Avatars appear with the Solar Avatar, just like some planets have many moons...

Jesus Christ was accompanied by John the Baptist. The latter's birth was foretold by the Angel Gabriel, just like the birth of Christ was. Moses was accompanied by Elijah and they both appeared to Jesus during the Transfiguration of Jesus. In India, Krishna was accompanied by Balarama. And Rama was accompanied by Hanuman.

Similarly, Parashurama was the Accompanying Avatar for Dattatreya. I do not intend to speak of the Parashurama Avatar in greater detail in this work, partly because He did not deliver a particularly abiding message to humanity either through His words or His acts. However, a few words on Lord Parashurama are not out of place here, especially since He was a firm advocate of what later became Vedic culture and Vedic Dharma. The word

Dharma can be loosely translated as "the righteous life" (the kind of life that is endearing to God) and the word appears in both Hindu and Buddhist literature.

The Parashurama Avatar was to a large extent subsumed by the glory of His teachers so to speak. I refer now to Guru Dattatreya and Lord Shiva.

Lord Dattatreya was the first great teacher to insist that spiritual interests and motivations that arise in humans occur because of the nudging (or grace) of God. He declared that all great things are wrought by God alone, such as the birth of rational, intellectual (and even non-theistic) thinking in individuals, and, even the very existence of non-dual doctrines is to be ascribed to God. If non-theistic doctrines such as Taoism, Buddhism, and Zen exist today, they exist says Datta Guru to save humanity from fear and give us inner strength. They are sacred, just like God-centered and faith-centered religions are sacred. However, there are some differences and I will cover them in a later section...One of the differences is that the effective lifetimes of non-theistic faiths will be somewhat limited. As an example, the Buddha Himself predicted His order would not last forever.

Lord Dattatreya also sensitized us to the grace of both "God and Goddess" in our daily lives. In His *Tripura Rahasya*, He gives us sublime teachings clothed in a delightful story of a man who had gone astray being led back to enlightenment by his resourceful wife. The wife tells the husband at one point, "Dispassion cannot arise in an individual except by the grace of God. If the mind becomes involved in the quest for truth it is by His grace alone. If it begins to move in the direction of detachment from sensual pleasures, it is by His grace."

Lord Datta was a supreme recluse. And this reclusiveness has continued even in many of His modern Avatars. Fortunately for us, a couple of His disciples gave detailed accounts of His teachings. Swami and Kartika were the disciples who recorded His teachings for the benefit of later generations.

Lord Dattatreya taught Ashtanga Yoga to Patanjali, who later wrote the famous Yoga Sutras. Lord Datta was also one of the originators of Tantra, which we will encounter in the next chapter.

This Avatar left home very early (while still a young boy) and wandered thereafter naked and with no possessions... He abruptly announced one day to His parents that He was leaving. This in itself is startling....who but a Divine Being could be so emphatic in His words and leave home before He was even ten years old... And before He departed from this earth, He filled us with His nectarine philosophy of absolute freedom from the mundane world...and how to obtain liberation from the cycle of birth and death.

There was no "beating around the bush" in the philosophy of Dattatreya. It was as if He foresaw the immense trials and tribulations that were coming in the future and wanted to liberate all deserving souls... He chose to be a naked ascetic (called a Digambara which means "Sky Clad"). Being a child He did not raise too many eyebrows by appearing naked in public. But He did attract attention. Later, even while He grew into manhood, His naked appearance continued, and was finally accepted as a true indicator of His asceticism. He roamed the forests and villages of Southern and Western India, for many years. Sometimes He would temporarily live a worldly life...but soon renounce it.

He was the First Avadhoota (an ultimate ascetic who wishes to have no possessions whatsoever like a Saint Francis of Assisi). An Avadhoot is one who is permanently anchored in spirit, and sees all phenomena around Him as a manifestation of Spirit.

Soon He began initiating people into the spiritual life and attracted many people...In a traditional and patriarchal society like India, a child captured the imagination of many and then went on to transform them. There is little doubt that He could perform miracles even as a boy. This same ability occurred in two recent Avatars of Dattatreya: Sai Baba of Shirdi (West India) and Sai Baba of Parthi (in South India).

Soon, He was a living legend. A pair of sandals that He wore are said to be housed in a temple to this day. Swami Vivekananda, a modern saint of India, was completely enamored by Lord Dattatreya. He described Lord Datta as a true ascetic, and said, "Like true ascetics, He could sit still and enjoy the bliss of Brahman (Universal Spirit), and not care or want anything else." Swami Sivananda of the Himalayas, a renowned spiritual master and guru of modern times, referred to Dattatreya as "the lion of Vedanta". Vedanta is said to be the pinnacle or the ultimate wisdom...Long before the word Vedanta was even coined, Lord Dattatreya lived and taught it.

The essence of Vedanta is non-dualistic thinking (called Advaita). In the ultimate analysis, Advaita means "Oneness" thus implying that everything is God, and there is naught but Him. Thus Brahman is Supreme and everything is just a manifestation or extension/creation of Brahman. In other words, Prakriti is a child of Purusha and so is Mind.

At the practical level, it implies that humans should live in a centered manner, avoiding extremes. This simply means that the individual, instead of getting "caught in the oscillations of life", such as pleasure and pain, should instead live in complete consciousness of these and be mindful of how each of these work and how they compete for our mind space... The seeker after truth should seek to integrate everything into one meaningful whole that *transcends* (or synthesizes) these opposites. An example would be a person who is not bothered by past or future...he neither runs away from anything nor is enamored by anything....he neither grasps nor is repulsed by anything. Rather he is a witness, alert and yet detached.

This does not mean however that one denies the existence of God or Avatars. In Hinduism, there is a way of integrating both faith and non-dualistic living. One surrenders both one's joys and sorrows to God. This is called Bhakti-Vedanta (Devotional Non-dualism) by some. For a Bhakti-Vedantist, his heroes (Avatars and Deities) are themselves non-dualistic in temperament. There is no question of a Dualistic or Conditional God. God is One, and Loves His entire Creation.

Avatars like Dattatreya and Sai Baba teach us to believe in the supremacy of Spirit, and to also believe that Spirit is omnipresent and more subtle than the subtlest phenomena in the Universe... However they also teach us to couple this with devotion to an Avatar, so that the love of the Avatar for the devotee, and the ability of the Avatar to grant liberation, will combine with the devotee's own will to transcend, and create a powerful combination indeed. When the devotion of the student and the grace of the Guru combine, that will take the devotee to permanent release from the cycle of birth and death and also more importantly, union with God. Bhakti Vedanta therefore is also high philosophy and devotional love working together in perfect unison. In other words, it is an exhortation to bring the Heart into the Intellect and the Intellect into the Heart.

If a person were to read Lord Datta's works, such as the Jivanmukta Gita and the Avadhuta Gita, he/she would immediately recognize that these belong to the category of the highest principles that remind one of the Transcendentalists of New England, and of the highest principles in Taoism and Buddhism.

In Hinduism, the entire span of history is divided into major epochs known as Yugas. The exact duration of the yugas is still a matter of some controversy... There are 4 Yugas:

- **Satya Yuga**, the first and most peaceful time on earth, when humans show a great amount of integrity and honesty, as well as fraternal affection for one another.
- **Treta Yuga**, the second major epoch, where corruption as well as weak-mindedness and selfishness begin to gradually creep in.
- **Dwapar Yuga**, when power struggles and political battles increase in intensity accompanied by gross selfishness.
- **Kali Yuga**, when chaos and cunning rule the roost and values are thrown overboard. Corruption is at its highest and humans are plagued with all kinds of mental cravings and ills.

Dattatreya is considered a Satya Yuga Avatar. However, this did not stop Him from pointing out basic human frailties in works such as the Tripura Rahasya and it did not stop Him from pointing out the need for human beings to strive for their personal liberation from the cycle of birth and death.

This might be a good place to diverge from the topic at hand to consider an important source of confusion: The Duration of Yugas. If one looks at the traditionally accepted duration of Yugas it boggles the mind. For example, Kali Yuga is said to last 432,000 years, and it is the shortest Yuga! The others are between 2 and 4 times as long...This is clearly an untenable doctrine given the spiritual history of humankind over the last 20,000 years...For example, Rama is said to belong to the Second Yuga and Krishna to the Third...

As this writer sees it, the Avatars are in complete control of the duration of Yugas and have speeded up the whole process. ...As mentioned before, Sathya Sai Baba announced one day that He had turned off Kali Yuga. The will of Avatars is infinitely strong...

The essence of the teachings of Lord Datta can be found in the work called the Avadhuta Gita. In it Lord Datta describes what the Ultimate Reality or Truth is, and exhorts the spiritual aspirant to follow Him into transcendence.

Let us now spend some time with the main teachings of the Avadhuta Gita:

This Gita begins with an enlightening line that helped to clear up some of the mist in this writer's head:

Through the grace of God alone arises the desire for non-dual consciousness in wise men to save them from fear.

The word fear includes such things as insecurity, despair, & hopelessness. This arises from a feeling of separation from everyone else, and so such feelings can be dispelled by realizing oneself as the All...Thus, sometimes in the evolution of man, there is a need to partake even of non-theistic doctrines, so that later the more heart based truths can be assimilated...in other words, the growth of the spiritual intellect can and will lead to a softening of the psyche and then the heart...

Even the growth of science is a benediction. For science, even though it is operating within a limited canvas and even though science has become as much a social activity as the search for truth, it has made us grow in awareness, as all consciousness based doctrines have.

Lord Datta then poignantly says, "How can I worship the All in All, when I am also the All." I'm reminded of a passage in one of the Shiva Puranas where Parvati observes Him bowing and worshipping. She asks Him, "O God of Gods, why are You (of all Beings) doing this? And the Lord replies, that He is bowing to the ultimate Godhead who has given birth to all things. I'm also reminded of Lord Sai who said in one of His discourses, "I too have come from Brahman."

The ultimate knowledge according to Dattatreya is "I am the all-pervasive formless absolute Self. I am that God who is the Self of all." Sai Baba once said to an audience: *You are all omnipresent.*

In verse 14 Lord Datta also says, "You exist everywhere..."! We are infinite and immutable souls who have embraced the mundane for the sheer sport of it. As Ralph Waldo Emerson said, "All life is only an experiment."

Lord Datta was of a Silent Mind. He says in the Avadhuta Gita: I have no mental activity, good or bad. And goes on to say: *While the mind is the past and the mind is all, in reality there is no mind.* It's a sort of twilight zone between Spirit and Matter. It is caused by Spirit colliding with Matter, leading to a bouncing off of energy (just like a waterfall bouncing off the earth). Mind now thinks it came from the body (or Matter) and completely identifies with it. Mind has therefore forgotten that it came originally from Spirit. This has led to Mind becoming completely delusional (or Mayavic).

The doctrine of no mind is echoed in Zen Buddhism and in other doctrines. Wallowing in the past and interacting with others and judging people, as also attachment and addiction to particular pleasures, all create the mind and appear to give it substantiality. But the mind is simply a mirage thrown up by our egos, our sense of separation. In the highest realization of Spirit, there is no Mind or Matter. Both are illusory. The realization of this leads to the knowledge that all thought is illusory, a point made by J. Krishnamurti in his discourses.

Lord Datta says with His Divine love and concern in Verse 11 of the Avadhuta Gita:

...Thus you are One. Why then do you not understand that you are the unchangeable One, equally perceived in all?

O mighty One, how can you, who are ever-shining, unrestricted, think of day and night?

He exhorts us not to divide the indivisible, and to realize that the supreme Self is everywhere and homogeneous everywhere. The individual is Brahman said Shankara who lived about 1200 years ago. Brahman is that Absolute that pervades everything. The concept however was first stated by Lord Datta, about 20,000 years ago!

Individuals are neither born nor do they die, says Lord Dattatreya which reminds us of the first verses of the Bhagavad Gita, where Lord Krishna says, "There is neither birth nor death". But since we run around deluded from pleasure to pleasure and from responsibility to responsibility, there appears to be a life, with a beginning and end. The answer to this however, does not lie in the renouncing of obligations but to offer them to the Divine. Our livelihoods and all our activities need to be offered to the Lord.

In a sweeping statement in Verse 15 the Lord says, *"There is no you, no me, and no Universe. All is the Self alone"*. So why this separation and suffering? Let us be filled with wonder instead....let us wonder at the material universe that seems at first sight robust and tangible, and yet is ultimately made up of atoms which are mostly empty space...let us wonder at the Big Emptiness before the Big Bang. Let us wonder at the power of Spirit that is invisible and yet fully participative in the unfolding of human consciousness.

The whole question of human suffering has given rise to entire religions, such as Buddhism and Jainism. But is there really suffering, or the delusion of suffering because of our ego's tendency to wallow in self-pity and forget what one has learnt...If the Highest Consciousness was a Witness to all our trials and tribulations, is it still suffering, or is it a process of annealing that is an inherent part of human evolution?

Perhaps Man has the ability to heal himself by thinking on those lines....Entire wounded civilizations (and there are many) have a chance to heal themselves by contemplating on those lines. Otherwise only self-pity will result. And sooner or later this self-pity will manifest itself in perverse ways.

The Avadhuta Gita contains the highest teachings in pithy language that makes it radiate light to the darkest corners of our hearts, if we will let it do that. I hope to convey to the reader that thousands of years ago, humankind was considered ready to receive the highest teachings on the nature of delusion and the illusory nature of the mind, by quoting another great verse, Verse 18:

Oh mind, why do you wander about deluded, like an unclean spirit? Behold the Self indivisible. Be happy through renunciation of attachment.

(Being "happy, happy, happy", is a principle that Lord Sai Baba has emphasized).

In other words, the mind has been seen as limited for eons. In this day and age, the limitations of the human mind appear even more obvious and garish. However, it is a mystery that we let the mind carry us hither and thither...

This Avatar was telling us that the mundane life can only give us so much satisfaction....sooner or later, in this life or a future life, we're going to be looking for a deeper and higher existence....and not long after that we are going to look at transcending life completely....especially when it becomes clear that coming back to earth in another body is hardly what one might call a risk-free option...especially in this day and age. Hindus believe quite strongly in the concept of Kali Yuga (the Dark Age), when human limitations will make the environment toxic to all...and negative karma easy to accumulate.

The Master implies in His Avadhuta Gita that ultimately the individual will want to rise above it all...and begin climbing a mountain so to speak. This mountain is the slippery slope of evolution. And karma can cause us to slide down...

So why even go up the mountain? Easy enough: Because God is there. God welcomes the climbers at the rarefied top, and then transforms them into "birds" so we may soar even higher.

But not all of us want the mountain that has the Lord at the top. We want to climb our own mountain, or even a mountain that others have created, without any expectation of Divine intervention or destination. Well, the Lord has no problem with that. He will provide you such a mountain if you so wish. Such people will be attracted to non-theistic doctrines and lifestyles, or perhaps to their own independent enquiry or efforts...

It is time for the world to rediscover Dattatreya, a colossus of an Avatar, who, if not for the overwhelming heroism of the Rama and Krishna Avatars that led to major epics written about their lives, would have been a very well-known and beloved Avatar today, not only in India, but all over the world...However, His legacy has stood the test of time. Shankara quoted Him in his Brahmasutra Bhashya (it is said Shankara did this after having Lord Datta's darshan in a cave in the Himalayas). This Lord is mentioned in several Upanishads, the later scriptures of Hinduism.

Rediscovering this Avatar has become all the more important because we live in the Age of Dattatreya, and that is one of the messages of this book.

The Age of Dattatreya began (once again) in the 14th century AD with the arrival of Sripada SriVallabha who was a delightful manifestation of Dattatreya and who I will be discussing in a later chapter. A New Line of Avatars began with Sripada, and this is continuing to this day. Both the Sai Babas are part of this illustrious line.

The implications of this are vast. Both the Consolidation and Evolutionary principles (i.e., both the Vishnu and Shiva principles) are now to be considered equally important and valid. Also important is the Goddess Principle as symbolized by their spouses, the Devis, who now form the third important pillar of this triumvirate. To strive for the Integration of these three is the message we have been receiving, and the message has been coming to us in different forms...

It's interesting to note that there indeed have been attempts to integrate things in the last 100 years or so, with attempts to bring science and religion together, open debates between leaders of various religions, integrative studies, the recognition of women's rights and the inclusion of women into higher education, and multiculturalism, etc. Terms such as Integral Spirituality, coined by Ken Wilber, and Integral Christianity as well as Integral Life Practice have come into usage. I can see Lord Dattatreya smiling.

The Feminine Principle beckons to appreciate the vastness of the energy the world is blessed with, both physical (material) and mental. It teaches us to appreciate the extraordinarily life supporting nature of this earth. Yes, while it is true that the lives of various living creatures, including man, are sometimes snuffed out by happenings in nature, the bigger fact is that billions upon billions of living creatures are inhabiting the earth right now, while the number of creatures who have to give up their bodies on any particular day is an incredibly small fraction of the total number of creatures roaming the earth...Appreciation of the arts and music (in other words esthetics) is also a way of bringing together Consciousness on the one hand and Matter, Energy, Space & Time on the other. The complexities of both art and music have grown exponentially in the 20th century with such movements as the avant garde in both the arts and music.

Lord Sathya Sai Baba revealed to us somewhat later in His life that He is Lord Dattatreya, manifested once again out of His love for humanity. Sai Baba is also an integrated Avatar, carrying with Him the potencies of Lord Shiva, Lord Vishnu, Lord Brahma, as well as the Goddess (or Shakti) principle.

In this Age of Datta, various streams of knowledge will come together and there will be an interest in an Integration of Knowledge as well as a revival of Spiritual Paths and Faiths. Knowledge itself will grow and be applied in various ways. In other words, various technologies will come into existence. However, life will continue to pose new challenges...

In the ultimate analysis, there will be an inevitable further integration of Purusha and Prakriti. While the consciousness/awareness levels of humans will increase, life will be no less precarious however. The silver lining is that a Golden Age has been promised by the most recent Avatar who left His physical body recently and who will reappear as Prema Sai Baba. He has also declared that Prema Sai will herald a new Age of the Heart by filling the earth with love and compassion.

Sages like Kapila may render somewhat incomplete teachings to humanity, but an Avatar like Lord Dattatreya comes in and more than compensates for that. The same I believe has happened in the case of the Datta Avatar, Sathya Sai Baba. His teachings leave no stone unturned. I will return to this Avatar when we look at 20th century spirituality...He was still a youth during World War II. Given His location in rural South India, it took Him until about 1960 to be noticed even by Indians...However, after 1970, the Worldwide Presence of this Avatar grew at an increasing pace. We shall return to this glorious Avatar in a forthcoming chapter. An Avatar that has visited many homes, including mine, all over the world in His subtle body.

Chapter Six

The Dawn of Tantra

Our biological body itself is a form of hardware that needs re-programming through Tantra, like new spiritual software, which can release or unblock its potential---*Slavoj Zizek.*

Some decades after Lord Dattatreya descended, an exalted being called Parashurama (who we have met before), the son of Sage Jamdagni and his pious wife Renuka, was constantly in confrontation with the rulers of the time. These feudal rulers, or Kshatriyas, also had only negative feelings towards Parasurama, and were looking for ways to take revenge… One day some of them stormed into his father's home when Parasurama wasn't there, and killed the old defenseless sage and also some of his chelas or students.

Karmically, this was such a serious crime that later, the Kshatriyas paid an immense price for it… It was a huge crime because Jamdagni had attained immense spiritual status, and was considered one of the most enlightened sages of his time. Many thousands of years later, the Buddha acknowledged that the original Vedas had been revealed to certain sages, and among these sages, the Buddha named Jamdagni…this passage can be found in the Buddhist text called the Vinaya Pitaka.

When Parasurama returned to his father's spiritual retreat (or ashram), he found a scene of chaos and mourning. As soon as His mother explained what had happened, Parasurama vowed to take revenge on the Kshatriyas. He was a fierce warrior, blessed with great powers, obtained from his guru, Lord Shiva. He was fearless and felt he could confront all his enemies at the same time if needed…

Concerned that the king and his men may come back looking for them in the ashram where he and his kin were more vulnerable, Parasurama decided to leave the ashram. He put his father's corpse on one shoulder and on the other seated his mother, and left for the forest.

On the way, they ran into a being who called himself Datta. He asked them who they were. The mother said she was Renuka, the wife of Sage Jamdagni. Knowing well her background and spiritual past, Dattatreya immediately knelt down and prayed to her, calling her a manifestation of Shakti, or the Female Principle. Dattatreya was a great Avatar and yet here He was, on His knees in reverence...When Renuka realized who He was, she told her son Parasurama to request Lord Datta to be his guru. This was not a big change in gurus for Parasurama, since Lord Shiva is more than associated with Dattatreya....Thereafter, Parasurama became a student of Lord Datta...Renuka is worshipped to this day in pockets of India, and that is at least partly due to the grace bestowed on her by Lord Dattatreya.

A Tantric would call this worship of Shakti a spontaneous Tantric act. During the time of Lord Datta, only males were allowed to practice Tantra...However, something of significance happened during the Datta Avatar...The wives (or consorts) of Shiva, Vishnu, and Brahma played quite an active role...They stayed around in the vicinity quite a bit... *Tantra, first and foremost, is appreciation and adoration of the Goddess Principle in Nature and in the Universe. The motivation here is to ultimately bring the Male and Female Principles together, (some may say. Purusha and Prakriti together) in a spirit of Oneness and Unity. This principle has reappeared in paths such as Taoism in the form of Yin/Yang harmony...*

However, this basic paradigm can be expressed in different ways, and this has led to some confusion as to what Tantra really is. For some, Tantra is a kind of "living on the border" where different energies intersect...and for some a spontaneous and even uninhibited set of practices. These may include experimenting with sexual energy, mindfulness, meditation, mantras, moving energy up the chakras, rituals of various kinds, etc. For others Tantras are texts that explore the highest spiritual philosophies, such as the Shiva Tantras, now mostly forgotten, but apparently destined to be resurrected, because as I have mentioned before, interest in Lord Shiva is increasing, especially among those interested in our beginnings... Incidentally, according to some, Tantra means liberation from darkness, the root *tan* meaning darkness, and *tra* referring to liberation.

Lord Dattatreya's transcendental teachings and asceticism, combined with His teaching, *Tripura Rahasya*, or *Mystery of the Goddess*, gradually led to the development of Tantric philosophy and practice. Datta's followers also began worshipping female forms...They did not worship only Renuka though. Quite naturally they gravitated towards the worship of <u>Durga, Lakshmi, and Saraswati who are respectively the spouses or consorts of Shiva, Vishnu, and Brahma.</u>

There has always been, and is present to this day, a very noticeable Goddess Principle in Hinduism. The fervent prayers of devotees to the Divine Mother took on many colors...Every village or large settlement began to have its own little goddess deity installed in the village shrine, which may be nothing more than a small earth dais. Humans are of course prone to giving names to their icons, and so the village deity was often given a name...and the number of such names grew quite large indeed. The phenomenon can be observed to this day in the rural areas of India...where there are as many village goddesses as gods.

Throughout this book there is an underlying "Quantum Theory of God" being propounded. At one point, I was contemplating adopting the phrase "And a Quantum Theory of God" as the subtitle to this book...However "Jacob's Ladders on Lotus Ponds" prevailed... In many quarters of the world, "idol-worship" is somewhat denigrated as a pre-historic practice. However in the Quantum Perspective a new picture emerges:

The power of prayer is often under-estimated... For example, what happens when a lot of devotees worship a female village deity fervently? Sooner or later the Divine Mother responds, as she must. As Sanat Kumara has said, "The Divine Mother is full of compassion for humanity." She deputes one of her agents, a Spirit Quantum, to take over the role of this village deity and to respond to the supplications of devotees to the extent she can…and thus a remarkable thing happens: the number of demi-goddesses on earth actually begins to grow…Why? Because human beings have "done the impossible"…they have made Quantums descend. Of course, the same process has also given rise to male demi-gods, other divine agents, and angels on earth. This too is implied in the term "Jacob's Ladder". For those of us who find the whole idea of God Quantums inhabiting statues a stretch may I humbly point out that the world of Matter and Spirit are completely intertwined…You and I are swimming in Brahman. But it takes an Adi Shankara to derive His bliss just from that. The rest of us need more mundane pleasures to keep us going…

There is also another process by which the statue of a deity can become occupied by a God Quantum, and that is through a consecration ceremony or ritual. All major temples in India go through a consecration function and only then opened to the public.

Sathya Sai Baba has also on occasion made reference to village goddesses and the fact that an idol can become consecrated and occupied by a God Quantum. Over a period of thousands of years, the number of God Quantums, angels, etc. that have been given positions of responsibility on earth has become quite large. And we humans are the cause as well as the beneficiaries of this.

Bringing Purusha and Prakriti together is of course easier said than done, and is a process that's going on to this day in increments. For example, the proliferation of patriarchal and male-dominated religions in the world has slowed down this process… Including more and more people from all social classes in higher education, teaching values, making people aware of rampant consumerism and materialism, and the importance of serving others, will all help. As Sathya Sai Baba has said, *"The combined power of Prakriti, Avidya, and Maya (Phenomenal World, Ignorance, and Delusion) makes people forget their true nature."*

However, there are flashes of silver linings so to speak. In these times, rather than direct worship of the Goddess or Devi, we appear to prefer approaching things in other ways. For example when we use the word GAIA for the earth, and liken her to a living entity, and express concern for the environment, we are in essence, embracing the Prakriti or Goddess Principle if indirectly. When we indulge in *life-supporting activities*, we are also embracing Prakriti. When we give time and attention to the raising of our children, and to creating strong families, we are enhancing Prakriti.

Spiritually this union occurred long ago. The ancient scriptures of India extolled the male-female relationships of Krishna and Radha, of Vishnu and Lakshmi, and of Shiva and Shakti. In each case, it was said the male counterpart derived His vital energy from the female counterpart...

Tantra is a *"dialogue"* between the Male and Female Principles in the Universe or in other words, a dialogue between Consciousness and Life Processes... Attempts to move energy between the chakras are a spiritual example of that. In one view, the lower chakras mostly represent Shakti (or Prakriti) and the upper chakras are closer to Purusha or Consciousness. The two somewhat converge at the all-important Heart Chakra... The various Tantric texts that depict Shiva (the epitome of Consciousness) and His consort Devi (who symbolizes Shakti or Life Energy) in dialogue are a manifestation of that. There are two kinds of Tantras: The ones where Shiva is addressing (or teaching) Devi, and the ones where Devi is addressing or teaching Shiva. In another view of the chakras, each chakra has a God and Goddess pair associated with it, with the Goddess standing as gatekeeper...

This has even resulted in a third kind of paradigm, or middle-ground, coming into existence: *Shiva and Shakti combined*, symbolized by Ardha-Naareeshwara (a Composite Being, carrying both the male and female principles). The latest Avatar Sathya Sai Baba is a manifestation of both Shiva and Shakti, in addition to Vishnu, thus leading to a very complex and powerful Manifestation indeed. A one-of-a-kind Avatar of Dattatreya has occurred perhaps for the first and last time in the spiritual history of Planet Earth.

Not long after this, a connection was made between the God and Goddess Principles to the two basic forces in Nature, Purusha & Prakriti. Shakti being the energizer of the manifest forms and movements in Nature, thus became Nature's upholder and preserver…Enter Vishnu the Preserver or Sustainer. It is not a coincidence that another name for Devi is Narayani, and she is considered the sister of Narayana or Vishnu.

Today, however, Tantra has more earthy meanings shall we say…many unfortunately relate it to mostly sexual practices, and/or rituals involving catharsis and intoxication, including the consumption of hallucinogens, etc. Rituals that lead to these have come into existence…but the ancients practiced it in a deeper sense, with the teachings of Lord Shiva and Devi in mind, while trying to move energy from the lower chakras to the higher, and striving for enlightenment…

Later Shiva and Shakti's spiritual progeny (Ganesha and Subramanya) became part of this Divine group of Deities. This was the age before Shiva and Vishnu worshippers went their separate ways, when things were actually more integrated….thus it is said that in that age, knowledge, religion, rituals, and rites of passage were "all one"…

Later, as religion became organized, the separation and the formation of various denominations began, and this process has been going on in every religion down to modern times…There appears to be no religion that has remained intact and not broken up into denominations. And Hinduism is no exception. The Shaivites had their Shiva Tantras and Yoga as well as Lingam worship to go by, while the Vaishnavites began to assert themselves, especially after the physical departure of Rama, with their more overt devotional practices…

During that idealized period, sometimes called Ram Rajya, the Puranas became more well-known, and the Vaishnavites basked in the glory of the Rama Avatar and included the Parashurama and Vamana (or dwarf) Avatars in their devotion towards Lord Vishnu. It has been called a Golden Period for Hinduism and lasted many thousands of years. Various schools of Hindu philosophy began to emerge, not all of them attractive to the Shaivites and Vaishnavites. This led to the formation of cults which were however usually short lived.

Thus, one ethos became two, and it didn't stop with that. As Goddess worship grew, it led to the formation of Shaktism, a third denomination in Hinduism. However, the Vedic period that accompanied this era was somewhat a dampener for Shaktism, as the Vedas were distinctly oriented towards male deities and avatars.

Things would stay that way for millennia until the advent of Adi Shankara who tried to bring the three together as described later in the book…Shankara the great 8th century Vedantist also extolled the Goddess Principle, composing hymns to the Goddess. In more recent times the influence of Ramakrishna Paramahamsa in the 19th and 20th centuries have resulted in a revival of the Goddess Principle. Ramakrishna was an uninhibited devotee of Kali, the strong and strident version of Shakti.

Quite in keeping with the dates stated for Dattatreya, the earliest Mother Goddess figurine unearthed in India (near Allahabad) belongs to the Upper Paleolithic, and carbon-dates to approximately 20,000 - 23,000 BCE. The practice of Tantra is therefore very old, much older than some people admit. Several manifestations of the Shakti Principle have been mentioned in Tantric texts. Not only do we have the well-known icons such as Durga and Kali. We also have goddesses such as Sheetala, Raktabati, and the Nava Durgas.

Since the Tantrics were convinced that Spirit is primary and all else has descended from Spirit, they began to look for signs that would suggest that, both in the body and mind. Sooner or later, a few gifted humans are born that are able to see things the majority can't... Some of the Tantric practitioners claimed they could see auras around all living creatures, and this is something that has been verified by Kirlian photography in the 20th century. The concepts of etheric body, astral body, and other metaphysical entities emerged. Some advanced sages insisted they could see vortices of energy in some parts of the etheric body and they said these looked like rotating wheels…the concept of chakras was thus born from the Tantric tradition. The chakras were each associated with one color of the rainbow, in order, from the base chakra (red) to the crown chakra which is violet. It is interesting that Violet rays in the spectrum of visible light have the highest frequency, while red rays have the lowest frequency…

Not long after Dattatreya was born a spiritual figure who was to play a big role in the life of the next Avatar the world calls Rama. This spiritual colossus was called Vishwamitra and he was born into a royal family and even became king for a while. Later, he renounced his kingdom and went through austerities in order to become a sage. He is perhaps the first figure of royal background that embraced the life of a renunciate. Many centuries later he would inspire another great soul Rishabha who was also born into royalty to embrace asceticism, and in the process begin a new faith: Jainism.

Vishwamitra's spiritual practices gradually led him to Tantra. His first Tantric teacher was Lord Datta Himself! Lord Dattatreya revealed the Gandharva Tantra to Vishwamitra. It is a conversation between Shiva and Parvati, wherein Parvati asks Shiva to be enlightened regarding certain spiritual matters. However, after satisfying her curiosity, Lord Shiva then proceeds to outline how the Goddess is to be worshipped, including mantras and yantras to be used. Lord Shiva also warns that Tantra contains in it all the opposites (i.e. it is both left-handed and right-handed, and to avoid the left-handed. We will see more about these terms soon).

Sage Vishwamitra soon became more involved with Tantric worship and perhaps this led him to compose what was to become the most well-known prayer in Hinduism: the Gayatri Mantra. However, what is not so well-known is that the popular form of the Gayatri Prayer is actually a shortened form of the original Tantric prayer. Before I give you the long form, here's the short form (or popular form) of the Gayatri with translation:
Om Bhur bhuva suvaha (*Homage to the Universe*)

Tat sa vithur varenyam (the ultimate light of wisdom that we Adore, personified by the Sun)
Bhargo Devasya Dhimahi (I pray that Your Divine Grace illuminates)
Dhiyo Yonah Prachodayat (and sanctifies my intellect).

The above is a simplified translation...It is today chanted by many. Here only the three lower chakras are mentioned.

However, the **long form** (or the *original form*) of the Gayatri Mantra includes a phrase for each of the seven chakras as given under:

Om Bhoo, (*Root Chakra symbolizing the Earth Plane*)

Om Bhoovaha, (*Sacral Chakra / "Astral Plane"*)

Om Soovaha, (*Solar Plexus Chakra / "Heavenly Plane"*)

Om Mahaha, (*Heart Chakra / "Spiritual Balance Plane"*)

Om Janaha, (*Throat Chakra / "Spiritual Knowledge Plane"*)

Om Tapaha, (*Third Eye Chakra / "Spiritual Austerities Pl"*)

Om Satyam, (*Crown Chakra / "Ultimate Truth Plane"*)

Om Tat Savitur Vareniyam, Bhargo Devasya Dhimahi

Dhiyo Yonah Prachodayat (*from the short form*)

And then the prayer concludes with:

Om Apo Jyoti Raso Amritam (*I am part of Universal Spirit*)
Brahma Bhoor Bhoovah Svar Om (*What I am, what I sense, and what I do are all part of it*)

A Tantric who chants those first 7 phrases, will touch the region of each of these chakras on the body as he/she proceeds from the 1st to the 7th chakra. *All the chakras are viewed as ultimately sacred*...An integral view of life as progressing at all these levels.

Tantra probably was being practiced before the Vedic scriptures of Hinduism were put into practice. Tantric practices were however handed down only to a select few through an apprenticeship or guru-student tradition. Vedic chanting however became much more widespread, and therefore has stood the test of time better...

For example, the chanting of certain single-syllable mantras, called Bija mantras, began in the Tantric tradition...There are specific sounds for each of the Goddesses and Gods. Instead of composing longer prayers to the Deities, the Tantrics believed in chanting one word or phrase many times... Some of the common bija mantras are:

Thoom for Durga (<u>th</u> as in <u>th</u>ere), *Shreem* for Lakshmi (the consort of Lord Vishnu), *Kreem* for Kali, and *Aa-eem* for Saraswati. However, to this day, Bija mantras are by and large ignored by the majority, who prefer to learn other mantras and coherent prayers instead.

Also, the use of Yantras or specific geometric patterns came from Tantra. We find a heavy use of triangles, with upside down triangles representing various Goddesses and right side up triangles representing spiritual aspiration or Shiva. A combination of mantra and yantra was sometimes used to calm the mind and focus it.

The most prolific Tantric guru is however considered to be Lord Shiva Himself. He is said to have directly imparted Cosmic and Transcendental Knowledge to His chosen devotees, who were invariably, advanced sages. Lord Datta is also therefore by extension, the father of Tantra. As we saw earlier, He has many attributes, being a combination Avatar. However, since Shiva resides on earth and blesses Tantrics on a regular basis, He is more directly linked with Tantra than Lord Vishnu...

THE BEGINNINGS of YOGA

The whole science of Yoga in some ways is meant to be a layperson's way of practicing Tantra. It is, in other words, a way of making Tantra more esthetic and more accessible to the public at large, or as elaborated below, more "right-handed". Yoga too is a dialogue of sorts between Consciousness and Prakriti.

There is after all, some overlap between Yoga and Tantra. For example, if one practices deep breathing while chanting Om under the instruction of a Yoga teacher, one is simply performing a Yogic exercise. But if one is chanting Om and visualizing the sound of the Om starting from the navel, emerging out of the lower back and then rising up the spine, and finally over the head, one is performing a Tantric exercise. Such an exercise is also reminiscent of Kriya Yoga techniques as taught by Avatar Babaji to Lahiri Mahasaya in the 19th century.

The above Tantric exercise is trying to move energy from the lower chakras to the higher chakras, *one of the primary aims of the Tantrics*. The Tantrics insisted that the Goddess Principle, (i.e., being, energy, motivation), resided in the lower chakras, and a student of Tantra was encouraged to move this energy first to the heart chakra, and thus create a home for the "Goddess" to reside in the heart, while also increasing the devotee's ability to emote and to love.

Now, a so-called dilemma appears: Do we continue taking this energy up even further (like they did in the old days), or should we instead bring Shiva down from the crown chakra to the heart chakra, thus creating a perfect union of Shiva and Shakti in the heart. The most recent Avatar, Lord Sai Baba, revived this meditation called Light Meditation, where one visualizes a light in the third eye region (Shiva) and after a few minutes, the meditator lets the flame move down to the heart, thus in a sense, uniting Shiva and Shakti. Some have preferred to call this a union of the Intellect and the Heart. Love is an important feeling in this meditation...

If one of the purposes of life on earth is to learn how to channel and manipulate our energies, the early Tantrics were the first to become adepts at it...In comparison, modern science and technology, which are also attempts to channel and manipulate energy, focus however mostly on the environment and not so much on the inner world of humans...the relatively recent field of psychology being a possible exception. Also, it must be admitted that in the modern age, the manipulation of brain waves (using technology) in order to create deep states of meditation is becoming fairly popular.

What we call Kundalini Yoga today also has roots in Tantra. The energy or Shakti that we call Kundalini is said to reside at the lowest chakra and it energizes our various instincts. It is the most primordial Prakriti. If the Kundalini is driven up the body, it unites with Shiva who is in the upper two chakras, the third eye chakra between the eyebrows and the lotus chakra at the top of the head... Thereafter, a practitioner's spiritual evolution can progress very quickly, such as the integration of head and heart .

While Tantra came from the Great Gurus like Lord Datta and Lord Shiva, spiritual hunger among humans sustained it. It is a system that later grew from the intuition of sages and seekers, some of whom were brilliant and blessed souls. In the case of the Hindu Tantra adherents, it was a longing for experiencing the fullest spiritual potential of the seeker and a longing for a blissful union with the Universe, and/or with one's preferred Deity or Avatar. It was also a longing for liberation from the limitations of the body/mind/ego complex and to bring about an end to mundane and crude living...

An extension of giving importance to the Female (or Goddess) Principle, is to give importance to any form of union between the Male and the Female Principles, including spiritual, psychological and yes, even sexual union. However, what was the real interest of the Tantrics? It was nothing less than preparing for complete liberation from the cycle of earthly birth and death.

However, in the present Dark Age, or Kali Yuga, Tantra has come to also include the "lesser knowledge" such as magic, potions, spells, exorcism, etc. So, yes, the overall picture is one that might well attract suspicion rather than respect. If one reads the original Shiva Tantras and the Shakti Tantras however, such as the Malini Vijayottara Tantra or the Netra Tantra, one gets a very different perspective. The perennial teachings of Lord

Shiva, long forgotten by modern civilization, give us much light. Fortunately, many ancient Tantras are in the process of being republished.

One needs to make a <u>distinction therefore between right-handed and left-handed Tantra</u>. The left-handed Tantra (Vamachara or Vama Marga) encompasses the less controlled or less esthetic practices such as the use of sexual intercourse and/or alcohol and/or meat in rituals, and later also the use of occult magic, or black magic, etc. On the other hand, the right-handed Tantra practices (Dakshinachara or Dakshina Marga) use more wholesome means, such as spartan living, yoga and breathing techniques of various kinds, mantra recitation, and meditation to achieve ends that are in keeping with the holy teachings of Dattatreya and Shiva.

Lord Dattatreya, in His work called the *Yoga Shastra of Dattatreya*, explains that Yoga is of four kinds: Mantra Yoga, Laya Yoga (or concentrated meditation, such as on some part of the body), Hatha Yoga (the one we are most familiar with) and finally Raja Yoga (which has many parts in it including the above three). According to Lord Datta, sages like Kapila practiced only Hatha Yoga... (It is clear therefore that Kapila preceded Dattatreya).

The science of alchemy which entered the life of Tantrics later is also to be considered a right handed practice, since it was a sincere attempt, not to transform base metals into gold, but to aid in the healing of the ill and the diseased, and to pursue bodily perfection and a long, healthy life.

The left-handed methods appear to have come into being because less adept and less advanced souls began desiring the powers of the right-handed tantrics and sages, but could not match them in austerity or spiritual experience/wisdom. As a result, more base methods began to be used, methods that in the modern age could be described as cathartic, or even wild. The worship of demi-gods by the left-handed tantrics sometimes resulted in powers being obtained by them, and these powers were often employed for material or monetary gain...

A serious spiritual seeker tries to transcend maya (the illusory world of matter, energy, and time). A tantric, on the other hand, when encountering a symbol of maya, recognizes it as the "play of the One". We might call this the "Everything is Holy" perspective...In the case of left-handed tantrics, this could also signify an "end justifies the means" perspective, and of course it has not appealed to everyone...A modern example of somewhat left-handed tantric methods is the 20th century teacher Osho Rajneesh. However, many right-handed Tantric methods are also practiced in the Rajneesh ashrams.

The tantric literature is so vast, and the techniques so numerous, that Tantra almost qualifies to be a religion in its own right. However, perhaps because of its controversial methods and somewhat murky reputation, most works that describe the faiths of the world do not mention Tantra...

Later, a Jain Tantra also came into being, and in keeping with Jainism's philosophy and tenets, the Jain Tantra is predictably mostly right-handed and began after the passing away of Rishabha, the founder of Jainism. Rishabha's deep connection with Lord Shiva quite naturally led to a Tantric offshoot...

The Buddhist Tantra can be regarded as "yet another Middle Way", somewhere between right and left-handed methods, much like mainstream Buddhism itself is. In the Buddhist Tantra one finds again a mention of male and female union as a vehicle of bliss, even if a more earthy bliss, as exemplified by the Tibetan practice of physical union meditation practiced by couples. The couple tries to move the energy upwards to the higher chakras and not indulge in pleasure-seeking however.

Also, the Buddhist Tantra suggests there are deities that can help the practitioner attain enlightenment or at least evolve spiritually and gain better control over one's energy dissipations. The school of Buddhism known as Vajrayana (sometimes called the Third Vehicle) is mostly a Tantric system, based on mantras, mudras (hand gestures) and mandalas (complex geometric shapes filled in with artwork, representing the cosmos, and reminiscent of yantras).

Left-handed tantric methods are usually frowned upon in Buddhism. The Buddha himself would not have tolerated any left-handedness amongst His monks. One of the great founders of Vajrayana, Saraha, was once expelled from a monastery for using alcohol in one of his tantric rituals...

The Thirumandiram, a text that originated in South India, is a very elaborate Tantric work full of mantras and other techniques. It is said to have been written in pieces after intense meditation. The author of this work is Saint Thirumular and it was written in the 5th century AD. The work is a concise description of the main precepts of Dravidian Shaivism with an emphasis on Divine Love, Philosophy or Teachings, the glory and acts of Lord Shiva, Yoga, Mantra, and Tantra Practices, significance of the Shiva Linga, stages of soul experience, and other topics.

There has been a revival of Tantra after the 10th century AD due to the efforts of the Tibetans and also to some extent, the Kashmir Shaivites. The former, who in their Mahayana tradition introduced goddesses such as Tara into their Tantric lore, followed the Tantrics of Indian Buddhism. Incidentally, the name Tara is said to be derived from the word *Tarika* which means the Being that Delivers or Saves.

Indian Buddhists, after the passing away of the Buddha, and following some of the Great Buddhist Councils, ended up creating a host of deities, even though they also spoke of the Void, or the "Nothingness". The Indian Mahayanists developed a dual approach to the Deities....one could meditate on them, or one could pray devotionally to them...This later influenced the Tibetans...

The Kashmir Shaivites, between the 9th and 12th centuries, also revived Tantra. In Kashmir Shaivism, Lord Shiva is considered the ultimate bearer of Universal Consciousness and the follower of this path attempts to merge with the Lord. This branch of Shaivism is also non-dualistic in nature, but differs somewhat from Vedanta. In Vedanta, Brahman or Universal Spirit is mostly passive and the world is Maya or illusion. For the Kashmiri Shaivite, Universal Spirit or Shiva is a bearer of supreme consciousness and is not passive but actively involved, if in an invisible manner. The phenomenal world is Shakti and is in that sense real, while being given meaning by Shiva who causes the whole of nature to evolve and finally merge with Him…thus, we are all limbs of Shiva and are therefore Shiva Himself. Shakti being also a part of Shiva, will always be by His side and do His bidding. In other words, Shiva also has a form and can be interacted with, one on one, while also being the impersonal Universal Consciousness…Vasugupta, the founder of this form of Shaivism is said to have received specific teachings from Lord Shiva…

In Kashmiri Shaivism, secret practices called Kaula practices are advocated for the serious aspirant, and these practices allow him or her to remain a householder, while evolving spiritually towards ultimate liberation. These Kaula practices originate from Tantra. Also, many new Tantric texts emerged and those that emanated from Shiva Himself were called Agama Tantras. Examples of Agama Tantras are the Malini Vijaya Tantra and Netra Tantra.

The Malini Vijaya Tantra in particular, drew the attention of Paul Reps, the author of Zen Flesh Zen Bones and also Osho Rajneesh. It contains 112 aphorisms dedicated to intense mindfulness. It was also a delight for Pandit Lakshmanjoo, a well-known 20th century Kashmiri Shaivite teacher. For these Shaivites the Shiva Lingam is reminiscent of Consciousness rising from the bedrock of Shakti or Prakriti Herself.

The advent of the Bhakti (or Devotional) sects over the last 500 years, especially dedicated to Lord Vishnu or Narayana, led to a diminishing of Tantric knowledge and practices. The balance began to shift towards devotion rather than the seeking of vehicles of transcendence or transformation…Historically speaking, India was being overrun by invasions and incursions, and this had a marked influence on the face of Indian spirituality after the 12th century…Vishnu the Protector and His consort Lakshmi became the refuge once more in the long spiritual history of India. It was therefore not a surprise for Vaishnavites to see the re-emergence of Krishna movements in the world. It seemed like the most natural phenomenon. For had not Krishna saved the world from demons and the Kaurava hordes? Was He not the paragon of Love?

More to follow in the chapter on Krishna...The rise of Krishna worship has led to the re-establishment of entire townships in India, such as Mathura or Dwarka. Saints like Meera have become legendary through their association with Krishna. The legends of Krishna have become common knowledge. And the Movie and Television Industries have reinforced all this quite noticeably.

Chapter Seven

Rama---The Eternal *Hero-Avatar*

Blow O wind to where my loved one is. Touch him and come touch me soon. I'll feel his gentle touch through you and meet his beauty in the moon. These things are a lot for the one who loves. One can live by them alone, that he and I breathe the same air and that the Earth we tread is one.---*Ramayana*

The story of Rama has been performed, danced, and sung in India and other East Asian countries for thousands of years. The most recent Avatar Sathya Sai Baba, was asked during an interview with some visitors from Europe and US, "When did Krishna live?" and the reply came forth immediately, "…5000 years ago". The next question was, "When did Rama live?" and the reply came just as quickly: "20,000 years ago". As if to further emphasize the point, Sai Baba said, "Yes, there was a gap of 15,000 years between Rama and Krishna."

These numbers of course fly against what conventional wisdom tells us. But 20,000 is hardly a figure to become skeptical about….especially when anthropologists tell us that modern man, Homo Sapiens, has been around far longer than that. There is no logical reason to believe that civilization is only a few thousand years old. In fact, such thinking is palpably unsound. I suppose the problem has arisen because for the longest time there were "no artifacts" from over 10000 years ago…but artifacts don't last forever …. Ultimately, all must turn to dust. To have an attitude of "If I can't examine it, it doesn't exist" is an unfortunate and perverse twist of science. One of the points of this book is that Avatars can literally "save us from Science". The ways of the world may be a fiction, but the Avatars are not fiction...

Quite recently, an underwater city was discovered off the west coast of India that has been dated to as far back as 32,000 B.C. And artifacts that are of that age have been found in the ocean bed. The sea sometimes preserves for eons what the land cannot…

The Rama Avatar is an intriguing one…Rama did not try and be a great guru or teacher. Rather, He was a doer and an upholder of noble values, and simply lived His message. Probably the only exception to that is His teachings to Hanuman called the Sri Rama Hridayam.

At times He came across as just another human so to speak….in fact many of the Avatars have that endearing quality about them…. He even appeared to make "errors" and sometimes had to pay a "price"…but when an Avatar is experiencing things one can only speculate whether He already knew the hurdles He would face on the earthly plane…

Anyway, Avatars have a wonderfully detached way of handling the most adverse situations. Adversity merely serves to bring out their message even more clearly, and serves to bring out the best in them and often also the best out of their devotees. The Sathya Sai and Shirdi Sai Avatars are also great examples of having no problem undergoing physical inconveniences, sometimes even to the point of severe physical incapacitation...

Rama became a hero who overcame odds, sacrificed much, and overcame all His rivals, using His considerable power. And later, as ruler He showed His immense compassion and steadfast upholding of the prevailing Dharma (code of righteous living).

He showed exemplary persistence and patience in overcoming His rivals. He was a formidable warrior, and also a renouncer of soft options, along with being an upholder of the highest values. All this ultimately points to the desire to bring about consolidation and preservation of life on earth by overcoming evil and thus creating an enduring legacy that would dissuade other potentially dangerous forces from taking arms against the forces of Good or in other words, the Lord Himself.

Rama was a manifestation of the Vishnu Principle… Not surprisingly perhaps, Rama proceeded to live a life of example rather than teaching. The more primordial Avatars of Vishnu, such as the Dwarf Avatar Vamana and the Narasimha Avatar were also task-oriented Avatars who "spoke through their actions"...The greatness in Rama shows up in His passion for righteous and whole-hearted living, which included a certain dogged persistence against all odds.

In His zeal to create the right environment for Him to teach by example, He approached Kaikeyi, whom history portrays as an evil woman, and said to her, "You are the only one who will be willing to do this, and I beg of you to do it for me. In other words, "You are the only one who will be willing to give up her name and reputation for my sake." He continued, "I want you to somehow convince the king to send me away to the forest for at least 14 years. And tell him Bharat (Kaikeyi's own son) should rule in my absence."

And the rest, as they say, is history... This twist to the Ramayana is not known to most people. It was revealed to the world by Sathya Sai Baba, and it makes perfect sense when one thinks about it...Otherwise, which queen would dare to be so blatant and brazen as to make her sister's son go away to the forest for 14 years, especially when He was already a beloved hero in the community...

And yes, there were tensions around Rama...almost throughout His adult life. Sita, his wife of several decades, at the end gave up her body out of frustration...this was preceded by a period of estrangement with His wife when she was asked to leave the palace and ended up living in a forest ashram...during this time Rama lived very frugally however. The way Avatars pursue perfection may seem intimidating to us in this day and age, but it always appears to come effortlessly to them...

While Avatar Dattatreya did not experience much turbulence in His life, Avatar Rama did, and plagued was He with demons and rivals of various kinds...leading us to feel there were changes going on in the environment even in that early era...Criminality and cunning were beginning to taint public life as society became more complex...However, Rama did have two very strong allies:

his brother Lakshmana and the so-called "monkey god" Hanuman.

By far His most beloved and ardent devotee was Hanuman, a mysterious figure with amazing powers who by many accounts is immortal and was seen by Goswami Tulsidas just 450 years ago. Another sighting of Hanuman happened in the presence of Sathya Sai Baba and some devotees less than 50 years ago.

And speaking of sightings, some people have claimed seeing Rama...such as Swamini Turiyasangitananda and the other being a devotee of Sai Baba who was shown a vision of Rama by Sai Baba's grace. Also it is said some Indian saints such as Tulsidas have beheld Rama.

The "earthly" way of representing Hanuman is to say he was a monkey but he has been described by Rama Himself as a scholar of the scriptures and of grammar, and he had no problem communicating with humans. Besides, Rama did not call Hanuman a monkey but a "Vanara" which means "Man of the Forest". His devotion to the Avatar is exemplary and one is convinced, completely Divine and "pre-ordained".

The other view is a celestial view of Hanuman as a potent Avatar in his own right, and full of celestial love for Lord Vishnu, and therefore for Rama. He belonged to a fairly large clan of Vanaras, who apparently were divine souls sent by the Gods to take the form of primates, and to help Rama in his campaign. The way these "primates" built that bridge from India to Lanka (a bridge visible to this day), it's not too difficult to accept them as divinely empowered creatures...It is also said by some that Hanuman was an appearance of Shiva, but he appears to be more a Shiva-blessed entity than a direct appearance of Lord Shiva Himself, who was endowed with powers by Shiva that proved to be useful at critical junctures in Rama's life.

He can be described as the "lunar partner" of Rama and what a partner He was. The tales of His devotion to Rama are legendary. They moved as one force... That Rama thought of Hanuman to be as worthy of His grace as any human was, is exemplified by the teaching called *Sri Rama Hridayam*, a short but compelling teaching that He imparted to Hanuman, wherein He emphasizes the Oneness of the Universe, by saying that the individual and the Absolute are one. The individual is but a limb of the Absolute, or the One Spirit, called Brahman by the Hindus.

The Sri Rama Hridayam is a simplified version of an even more elaborate and transcendental work, called the **Yoga Vasishta.** One of Sri Rama's gurus was the sage Vasishta, who is credited with teaching Rama when He was a young man, all about the essence of life and emancipation from it. It may seem odd to some readers that a god has to take lessons from a human, but when Avatars descend, they often wish to make their sojourn as typical as possible. Krishna had a teacher for a while, and so did the Buddha, as well as Jesus, in His travels into India. But more of that later in the chapter dedicated to Jesus Christ.

The Yoga Vasishta is one of the oldest teachings in the spiritual history of humanity, preceded only by the works of Dattatreya. It is amazingly explicit in its message to humanity. The Yoga Vasishta is given to us in the form of a dialogue between Rama and the sage, with Rama asking some pointed questions and receiving profound replies from the learned one. We are fortunate indeed that this sage's teachings have been passed down to this day through the oral tradition of Hinduism...

Three great sages played a big role in Rama's life on earth....Vasishta, Vishwamitra and Agastya...Of these, Agastya is perhaps less known than the other two. He was a witness to the battle between Rama and Ravana. The *Aditya Hridayam* composed by Sage Agastya, represents both a prayer to the Sun God, and also the spiritual teachings of the renowned sage that were imparted to Rama, when Rama was in a tight situation. The great battle between Rama and Ravana was going on, and after days of intense fighting, Rama was exhausted...He needed to muster up His strength once again, and Agastya showed Him how to win the sympathies of the Sun God through prayer. The subtle message of this entire episode is that if Spirit and Mind collide, initially it might seem as though Mind is "winning." But it is always ultimately going to be "Spirit over Mind over Matter."

The first two sages, Vasishta and Vishwamitra, were equally dear to the Avatar, even though they were very different individuals, with Vishwamitra having less experience in the spiritual ways than Vasishta (Vishwamitra having been a king at one time, and a relative newcomer to the hallowed life of a hermit).

Apparently there was no love lost between these two sages...they collided somewhat abrasively with each other when Vishwamitra was still a king and had a lot of military power...After suffering defeat at the hands of Vasishta, Vishwamitra is said to have realized the superiority of "spiritual weapons" over material weapons...he then took up the life of an ascetic, and after many years of prayer and penance he was accepted as a "Great Sage" by Vasishta himself.

The Lord however, does not take sides in a situation like this. Instead He reveres both these enlightened figures...one because of his experience/pedigree and the other because of his ability to transform himself radically after pursuing the requisite knowledge and skills (as Vishwamitra did by approaching Lord Dattatreya for assistance). If Vasishta was the thesis and Vishwamitra the antithesis, then Rama was the grand synthesis between the two. In short, the opposites were within him. For example, while showing worldly acumen and even guile when dealing with rivals, He also showed great detachment from worldly comforts, even after regaining His lost power. When His wife had to be let go from the palace because her reputation was tainted, He proceeded to run the gamut of anger, sadness, and humaneness and stop sleeping on His regular bed and instead slept on the floor...In the forest too, He lived very simply for many years, like other forest dwellers.

Did Rama show extraordinary powers such as what one might expect from an Avatar? Did He show unusual powers? One of the first occasions He had to show His supra-human nature was when He not only strung but broke Shiva's bow, which had been placed before Him as a result of a contest between men for the hand of princess Sita. He also ended up killing many demonic creatures that were bigger and stronger than Him, and finally the demon king Ravana, who was considered unconquerable.

But this was not an Avatar that performed miracles or healed the sick or revived the dead. Every Avatar, as Sai Baba has said, chooses His own format. The format can be quite "low-key" for some Avatars...and sometimes the format used is a camouflage, either temporary or long lasting. Sometimes the Avatar starts in a very humble life situation, but ends up making his presence felt in the world.

During Rama's life hardly anyone knew His origins let alone His mission on earth...only a few sages are said to have known who He really was. It took a long time for the word to get around so to speak. Only by the end of His life, did a significant number of people come to know a little about who He really was...an Avatar of Lord Vishnu, who had come to earth to send a clear message to those who stood against the higher and nobler urges that all humans inherently possess, and seek to stunt their development and even throw mud on Divinity. Ravana, the chief villain, is known to have put spiritual hermits and ashram dwellers to death. What he did not realize is that many of these people had already surrendered to the Lord and were therefore His chelas...One of Rama's missions was indeed to make the world a safer place for sages and hermits to conduct their elaborate and long-lasting rituals, without fear.

His wife Sita was considered to be one of the incarnations of Lakshmi. Sita had previously descended as Vedavati, and the evil kind Ravana had tried to abduct her, but Vedavati broke away from him, and cursing him she said she would reappear on earth later and be the cause of his death. Ravana and Vedavati were thus destined to meet in her next life as Sita. And this could be the reason Ravana found himself irresistibly drawn to abducting her from the jungle...One could also look upon the whole thing as a "karmic trap" laid by Lord Vishnu to justify the killing of Ravana later.

The gist of the Ramayana is that Rama was born into a royal family and was the oldest son and therefore the rightful heir. His father, King Dasaratha, had 3 wives and Rama was the son of the oldest wife, Kausalya. However, another wife Kaikeyi wanted her own son Bharat to be crowned king instead. She used all her wiles with the king and got him to agree to banish Rama from the kingdom and live in the jungle for 14 years. She could do this because she had once saved the king's life for which he had said she could ask him for anything at any time in the future, and he would give it to her. She apparently postponed the offer until the time was right….Harmonic convergence (of the situational kind) is very common in the presence of an Avatar.

Rama and his wife Sita, along with his brother Lakshmana, set off for the forest. After some travels and dislocations, Sita was kidnapped by Ravana, who fled with her to Lanka, and imprisoned her in a garden. After a long wait, Hanuman discovers her in the garden, and then is off to tell Rama about her safe whereabouts, following which a plan of attack is developed and then executed, and a long story comes to a partial end with the killing of Ravana.

Both Rama and Ravana were devotees of Shiva. While both had the grace of Shiva, Rama also had the love of Shiva….and of course that wins out in the end. The grace of Shiva is also showered on Rama in the person of Hanuman, who embodies nicely the Shiva principle of selflessness and simple living.

Both Rama and Hanuman are considered cosmic potentates and accessible to this day through prayer and meditation. Yes, even in this Kali Yuga (or age of spiritual and psychological limitations), many saints have claimed that they have managed to have a "darshan" (or visual encounter) with Rama, as well as Hanuman.

The impact of the life of Rama on Hindu culture cannot be overestimated. This 20,000 year old hero has made frequent comebacks into public consciousness, through the lives of saints, seers, and yes, even modern media. The number of Rama temples in India can scarcely be determined because they run into the hundreds. Hindus are convinced that the Rama Avatar is one that inspires us to live lives of trials and tribulations with vigor and unflagging spirit.

If anything, Rama's life tells us that Avatars don't come down to relieve all our burdens and make our lives pleasant. Instead they make us realize that before Good can triumph over Evil, the Good will have to be annealed and strengthened... The eventual victory of good over evil is almost a foregone conclusion, but the time needed is not, and the good will need to make sacrifices, and even fumble and falter sometimes, and still come out smiling. The spiritual evolution of humanity is to a large extent all about just that...Hard lessons can be expected sooner or later.

During His sojourn on earth, Rama went from being a prince/ protector to a wanderer through forests and inhospitable terrain and then through various challenges and triumphs. During His wanderings He never once declared His Divine pedigree. With the result that most people did not know they were in the midst of a spiritual phenomenon, a Divine visitor, who knew that His real days of glory would return only after He left his body...

The Good of Rama is a multi-dimensional Good that covers all planes of existence. Accepting noble mentors on earth was part of that...His chief guru and preceptor, Sage Vasistha, was an enlightened teacher whose student was an Avatar. The combination was dynamite. It resulted in predictable success.

Valmiki, the sage and scribe, through whose writings the world has come to know of Rama, was a contemporary of Rama, and such potent scribes that come into being at the same time as an Avatar are not coincidences. Rather they represent harmonic convergence of the highest order. The presence of other noble souls who descend along with the parent (or Solar) Avatar are also incidences of harmonic convergence.

Similarly the birth of Hanuman and His eternal devotion to Rama can hardly be called a coincidence...This Neanderthal's devotion to Rama was so profound that Hanuman was granted eternal existence on earth. As long as the earth lasts, Hanuman will be with us, according to the scriptures. He has become a beloved icon indeed, embodying the somewhat opposite characteristics of great power and great devotion and earning the title of "most beloved devotee" from Sai Baba.

The essence of the Ramayana according to the renowned sage of the Himalayas, Swami Sivananda, is quite simply, this: the attainment of liberation through the control of the mind. No matter how adverse the situation, a human being must *act,* rather than become overwhelmed by the morass of thoughts, emotions, and lamentation that so many of us are apt to get into. In order to overcome adversity, action is needed. But it needs to be performed with the best of intentions. "Fearlessly doing what is right", is another message of the Ramayana.

The ends never justify the means. Having said that, there is one exception and that is when *one is fighting evil itself.* When one is fighting the forces of evil, both tact and skill have to be employed. The same point is made in the Mahabharata. In the armed conflict between the forces of good and evil, dubious methods are used by both sides. However, ultimately the Avatar Krishna ensures the victory of the forces of the good. Similarly, the Ramayana depicts vividly the victory of the good over the forces of evil, and promises nothing short of the *ultimate* victory of Good over Evil in the future. In fact, this is one of the major aims of all Avatars.

What about karma? The law of Karma is in perfect harmony with the above. The doer of evil will pay the price in the future, though not necessarily in the same lifetime... The fighter against evil does not need to fear, as long as evil makes the first move and refuses to give in...by killing Ravana, Rama did not incur any karma. Rama's prayer and worship of Lord Shiva before embarking on His mission of killing Ravana also protected Him. The power of prayer in mitigating the effects of karma should not be under estimated. All acts, including the campaign against evil, should be offered to the Lord and then the karmic effects will be minimal.

Rama sacrificed so much and did so much to promote righteousness on earth, that His name now has the potency to make us resonate with that ethos that He helped to set up, with the result that we now stand to benefit from His name just by chanting it. This form of human evolution as a consequence of spiritual resonance, is something that has been revived by the most recent Avatar, the omnipresent Lord Sai Baba, who said:

In your heart there is the Soul we call Rama, the Rama who will confer eternal joy upon you. So repeat the Name of the Lord. The Lord's Name is the Sun, which can make the lotus in the heart blossom in full. Lord Rama is not merely the son of emperor Dasaratha, but is the Ruler of Dasa Indriyas (the ten senses). The recital of Lord Rama's Name must become as automatic and as frequent as your very breath. The Lord's name will endow you with power and all the spiritual capital you need. (Many devotees of the most recent Avatar chant the mantra "Om Sai Ram" as they go about their daily lives....Truly all three of these words are potent....)

Swami Sivananda goes on to say: *Mind merges in Brahman by concentration and incessant meditation on Rama. This is the esoteric teaching of the Ramayana. Constant repetition of the two-lettered Mantra RAMA (RA+MA) with Suddha Bhavana and perfect concentration leads to the control of mind and Samadhi.*

Through sensory and mind control, the goal is reached. According to Swami Shivananda of the Himalayas, the secret of Ramayan is the attainment of liberation through control of the mind. Ravana represented all the defects one can find in individuals. If there was a vice, he had it. If there was a mental shortcoming, Ravana manifested it.

Here is another quote by Swami Sivananda: *Sita represents mind. Rama represents Brahman. Sita unites with her husband Rama. Mind merges in Brahman by concentration and incessant meditation on Rama. This is the esoteric teaching of the Ramayana. As you think, so you become.*

The shorter the Mantra, the greater is the concentration needed. So repetition of Rama brings about greater amount of concentration. Several saints have had a darshan of Rama by repeating His name.

Chapter Eight

Hermes: King of the Egyptian Mysteries

Leap clear of all that is corporeal, and make yourself grown to... that greatness which is beyond all measure; rise above all time and become eternal; then you will apprehend God—***Hermes Trismegistus***

Around 8,000 BC, a great soul appeared on the sands of Egypt. This was Hermes Trismegistus, who taught of the One God, and inspired people wherever He went. He was a great and effortless polymath (a being that possesses great talents and/or knowledge in many areas) and was perhaps one of the first polymaths the world has seen.

He was an early alchemist, long before alchemy became fashionable...He was one who effortlessly manifested a high level of subtle knowledge and expertise in many diverse fields,...He taught people around him various things, including science and non-science, and He also pointed them in the direction of Spirit, thus prompting some writers to insist He was a very special case of God in man...About His previous lives and background, few have ventured to say much except that He was, according to Edgar Cayce, one of Jesus Christ's former incarnations... His writings and pronouncements more than suggest that He was the recipient of the ultimate grace of the Lord. He became both God and Guru to His fellow-Egyptians.

The term Trismegistus, meaning "thrice-greatest", was a term of honor to this great soul and the name has stuck, and even created confusion, with some people thinking there were three Hermes', all reincarnations of the same Hermes...Some writers have called Hermes a prophet who saw the coming of Christianity. He was considered to be well-versed by his contemporaries in the fields of astrology, astronomy, and alchemy as mentioned earlier. He urged "purification of the soul".

The Great Pyramid at Cheops is ascribed to this venerable Being and He is considered one of the primary forces behind the design and execution of this and other pyramids. Most pyramids were built on astronomical principles.

Some Egyptologists who have been trained in the West tend to take a conservative view regarding the age of the pyramids. They often claim that the first pyramid was built only around 4000 BC. Spiritual mediums such as Edgar Cayce however, have a different story to tell... The great Pyramid at Cheops is about 10,000 years old, and that is not an outlandish figure because the first Pharoah or king of Egypt was born about the same time. As we know, pyramids are tombs of Egyptian royalty....Perhaps because a pyramid can be described as a "sealed container", the term "hermetically sealed container" is used for any container that doesn't allow heat to enter or leave it...it's a term used in science to this day.

Hermes was probably born in Atlantis, but later migrated to Egypt, as did many others before and after Him. In those times, the valley of the Nile was an irresistible destination for people because of the fertility of the valley and the consequent abundance of food. Many of the Egyptian Pharaohs were spiritually evolved beings who encouraged temple building and spiritual practices. Thus, the Egyptian Mysteries are very ancient indeed. In trance readings Edgar Cayce suggested that thousands of people between 28,000 BC and 10,000 BC migrated to Egypt from Atlantis and surrounding areas. Over a period of time there developed among them prophets, philosophers, poets, etc. The Egyptian civilization was one of the cradles of all the Middle East and North Africa.

The whole philosophy of Hermeticism has seen much resurgence through the ages. In recent times the renewed interest in Gnosticism after the discovery of the Nag Hammadi scrolls has also renewed interest in Hermeticism, since they share similarities... Both Gnosticism and Hermeticism share a love of the personal experiencing of God and of the soul within, and an acknowledgement that liberation from the clutches of the earth only comes through surrender to the Divine and a merging with the Divine...This view of liberation appears destined to make a great comeback over large parts of the globe.

Both Intuition and Direct Experience are emphasized and the role of organized religion is de-emphasized. Hermeticism espouses (as described below) a reconciliation of the opposites within us, and this is an important factor in human spiritual evolution. Hermes was perhaps the first being to openly state the following:

Find your home in the haunts of every living creature; make yourself higher than all heights and lower than all depths; bring together in yourself all opposites of quality, heat and cold, dryness and fluidity; think that you are everywhere at once, on land, at sea, in heaven.

Hermes is a great embodiment of the Shiva Principle of transcending opposites. The great Rishabha, Founder of Jainism, who will be introduced in the next chapter, shares many commonalities with Hermes, and they lived at approximately the same time too. They form the Second Cluster of Divine Descents.

Another Being that belongs to this Cluster is Dipankara Buddha, an embodiment of Sanat Kumara and yet non-theistic in His approach, just like the other two in this Cluster. It was time for some "non-theistic spirituality" and so the world got its first real dose of that...I have put non-theistic spirituality in quotes because all the three embodiments of this Cluster could be very theistic if the situation demanded it. They merely wanted to empower humans in a different manner...

As we have seen before, the First Cluster was made up of Lord Dattatreya, Kapila, Parasurama, and Lord Rama and they form a theistic cluster. And much later, we had the second cluster made up of Hermes, Rishabha, and Dipankara Buddha which was a non-theistic cluster.

Perhaps predictably, the next major Cluster was a theistic Cluster. This 3rd Cluster in human history was made up of Krishna, Vyasa, Melchizedek, Abraham, and Zoroaster. This cluster began around 3000 BC, but went on for a long time (about 1000 years).

The Fourth Cluster was non-theistic: Buddha, Lao Tzu, Confucius, and Mahavira. It was also the time of the Greek philosophers... The influences of this Cluster as well as the Third Cluster are felt widely to this day. However, Clusters 1 and 2 have all but faded out of public memory...

The Fifth Cluster was a theistic one: Jesus Christ, Avatar Babaji, and the prophet Mani. We will see more of them in subsequent chapters.

The next Cluster, a non-theistic one, is made up of Bodhidharma (the founder of Zen), Adi Shankara, Matsyendranath, and Gorakhnath. It would be appropriate to put Shankara into a non-theistic fold because of His emphasis on non-duality and His great debates with scholars, in which He invariably emerged victorious....however, Shankara had a theistic side to Him also, and this side emerged when He interacted with lay people...For example, He installed deities in temples.

The Seventh Cluster is markedly theistic, and in this Cluster we have Heart Masters such as the early Avatars of Dattatreya, Chaitanya Mahaprabhu, and Kabir. This is the longest-lived cluster and in some ways, continues to this day... Ramakrishna Paramahamsa, Shirdi Sai Baba and Sathya Sai Baba can be thought of as belonging to this theistic cluster too, at a time when the number of great Beings has increased in the world. The last two have consolidated greatly the Age of Dattatreya along with others who have been named elsewhere in the book.

Some might say there is yet another cluster in the 20th century, comprised of non-theistic (or perhaps quasi-theistic) beings such as Ramana Maharishi, J. Krishnamurti, and Osho...However, this cluster has not appeared robust enough yet to be recognized as such...for example there are no Avatars in it.

And so we observe a pattern of sorts when we examine the above Clusters don't we: Theistic and non-theistic clusters alternating! This intriguing pattern seems to suggest Balancing

Forces at work... Where there appears to be a balancing force, one could well attribute that to Karmic factors...

Hermes Trismegistus was a legend in His lifetime and was described as "having all the knowledge of the world". He was a very prolific writer and is credited with many works that covered subjects such as the training of priests, science (alchemy, in particular), astrology, philosophy, and spirituality. There is little doubt that other powerful and spiritually evolved Beings also descended on Egypt in even more ancient times. But due to the absence of a strong oral tradition in Egypt, they are lost to us...

According to some, Hermes' writings spread and ended up influencing the spirituality of other cultures in various parts of the world, including India. This is more than likely, since in His writings (such as in the Kybalion which is discussed below, one can see how it could have influenced Buddhism for example). Whether He himself was in turn influenced by the more ancient Dipankara Buddha or by the sages of India is not clear.

He is also credited with authoring the Emerald Tablet, or the Smaragdine Tablet, and some of the more famous statements therein are:

What is below is like what is above.

All things are produced by the mediation of One Being. It is the cause of all perfection in Nature. Its power is perfect if it is changed into action.

Hermes advises us to ascend with wisdom and then again descend and unite the world. This hints at Bodhisattvic reincarnation, later found in Mahayana Buddhism, wherein advanced beings postpone their own salvation to save other beings. The Ancient Egyptians did accept reincarnation. Hermes looked upon the Sun as the mother of all and claimed that its energy "penetrated all things". He looked upon the Sun as the chief representative of the ALL, but also admitted the ALL is beyond true description or ultimately Unknowable. A similar idealization of the Sun has always existed in Hinduism.

In the Kybalion, we have various Principles being enunciated by Hermes. The Principles are:

1. The Principle of Mentalism: All is Universal Mind or Spirit. In the Mind of The ALL, we move and have our being. There is no one who is Fatherless or Motherless in the Universe...and Energy and Matter are subservient to the Mastery of Mind. (In modern times some have called this principle "Mind over Matter"). A Buddhist might relate well to such a Principle.

2. The Principle of Correspondence: As above, so below. As below, so above. Even though there are planes beyond our knowing, applying the above principle we can infer much about these higher planes. It is said the ancient Egyptians used this principle to understand the Goddess Isis and other Goddesses like Hathor. This principle has so many potential applications it would take many pages to discuss them in their entirety...

3. The Principle of Vibration: Everything is in motion. Nothing is at complete rest, because everything vibrates. As Fritjof Capra noted in his book The Tao of Physics: The Dance of Shiva pervades the whole Universe and never stops. Spirit vibrates at the highest frequency of all, and this vibration is undetectable by us and it makes Spirit invisible. Gross matter vibrates at the lowest frequency. Mastery of Life, said Hermes, is using higher frequencies such as mind to overcome the deleterious effects of lower frequencies such as body...

4. The Principle of Duality: Every phenomenon has poles or opposites contained *within* it. Opposites are the same, differing in *degree* rather than in kind...There are two sides to everything... Everything exists and does not exist at the same time. Thesis and Antithesis merge into each other and it is impossible to say where one ends and the other begins...for example, where does "Cold" end and "Warm" begin? Where does Hard end and Soft begin? All are degrees of the same thing...Non-duality aside, this also reminds us of the doctrine of Relativity, and warns of the subjective nature of all judgmental statements regardless of how "true" it may be.

But another important application of this principle is that it is possible to change hate to love, a bad mood into a good mood, etc., by acknowledging that by altering the vibrations or frequency of vibrations we can smoothly go even from one extreme to another…Thus, Alchemy can also take the form of Mental Alchemy and this is the further study of how things like changes in mental states could be achieved. Hermes was a mental alchemist even more than a physical one.

5. The Principle of Rhythm says that everything oscillates in the Universe from one polarity to another. Thus there are action and reaction and they tend to equally compensate each other…Isaac Newton (who was deeply interested in the teachings of Hermes) was inspired by this Principle to come up with his 3rd Law of Motion….To stay in the middle and control one's own inner oscillations is one of the keys to mastery of life itself. Again, this is something that reminds us of the teachings of Buddha. Buddhist meditation seeks to center the meditator between opposing pushes and pulls...

Through understanding this Principle the student of Hermeticism also comes to understand that nothing stays the same, whether the forces of nature, or the rise and fall of nations. Thus emerge the principles of flux and impermanence, the middle ground, and the avoidance of attachment, etc.

6. The Principle of Cause and Effect is stated as: Every Cause has its Effect and Every Effect has its Cause. Everything happens according to Law. By mentally rising above mundaneness, a person can become a Cause rather than an Effect…Also, since every Effect has a Cause, the Effect cannot be more subtle or of a Higher Energy Level than the Cause. Life and Mind cannot rise from the rubble of Matter or even from mere raw Energy or Force. That which is more subtle cannot rise from that which is less subtle, for nothing manifests in Effect unless it is inherent in the Cause…

7. The Principle of Gender: Everything can be looked upon as belonging to one gender or the other, but both genders are present in everything and only their relative amounts vary…thus

Hermes stated the Yin Yang Principle long before the Chinese did (The yin yang perspective was born in China sometime after 100 BC)…Both men and women have elements of both genders within them and so does God, for God created humans in His own image…

The writings of Hermes remind us of some of the perspectives of Gnosticism, and in all probability, the Gnostics took their inspiration at least partly from Him. Also, the old idea that Purusha could not have come from Prakriti and so Purusha precedes Prakriti is something that Hermeticists would relate to. The ALL of Hermes corresponds well with the Brahman of the Hindus.

Was Hermes influenced by Hinduism which had matured in India by then and had probably traveled along trade routes to the Middle East and Egypt. Given His wide-ranging interests and spiritual proclivities, it would not at all be surprising if He was familiar with Hindu spirituality. In fact, concepts like Maya and non-attachment to the body appear in His writings.

Another example of this correspondence:

From a work attributed to Hermes called the Pymander we find the line: "The Father of all things consists of Life and Light, whereof Man is made." A follower of Kapila's teachings might well read this as: The Universe consists of Prakriti and Purusha, and Man is a combination of these two".

From the Pymander: Holy is God Whose Will is Performed and Accomplished by His Own Powers. In the Hindu scriptures God is said to have these three attributes (or energies): the Will to create, the Ability to create, and the Knowledge to create.

In His Pymander, Hermes claims that Cosmic Ignorance is actually to be viewed as a blessing of sorts…for He says: Man is prone to maliciousness and if there is Ignorance, people may actually be wary of doing malicious acts for fear of what is hidden and kept secret…

In a related work, called the Poemander (which is considered the Second Book of the Pymander), Hermes describes having a Blessed Vision of an Angel-like creature that appeared to Him surrounded by light, and spoke to Him, asking Him what He wanted. When Hermes said, "To understand the nature of things and to know God", the Being replied, "I will teach thee". And the Being went on to say, "The Union of Consciousness, the Word of God, the Mind, and the Father (God) is the (goal of) Life."

And so, declared Hermes, "I decided to go and teach Piety and Knowledge." He considered Himself to be a lifelong learner.

Both Gnosticism and Hermeticism are seeing a rebirth of sorts following the discovery of the Nag Hammadi scrolls. We will see more about Gnosticism later. Both movements believe in the final release of the soul as following an ecstatic understanding of God. Until then the soul is bound to the earth...

I'd like to end this section with a quote from Francis Barrett who in his *Biographia Antiqua* said, "If God ever appeared in man, He appeared in Hermes Trismegistus."

Ancient Egyptians---Old Atlantean Souls

I wasn't sure at first if I should include the ancient Egyptians in this narrative. But my interest in them was piqued when I heard of the resurfacing of an ancient Egyptian Goddess into the public eye, and also when I heard of their underlying monotheism...

I am aware of the immense controversy the ancient Egyptians have generated in modern times. Regardless of their racial makeup, it is clear they were a spiritual people who appear to have been greatly influenced by Hermes, though they later had "their own Hermes", in the form of Imhotep, the great polymath and physician.

The spiritual ethos of the Egyptians is considered to be older than Zoroastrianism, Judaism and Christianity. Quite mysteriously, we have what appears to be a culture of pantheists and Nature worshippers also professing a belief in a Supreme

Father... How this "umbrella monotheism" came about is a mystery. According to one writer, Iamblichus, they actually believed in a Supreme One, who was uncreated and omnipotent and all other gods were only attributes of the One... Whether they were also influenced in this by the people of Atlantis is an unresolved question at this point. It is unlikely they were influenced by Hinduism either. So for this writer, there is a missing link or links, that we don't know about, that caused the ancient Egyptians to believe in an Uncaused Cause. If there was an Avatar or Master that actually did this, He is lost in the mists of time...

During the period before Jesus Christ was born, the Egyptians were regarded as a spiritually oriented people, who sought to implement the Hermetic principle of "As above so below" in many aspects of their lives. For example, pyramids were designed to reflect the location of stars in the sky. Thus, there was little difference between the sacred and the worldly or mundane. Everything took place (or could take place) under the gaze of the gods...who were always watching.

For the Egyptians, when nothing existed except the One, the Universe was brought into existence by the Word, or the voice of God. Madame Helena Blavatsky was impressed enough by the ancient Egyptians to write about them. Her book Isis Unveiled is especially well known in this regard...

Recently the Egyptian Goddess Hathor has "resurfaced", and according to the book *The Divine Mother Speaks*, is working closely with Avatar Babaji. This caught me by surprise and I found that even seasoned spiritualists had only vaguely heard of Hathor...Perhaps we should not be too surprised if ancient goddesses resurface, however. Any God Quantum can apparently be called into service at any time...you and I could be called to Divine Service after we leave our bodies...The Goddess Hathor was once worshipped in Egypt by royalty and commoners alike. In this book, the Goddess reveals some of the wisdom of the ancient Egyptian Mystery Schools...

One Egyptian Deity from ancient times was Serapis, now linked to the Ascended Master Serapis Bey. Serapis Bey is a member of the Great Brotherhood and apparently interacted with Colonel Olcott, who was Madame Blavatsky's partner in starting the Theosophical Society. Serapis Bey is said to have lived more than one life in Egypt after having originally incarnated in Atlantis...

Egypt of course is the place where Joseph and Mary sought refuge with their infant Jesus. They lived there until the death of King Herod. The Egyptian Church is almost 2000 years old and is also called the Coptic Orthodox Church. It was established by Saint Mark, one of the apostles. One of the characteristics of this Church is the early development of Christian monasticism which is said to have been born in Egypt...its large areas of desert were considered a place of refuge for the monastically inclined. Great devotees of Christ like Anthony the Great established small spiritual communities in the desert starting from the 3rd century AD...they were apparently followed by hundreds of like-minded people who spent the rest of their lives in contemplation of the Divine, thus leading later to the formation of monasteries. Anthony viewed the desert as a perfect place for purifying the spirit and to become detached from luxuries and possessions... Silence and prayer in addition to spartan living became the hallmark of these early Desert Fathers. By the time Anthony passed away, there were so many people with Him that the desert "became a city" according to writers of those times.

One Coptic of note in recent times was Hamid Bey, who was raised in Cairo, and was trained in an Egyptian Coptic Temple. By the time Hamid Bey traveled to America in 1926, he was already known for feats of mind over matter that even a Houdini would be unable to explain. Hamid Bey met with Yogananda Paramahamsa and they both resonated so well with each other that they began touring the country together. Yogananda would first deliver a speech and later Bey would cause a sensation with his public demonstrations, including multiple live burials, permitting skewers to be stuck into his flesh, and mesmerizing animals, all of which are apparently well documented.

In 1937, Bey moved to Los Angeles and founded the Coptic Fellowship of America. Prior to that year, He had already been ordained as a minister of the Self-Realization Fellowship that had been started by Yogananda. Paramahamsa Yogananda was generous in His praise of Hamid Bey and called Bey an Old Soul and an accomplished Yogi who could demonstrate the power of mind over matter to anyone...Yogananda introduced Hamid Bey as a Master from Egypt and one who could touch someone's pulse and read his or her thoughts...and as one who could remain buried underground for 24 hours in an airtight casket, or even hold a thousand pounds on his chest.

Both these souls are now Ascended Masters. Paramahamsa Yogananda displayed a deep knowledge of Christ Consciousness and even wrote a book entitled The Yoga of Jesus, a fact that was acknowledged by Jesus Christ in modern times during channeling sessions. Hamid Bey is also one who ascended in recent times and is working alongside Masters who ascended centuries ago. There appears to be a wonderful egalitarianism about ascension...

The Mystique of the Australian Aborigines

The Aborigines are a very old race of people and have been on the Australian continent for at least 80,000 years and probably much longer than that. Many spiritual writers, including Blavatsky, have written about a continent-sized land called Lemuria that once lay in the Indian Ocean and extended all the way to Australia and beyond. Certainly the aborigines look like they could be of African descent...One theory is that they migrated along the coast of the Indian Ocean all the way to Australia eons ago.

They are a uniquely spiritual people, practicing spirituality in every aspect of their lives. There are indications they might have interacted with Asians (especially people from India) about 4000 years ago...Even though they had been nomads for thousands of years, they held a deep connection with the land and considered themselves children of it, while at the same time realizing it was a relatively dry and arid land for the most part and not very hospitable...and so one had to move on, and on... There was a sense of oneness with the entire landscape and not just a local spot...

The aborigine had to share everything with everyone else, and that led to a high level of consideration and tolerance. After all, the earth was mother and the earth was always there as a witness...No matter where he walked, the aborigine was at home...All the wonderful things in the landscape were created by ancestors who came from the land, and kept reincarnating so they could continue their good work and participate in the upkeep of the land, thus leading to constant renewal...

If the Aborigines have been around for so long, why should we think of other cultures, such as the Indian or the Chinese as much younger, as the Anthropological Establishment would have it? It's a fair assumption that both Indian and Chinese cultures must be at least that old, if not more. It is becoming increasingly clear that all Asian civilizations are extremely old, and if one is obliged to put a figure on it, one could say at least 50,000 years old.

An aborigine when asked about aboriginal spirituality said:

It is a state of being that includes knowledge, calmness, acceptance and tolerance, balance and focus, inner strength, cleansing and inner peace, feeling whole...

Chapter Nine

Rishabha & Dipankara---Fathers of "Indie Enlightenment"

Equanimity of the mind is the one thing you should strive for. You should learn to receive gain and loss with the same frame of mind. Anger should be conquered and the mind should be brought under control---***Lord Rishabha***

Lord Rishabha, who lived at the dawn of the Agricultural Age, is famously considered, especially by people who subscribe to the Jain religion, to be a father of modern civilization and spirituality, so strong was His earthly presence. The Agriculture Age in India, and in the Middle East, is said to have begun about 10,000 years ago. The Vedas (ancient Hindu scriptures and considered the primary scriptures of ancient Hinduism) had been around for a while but in an amorphous or unorganized form… The Vedas had probably been consolidated during the time called "Ram Rajya" in India, following the departure of Rama from His body. In those pre-agrarian times, life and society were not as structured as they are today…It is not surprising that therefore that Hinduism has never been known for a cohesive and coherent structure or practice…rather it is an undemanding, if unorganized, religion.

Apparently, the time was right for a new approach…An approach that was based more on the emancipation of the spiritual fire in the hearts and minds of individual seekers, who after evolving for several lifetimes, needed a springboard of sorts that would be internally satisfying and bring out one's potential…in other words, the time was right for the likes of Lord Rishabha to flower. And thus was born an emanation of Lord Shiva. I will stop just short of calling Him a Super Avatar though…He just doesn't belong in the same category as full Avatars who revealed truly Divine attributes such as Omnipresence.

A companion avatar in the same Cluster of Divine Beings was Dipankara Buddha, the First Buddha for all practical purposes, who was an avatar of Sanat Kumara, or Subramanya, and who mentored Gautama Buddha (whose name was Sumedha then), and predicted that this Brahmin disciple of His would one day become enlightened and teach the world…He also predicted that Sumedha would be known as Gautama in that lifetime. Sumedha was embraced in this manner after he renounced his wealth to follow Dipankara and also performed numerous acts of love and service to his guru. The legends about Dipankara Buddha are present both in Theravada and Mahayana Buddhism.

Rishabh Dev (as He is sometimes known) was born into a Hindu royal family, and was even king for a while, but later effortlessly renounced His worldly ties and embraced the life of a hermit…He retired to the forest and became a "Sky Clad" seeker of the Absolute, and also a teacher. He was one of the great Spiritual Mavericks the world has seen…and a great exponent of the Shiva Principle (a creative and progressive thinker, willing to initiate change and also embrace a spartan and spiritual life for the sake of human evolution). A "profound and powerful" prayer to Shiva, called the Shiva Kavach, is ascribed to Rishabha. More about this prayer is given below.

Rishabha was a polymath just like Hermes, and is said to have taught His people the rearing of crops and farm animals, the cooking of food, and various arts and crafts. He also taught them warfare, writing, and business principles. Truly a man of many parts and talents (One is reminded of a saying of Sathya Sai Baba: Talent is not a gift from God, talent *is* God), Rishabha quite simply altered the environment around Him, at a time when such a Being was needed… This "many-sidedness" is one of the characteristics of Beings manifesting the Shiva Principle and was also displayed by Shiva Descents such as Adi Shankara. The many-sidedness appears because of a highly developed evolutionary impulse within them…an impulse that causes them to become prime movers of society and literally steer people in a different direction.

Thus, apart from Darwinian Evolution, we have this kind of much more speedy evolution of mankind, caused by the Grace of Deities and Avatars or Spiritual Mavericks. Other polymaths who have appeared throughout history in all parts of the world are Aristotle, Leonardo Da Vinci, Copernicus, and Michelangelo.

Lord Rishabha has been linked by some to Lord Vishnu, but His incredible austerity and ultimate enlightenment remind us of Shiva, the most austere and ascetic Lord, who has lived for eons in the snow-clad and pristine wilderness of Mount Kailash in the Himalayas... Rishabha's tenure on earth at around the same time as Subramanya's Descent as Dipankara Buddha is also in keeping with the nature of like-minded Avatars to appear together...We will see more about Dipankara Buddha when we look at Buddhism. Dipankara Buddha also led a very austere life indeed.

The royal period of Rishabha's life is hardly known but the period of His wandering as a renunciate is, following which he was able to teach and inspire many lay-people. So many people were spiritually influenced that He ended up starting a movement which later blossomed to become the world's first non-theistic religion, Jainism.

Rishabha is called the first "Tirthankara" or Enlightened Master of the Jain religion. He was followed by 23 others, the last being Mahavira, who lived during the time of Gautama Buddha. Perhaps quite predictably, the number of Jain Tirthankaras and the number of Buddhas before Gautama are about the same...

Jain spiritual history is therefore long and was reasonably well-documented in a tightly preserved oral tradition. Jains are strict vegetarians and often exhibit philosophical and transcendental interests to this day... That the Jain religion takes spiritual growth very seriously is evident from passages like this from the Saman Suttam, a Jain text:

There are... stages in the path of gradual spiritual development and final emancipation... (Some of the critical steps are): Moving from faith to the observance of vows, then moving to vigilance, then to new forms of bliss never experienced before, then to meditation, and then to destroyed delusions and finally to omniscience...It should be understood that emancipation is attained in stages.

One of the critical phrases in the above is the injunction to move from faith to the observance of vows. Thus, in the Jain view, faith can lead to complacence but observing vows strengthens one's resolve...The reference to "new forms of bliss" is akin to "minor enlightenments" (a term also used in Buddhist literature) and insights into the workings of life and also the higher consciousness inherent in man. In the Jain view, one who can successfully go through all these stages, can reach the state called Kaivalya, which is a highly empowered and independent state, where the soul has also become free of karma, and thus attains freedom from "the inanimate and the soulless", or in other words, is no longer subject to reincarnation on earth, and gains the Absolute, which is Soul or Spirit. Such a being instantly moves to a heaven where there are similar souls and resides there permanently.

Rishabha is said to have attained "final bliss" at Ashtapad Mountain in the Himalayas, i.e., He left His physical body there. *Ashtapad is a mountain located next to Mount Kailas, the home of Lord Shiva...* Incidentally, the word Kailash means crystal, and the mountain is one of the first and greatest spiritual vortices on earth. This mountain is revered by people of the Hindu, Buddhist, and Jain traditions. Many people have reported seeing mysterious lights floating in the air in the middle of the night above Lake Manasarovar which is at the foot of Mount Kailash at a height of about 15000 feet above sea level. The peak of Mount Kailash is about 21,000 feet above sea level. The area, in spite of being very remote, is beginning to attract an increasing number of pilgrims and seekers from all over the world.

There are Jain scriptures that describe some of the previous lives of Rishabha...and one can therefore ask the question, was Rishabha an avatar or was He more a great Chela (or protégé) of the Lord. A Chela typically tends to evolve over lifetimes like an Ascended Master of the Great Brotherhood does. In any case, the great Chelas or Spiritual Mavericks in this 2nd Cluster were formidable beings indeed.

One might venture to say that other examples of Cosmic Chelas or Spiritual Mavericks are the various sages of old such as Sage Vyas, Avatar Babaji, Bodhidharma, Gorakhnath, Ramana Maharishi, Nisargadatta Maharaj, Meher Baba, and many others. In a sense, they are neither Avatars nor Ascenders...at least within the limits of our understanding.... and yet all the figures named above have made unique and significant contributions...they all appear to be recipients of uncommon grace and mentorship even though on the surface they may appear to be very independent beings. We shall see more about that later.

Saints of every religion, like St. Teresa of Avila, Hildegard of Bingen, Rumi, and Ramakrishna, are also examples of Mavericks who have displayed higher sensitivity. Without trying to be prime movers, they end up being inspirational, and bring a new and heightened flavor to the spiritual life of the people around them.

In all of the above individuals one can see the power of the Highest Consciousness that is closest to Spirit. Many sages fall under this category, and they have appeared through the ages. Included are people who spontaneously develop marks of the Crucifixion of Christ on their palms (called Stigmata).

Mavericks usually display one or more of the following characteristics:

- They tend to show transcendental tendencies or uncommon devotion from a fairly early age.

- They tend to be guileless and yet mentally strong. They tend to avoid being worldly wise (i.e., tend to not indulge in any manipulative behavior or "street smartness" in modern parlance).

- They tend to live effortlessly and spontaneously. They appear to achieve all things effortlessly...and receive uncommon grace from a Deity or Avatar.

- They tend to have many sides to them, or in other words, they tend to be made up of many parts…and yet they display detachment from the world at large. They care little for recognition or more mundane forms of self-actualization. In fact, renunciation seems to be "built in" to their fundamental make up.

- They tend to be original and non-conformist in their approach to the Higher Life.

- They often have an astrologically auspicious birth and are the recipients of both Divine Grace as well as "Divine Trials", extending to sometimes rather severe tribulations, especially of the body. Really advanced Mavericks will even embrace such trials effortlessly, because their Spirit is driving that impulse from within…

Leading a spiritually exemplary life, Rishabha was worldly and other-worldly at the same time. Another indication of his strong connection with Lord Shiva is Rishabha's teaching a prince who had lost his kingdom to rivals how to chant a special prayer to Lord Shiva called the Shiva Kavach (or the Armor of Shiva), and as the legend goes, that prince succeeded in winning back his kingdom. The Shiva Kavach is a wonderful prayer to Lord Shiva interspersed with meditation to increase the potency of the prayer. Some of the phrases that Rishabha uses to describe Shiva are:

- He who gives all powers.

- He who is full of eternal joy and lives in the lotus of everyone's heart.

- He whose innate luster spreads all over the sky.

- He who is beyond the senses.

- He who is endless and beginning less.

Today, even some Jains acknowledge his link with Lord Shiva. He has all the hallmarks of Lord Shiva, in the way He displayed great detachment, embraced silence and meditation, and became a flag bearer of societal change. Any Manifester of the Shiva Principle will exhibit the tendency to shake the status quo and not accept conventional roles. And He will embrace great austerity and fortitude. Lord Rishabha exhibited all these characteristics.

It is fairly clear that Rishabha considers Lord Shiva to be as close to the ultimate Godhead as any deity can possibly be. This awe-inspiring prayer was not made available to the masses of the time however. Instead it was taught to only a select few...to this day it is a not very well-known hymn, either among Jains or Hindus...

According to the Bhagavata Purana however, Rishabha is said to be an Avatar of Lord Vishnu... The Bhagavata Purana is a Vaishnavite text, which means it came from devotees of Lord Vishnu. The divisions between Vaishnavites and Shaivites have unfortunately reared their head over the centuries and continue to this day. Adi Shankara saw this long ago and tried to bring the two sides together with his Smartha Sect which we will examine later. This rivalry has spilled over into modern times and the media also. TV series have been made on both Lord Vishnu and Lord Shiva and have tended to be biased in the coverage of their own Lord's Divine status and potency...

In the Jain religion, Lord Rishabha is the First Tirthankara or First Enlightened Sage, and this religion became the "Religion of Sages and Saints". The Enlightened Sage became, for the first time, a personage of so much sacredness and importance that He began to be seen as a substitute for Divinity itself. Suddenly, to at least a limited cross-section of people, He became a God and even surpassed God in relevance. He became a refuge, a practical guide, and also a transcendental guide, who had merged with the Absolute, in spite of having been subjected to worldly pleasures and wealth from a young age.

The fact that such an impetus comes from the God Quantum within (or the Shiva within) was lost on some people, who, quite reasonably, thought of all such overt human effort and accomplishment as an Isolated Phenomenon. And thus the Jain religion was born which honors such "Newly Born Lords". This religion has never had more than a few million adherents at any point in time, but the main point is, it has stood the test of time, and is now a respected and stable religion in modern India. The Jains are known for their piety, their strict adherence to vegetarianism, and their great regard for all living entities, no matter how humble the life form may be…

Lord Rishabha, after many years of meditation, reached the highest state of consciousness, called at that time "Kaivalya", and attained liberation, even while in His physical form.

So, it seems somewhat ironic to us….the Inner Guru Shiva prompts Lord Rishabha to teach the Shiva Kavach to only a few ….with the indirect result that Rishabha begins to be seen as a "self-evolved" saint by the masses…He then becomes the Founder of a non-theistic religion grounded in the exaltation of beings that renounce the world and enter into the meditative life…. But it's all part of the Divine Sport, for the Lord who sports within us. Since Lord Shiva is the Lord Transcendent, and oversees everything, we don't have to worry about such ironies. Everything is for the good ultimately. The Jain religion has played its own role in bringing us closer to transcendence.

Meanwhile this religion is now making its presence felt in the western world also. However it is seen as a somewhat austere and other-worldly religion and not so much as a religion that is accessible to one and all…It is a religion that is founded on compassion, restraint, a love of knowledge, and finally, a search for enlightenment.

I would like to emphasize that <u>neither Avatars nor Mavericks want to start a religion.</u> <u>It is their earthly followers that end up bringing in a structure, organizing things, and thus creating a religion.</u> The religion invariably emphasizes only some aspects of the founder, and downplays others. Also, a hierarchy is often created and middlemen spring up, purporting to be the true ambassadors of the founder. Sooner or later, factions spring up and the religion splinters into two or more groups. Over time, the founder's charisma and message can even diminish, and the spirit of the original teachings become somewhat tainted by more earthly considerations.

I would like to conclude this section on a momentous Maverick and Old Soul, by noting his stirring words regarding Lord Shiva:

He who is the form of "Om", He who is the divine ether...He who is the teacher of the world, He who is a witness of the world, and He who is hiding in all reasoning, may He protect me.

In this quote we find a stirring description of the one who Rishabha thought was the Ultimate Deity of Consciousness and who could therefore nurture any soul that He wished.

Chapter Ten

Zoroaster---Clarion Call for the One God

Doing good unto others is not just a duty; it is a joy---
Zoroaster.

According to more than one source, Zoroaster lived well before the time of Abraham. His native (Iranian) name was Zarathustra, and He was one of the first great Prophets of the Middle East and a great mono-theist who adored His God, Ahura Mazda (one translation of this name is: Wise Lord). Zoroaster has been recognized as an Ancient Prophet and a Devoted Visionary by both Sai Babas.

It is fairly widely accepted in esoteric circles that Ahura Mazda was none other than Lord Sanat Kumara (or Lord Subramanya), and Zoroastrianism was perhaps the first religion that originated from Him, though as we have seen, the seeds of His teachings had been on earth since the time of Dipankara Buddha...

Lord Sanat Kumara (who it is said, descended again as a son of Lord Krishna around 3000 BC), was "more successful" however, with His second world-recognized religion, Buddhism, if in an indirect manner, and was even more successful, in terms of the sheer number of souls influenced, with Christianity through His Cosmic Brother Jesus Christ. These three religions came into existence in that chronological order, thus suggesting a Growing Presence on earth for Lord Sanat Kumara...It is not a coincidence that Buddhism once had a fairly strong presence in Iran and the Middle East and reached there fairly quickly after the Buddha left His body...

Zoroastrianism took the Middle East from tribalism to becoming a more introspective and organized society, thus paving the way for the evolution of Judaism/Christianity on the one hand and Islam/Sufism on the other. It is reported that Ahura Mazda revealed to Zoroaster that in the future the Christ would come and save many souls...

Zoroaster is a Prophet and Master belonging to the Third Cluster of Beings referred to earlier. He was in all probability chosen because of His ascension over lifetimes, thus making Him an Ascended Master of sorts... Lord Sanat Kumara, now wearing a more theistic hat, guided and gave His energy to this new religion and so it's not surprising that it has stood the test of time and is practiced to this day, if in modest numbers.

Legend has it that one day when Zoroaster was at the Daiti River bathing Himself, a being of light (in all probability an angel) appeared to Him and led Him to Sanat Kumara, who was quite open to teaching Zoroaster directly and this made Zoroaster a Master quite rapidly and then a teacher of the masses...and an author of the Avesta, the religious scripture of the Zoroastrians.

Zoroaster was introduced to Archangels, to the importance of a pure life, and also to the purifying rites of fire worship, and thereafter Zoroaster was particularly attracted to both purity and to the purifying nature of fire and also reportedly saw things in fires that no one else did...This is not uncommon...in modern times photos have been taken of Deities and other celestial beings appearing in sacred fires...For Zoroaster, the homogeneity of all fires attested to the purity of fire itself. In what is now called Chak-Chak in Iran, Zoroaster lit a fire that burns to this day.

It is apropos to note here that in the Vedic religion too, fire has a special meaning, and the influence of the Vedic religion on Zoroastrianism is very apparent. Fire, in the Vedic lore, is literally the "mouth of God", and it is said that if the appropriate mantras are chanted, a fire can be used to send things to one's chosen Lord or Heaven-occupants, simply by letting it burn to ashes in the fire...The very first line of the Rig Veda says: "Let us venerate Agni, God and minister of the Fire Ceremony, and a bestower of treasure par excellence."

Perhaps because He strongly believed in the potency and purity of fire, Zoroaster taught that fire would become impure if bodies were cremated, and nor was it appropriate to tarnish the earth by burying the dead, and so was born a unique way of disposing off the dead: Corpses are deposited in a remote and/or high elevation such as a hill top, where vultures and other birds of prey or even wild animals consume the body…

While Zoroastrianism has had to bear the burden of subsequent alterations through the millennia, Zoroaster's teachings reflect the Shaivite influence of Sanat Kumara. For example: Time is not to be viewed as just the rise and fall of cyclic seasons…The Universe has a beginning and an end…(since <u>Lord Shiva will one day destroy the Universe, calling the Great Experiment to an end</u>). Meanwhile, it is the responsibility of the Good to ensure that a victory over Evil is attained, and so man needs to "side with God" in more ways than one. Moreover, God is accessible to all who embrace Good and avoid Evil. Thus, leading a moral life is one of the kingpins of this religion, and Zoroaster was the first Prophet to emphasize this, and long before Moses came down the mountain carrying the Ten Commandments. Zoroaster took the focus away from ritualism to personal conduct as a way of getting closer to God.

Zoroaster preached that the best desire to have is to desire God. Thus He says in His Gathas (or Teachings):

"…Tell me truly, O Ahura Mazda, the religion that is best for all mankind--the religion, based on truth… the religion which establishes our actions in order and justice by the Divine Songs of Perfect Piety, and which has, for its intelligent desire of desires, the desire for Thee, O Mazda!"

While an emphasis on monotheism was apparently needed during those tribal times, the way it panned out was that all other Divine figures were construed as being automatically separate from Ahura Mazda, and in a sense pretenders, and therefore "anti-Ahura Mazda". Thus the very word "Daeva" (from the Sanskrit word for God: Deva) became turned around and instead was used to refer to a devil…There just wasn't room for more than one Divine Being…

It may be worthwhile to point out here that the monotheism of Zoroaster was more functional and ethical while the monotheism of India was more contemplative and spiritual. Such an active form of monotheism combined with the notion of continuous battle between the forces of good and evil, leant Zoroastrianism a certain aggressive hands-on flavor… Zoroaster frequently prayed to His God for victory over His enemies. Man's role became defined as "active collaborator with God."

Another Iranian prophet, Mani, who founded Manichaeism, lived around 250 AD. There are commonalities between Zoroastrianism and Manichaeism. To his credit, Mani was an integrator of various religions including Hinduism, Buddhism, Christianity, and Zoroastrianism. His religion actually flourished for quite a while after his passing away… However when he began promoting himself as a superior alternative to all the above religions, he ended up with more detractors than devotees. His insistence that he was another apostle of Christ did not help matters…He was incarcerated and later put to death. His very existence came to light only in the 20th century upon the discovery of some ancient scrolls… While he has attracted the attention of some religious scholars, he remains largely an unknown and unsung prophet who however had the gift of speaking and writing, both of which he apparently did quite copiously. On being persecuted, many of his followers fled to China, where apparently his movement lasted until about the 15th century.

Manichaeism is an example of a religion that did not have a Divine sponsor such as Lord Sanat Kumara and therefore petered out. It takes a lot of energy to begin a path that stands the test of time…and we are mostly talking about spiritual energy of the kind that can be provided most effectively only by a true Master or Deity…

Zoroastrianism lives on, mostly in India and in a few pockets in Iran and the West. The Zoroastrians in India are known as Parsis. When they migrated to India from Iran about AD 900, they brought this already ancient religion with them. In a sense, this was a Coming Home, because they were coming to the home of Lord Sanat Kumara. The Parsis have definitely brought with them a flair for the spiritual life.

Chapter Eleven

Lord Krishna---Heart Master and Hard Master

Develop thirst for Krishna, and you will discover the cool spring of bliss within you. The name of Krishna makes you strong and steady, it is sweet and sustaining. Whoever has the thirst, Krishna will quench it---***Sai Baba***

Avatars inspire us because they often are a perfect combination of head and heart. And so, the story of Krishna continues to this day. His spiritual presence and influence on earth will never cease, because His devotees are continuously calling on Him…

One can think of at least 4 Beings who have had direct contact with Krishna in the last 500 years: Meera the Indian saint, Narsi Mehta, who lived in Gujarat, Chaitanya Mahaprabhu who was born in Bengal and who was a devotional lighthouse, and Srila Prabhupada, who in the 20th century did what appeared to be almost impossible at one time: Resurrect the name of Krishna all over the world.

Real contact with Krishna is rare of course, but not uncommon. George Harrison of the Beatles was once convinced that Krishna heard him refuse a sum of money to a devotee that was needed for publishing a Krishna book, and at that very moment a bolt of lightning made a loud noise just outside the house, and made George's home completely dark for some time…when the lights came on again a couple of minutes later, George smiled, and immediately agreed to sponsor the book, saying, after this kind of event, what else could he do?

The saint Meera of Rajastan was a remarkable devotee of Krishna, and was often seen not just singing about Krishna, but describing her frequent encounters with Him, including things like somewhat mundane indoor board games, card games, and the like, with Krishna as her sole playmate. An attempt to kill her failed, as nothing happened to her even after she drank a poisonous brew…

As we have seen before, Krishna belongs to the "Kapila Stream" of Avatars. What then about Krishna's links with Rama one might ask, as is traditionally presented...? After all, Kapila and Rama were quite unlike each other....one was a great spiritual teacher, and the other a great Dharmic king, a supreme vanquisher of evil beings and an upholder of idealistic living. If Kapila is the "thesis", and Rama the "antithesis", then Krishna is the grand synthesis between them...He was (literally) both Guru and King. Krishna was a great "summative" Super-Avatar of the era before the Modern Age of Darkness began (i.e., the era before Kali Yuga).

The legends surrounding Krishna are so colorful, and His teachings so inspiring, that in many enclaves of the world (due to the efforts of some organizations like the International Society of Krishna Consciousness founded by Srila Prabhupada), the adoration of Krishna never ceases. Given that He lived 5000 years ago and long before the advent of recorded history, this resurgence is quite remarkable, to say the least. However, it is not surprising because this Avatar displayed extreme potency and astonishing extroversion. And also, the timing of all this appears to be no accident or coincidence but rather a ripening of spiritual vibrations whose time has come...

Books and other writings about Krishna have seen a new resurgence...His devotees are also now beginning to branch out into other fields, and trying to relate the old with the new...spirituality with science and revelation with rationality, with well laid out arguments...Some decades ago, the Science and Religion Conferences began to be held, and we also had the ISKCON movement try and do the same thing during the second half of the 20th century...

Lord Krishna's life-story has been told and retold through the centuries a myriad number of times, and yet seems to remain fresh to this day. His antics when a child, His playtimes as a teenager, His grand umbrella of protection bestowed to the people around Him, His killings of unholy beings of various kinds, and His teaching of Arjuna on the battlefield, all spark awe and delight at the same time. He is the folk-hero par excellence among Hindus all over the world.

His life and message appear to advocate a multifarious relationship with God. The devotee is exhorted to look at Krishna as a nurturing mother, a benevolently stern father, a spiritual teacher and guide, a friend, and also Godhead descended in human form. During His life He gave people all these signals…

The recent efforts of Srila Prabhupada and Kripalu Maharaj to bring Krishna into focus have borne fruit in various parts of the world. The Festival of Chariots is now celebrated enthusiastically in many countries and in all continents. Krishna is fondly worshipped not only through ritual, but also song and dance. However, the tendency to over romanticize is quite apparent, even in modern times. This often leads to certain wisdom aspects of the Avatar's teachings not being given enough importance….This is perhaps due to the emphasis on a certain Innocent Faith and Devotion when it comes to Krishna, rather than an analysis of His teaching or a desire to get into His more abstruse teachings such as those found in the Uddhava Gita…

Any discussion of Krishna's life is somewhat incomplete without a mention of some great Beings that accompanied Him to earth, such as Radha the Great Gopi and Devotee of the Lord, the great Sage Vyaas, and Krishna's brother Balarama. They were all special in their own right…Radha was the ultimate devotee (and not romantic lover), of Krishna. In fact, she was older than Krishna, and first spent time with Him when He was very young indeed. Why is she held in such high regard? There have been some amazing signs of their Oneness. For example, Radha was born blind. For the first few years of her life, she lived in darkness. One day Krishna and His parents visited her family when Krishna was about 4 years old….and then she opened her eyes for the first time…When the Cosmic Soulmate appeared, the eyes opened to behold Him.

She would spend most of her waking hours with Him after that…Krishna lavished attention on her, and kept reassuring her that one day the world would hold her in high regard and remember her devotion. There are some devotees today who insist that Radha was a manifestation of Shakti or the Goddess of the Universe (one of whose manifestations is Parvati). Interestingly, Shakti is also called Narayani, i.e., sister of Narayan (Lord Vishnu). Thus, Narayani is another name for the wife of Lord Shiva, and she is also called by the more well-known names of Parvati and Durga.

After what seemed like an Eternal Youth of playful pastimes in their village, one day, Krishna moved away, because He had much to do...Radha was heartbroken but continued her life with courage...Now and then Krishna would send her a missive or a messenger...but they did not see each other much again. The Lord left His beloved Devotee behind for the sake of humanity, content on being reunited with Her after their physical sojourn on earth.

In the ultimate analysis though, the Bhagavad Gita, considered to be Krishna's primary teaching is perhaps not as well known or appreciated as one might expect...Even in India, the Gita is not so widely read, and that is of course disappointing to more enlightened Hindus. And why is this happening, one may ask. There are several possible reasons... For a long time (for several centuries) it was very difficult to even get hold of a teacher or transmitter of the Gita, since spiritual works were often over-zealously guarded. India's caste system ultimately led to the scriptures being the privilege of the few rather than the many.

One of the ways the Gita might have found its way into public consciousness is through discourses given in temples by various sages and gurus. But Krishna's life and pastimes were so much more interesting to a semi-literate population than intellectual stimulation that they overwhelmed public discourse about the Gita. This phenomenon exists in India to this day...

Hinduism has done a poor job of disseminating the spiritual riches that it possesses. There was a tendency to hoard spiritual knowledge, and even to consider certain human beings as being "unready and unfit" to receive spiritual knowledge. The most recent Avatar, Sathya Sai Baba, however, has been found to talk to even poor peasants about the highest spiritual principles. Once when some of His devotees asked Him why He did that, Sai Baba responded that even though talking about the soul and spirituality may not appear to make an impression on such simple folk, some lifetimes from now, the spark lit by Him would manifest itself...I am reminded of what Krishna says in the Bhagavatam, *"I have lit the flame and implanted the sound of Om in all living creatures."*

And now, in the post-modern world of today, the Bhagavad Gita and its transcendental teachings seem remote and archaic to young minds that long for other sources of satisfaction and fulfillment...efforts to put the Bhagavad Gita in motel rooms in the US notwithstanding.

Even less known than the Bhagavad Gita is the Uddhava Gita, a more spiritual work than the former, and Krishna's final teaching, imparted to His friend Uddhava, shortly before He left His body. The Uddhava Gita is replete with spiritual wisdom as well as revelation. There is a tone of authority as well as austerity in the Uddhava Gita that is awe-inspiring. These words could only have come from a supremely Divine Being.

Throughout this teaching, the Lord makes frequent references to the Self, or Universal Self. What is this Self? Lord Krishna explains, like Lord Kapila did many centuries before: *The Self or the Purusha is the One who has pervaded the entire universe. He is causeless and attributeless.*

The setting is as follows: Uddhava implores Krishna to take him along when He leaves the world to go back to His Heavenly Abode, but Krishna gently refuses. He tells Uddhava to instead become a spiritual ambassador. He then proceeds to impart a profound teaching to one of His favorite devotees, and in so doing, leaves no stone unturned...

The transcendental and materially simple life is vigorously promoted in the Uddhava Gita, and that is both its attraction as well as an intimidating factor for a lay person....If the book is persisted with however, its value is immense. The Uddhava Gita has become, unbeknownst to many, a pivotal text in the spiritual history of mankind. Here are a couple of examples of its influence:

In one section of this Gita, Krishna makes reference to Dattatreya. This simple act has done much to resurrect and sustain the name of Dattatreya in India. 15,000 years after the passing of Lord Datta, an Avatar resurrected His name. Also, in the Uddhava Gita, Krishna speaks of the limitations of heaven itself, and describes it as having its share of envy and rivalry, and He even describes heaven as being a place of contamination, waste, and decay! Such words from the Lord make it appear as if Krishna's intentions were to draw His devotees to Himself, rather than the heaven inhabited by miscellaneous beings in various stages of spiritual evolution...

Krishna also says, once the karmic effects of heaven wear off, one would return to earth... A wise person, Krishna says, "prizes neither heaven nor hell", but rather to merge with the Lord (i.e., a Super Avatar like Himself) who is virtually the same as Universal Spirit. Krishna then speaks of the presence of worlds that are more pure and transcendental than heaven itself. He even names these transcendental worlds and declares them to be the final abodes of great yogis and sages...

Krishna's words in the Uddhava Gita suggest that any pure and spiritual person can attain liberation, with or without the direct grace of the Lord. However, given the limitations of the age we live in, the path of Devotion to the Lord is considered by many to be the most prudent and the swiftest.

The Buddha also appears to have been fully aware of the worlds "higher than heaven" and also fully aware of the limitations of heaven. It is popularly believed that the Buddha was an atheist or God denier. Far from it, the Buddha actually openly acknowledged the presence and existence of gods, even making statements like, "Indra became the king of the Gods because of His powers of discrimination." We will return to this topic in the chapter on Lord Buddha.

In the Uddhava Gita, just as in the Bhagavad Gita, Lord Krishna asserts that the world is not to be taken too seriously, since it is really of no great consequence at all... Speaking from the vantage point of Spirit, Krishna says, the immortal Universal Self alone exists, or if you will, God Alone Exists. And so, the path of Love becomes a sufficient path....Devotion and Surrender to the Lord will lead a person to salvation, by the grace of the Lord....Krishna was looking at the Kali Yuga which was looming ahead when He taught these principles to the world...

In the Uddhava Gita, Krishna declares Himself to be Vishnu, the ultimate Preserver of the Universe and its Consolidator. He speaks about Evolution and alerts us all when he says: *The devotee who aspires to Divine heights will be tested.* The body and mind of such a devotee will be made to go through certain rigors and that is all part and parcel of the evolutionary spirit in which the lord moves. In fact, the more evolved a devotee, the more extreme the tests and hurdles usually become...Out of compassion for the rest of humanity, and in the spirit of service, the more evolved souls have to be willing to take the heat...

As mentioned before, one of the self-professed aims of Krishna was to prepare humanity for the tumultuous times that He knew lay ahead. The Hindus call the current Dark Age "Kali Yuga" and it began 5000 years ago during the last few years of Krishna's physical presence on earth. And as if a premonition of things to come, this Avatar's life was almost always spent in overcoming petty rivals, non-believers, and outright enemies, who were out to cripple Him. If the non-believers beheld an inexplicable miracle by Him, they declared Him to be merely a sorcerer, seeking fame and temporal power. Such practices continue to this day, but the people who say these things hardly ever go into the teachings of the Avatar...and they don't speak with the direct disciples or apostles of the Avatar. Later, when the Avatar outlasts all His detractors and continues to go from strength to strength, His inherent Divinity becomes more clear.

And let me hasten to add that just like there were exemplary devotees of Krishna during His life on earth, there are exemplary devotees now, and they have sprung up throughout the ages...But the number of pitched battles and wars that Krishna was involved in is quite high indeed.

So it was no bed of roses for this Avatar. Much was and is, said of Him: that He lived in a palace, that he had thousands of wives, and that He was a war monger as well. But when the Universal Spirit itself descends to earth, can we demand that such a Being follow the practices of ordinary human beings? Indeed not…for the morality of convenience that society weaves unto itself is not something that should be thrust upon an Avatar, who has descended out of Love for humanity. Like Jesus, He had no qualms about bringing on the heat: Fire, sword, and war. His so-called thousands of wives resulted from liberating women who were in the harems of His powerful enemies who were invariably kings and/or scoundrels.

It was around 3000 BC that Krishna left His physical body, and it is one of the great "transition times" in human spiritual history, according to both the Mayan and Hindu calendars. In the years after that, Kali Yuga (the dark age of moral decay and corruption) began to take hold, reaching its nadir during the Dark Ages in Europe and other parts of the world. Following the decline of the Roman Empire, Europe (and most parts of the so-called civilized world) plunged into a state of intellectual darkness, intolerance, a growth in invasions and conquests, forcible proselytization, corruption, etc. The Renaissance in Europe provided some respite. Similarly in India, the growth of devotional cults such as the Vishnu and Krishna worshippers led to a spiritual renaissance in India.

This chapter on Krishna would not be complete without spending some time on a great accompanying soul who showed spiritual potency and also great humility in the presence of Krishna, and that is the sage called Vyas (pronounced Vyaas) . Ved Vyas' birthday is celebrated as Guru's Day by many sects in India regardless of who the Guru might be.

Vyas is considered the Teacher and Messenger of the Kali Yuga, and was an integral part of the Mission of Krishna. He is the great link between the oral tradition and the written tradition of ancient Hinduism, because he put all the scriptures down in writing. This sage worked on the Vedas and separated them into four books for easier absorption by lay people. Before that the

Veda was just one very large scripture...with too much diversity in it...Vyasa named the Vedas the Rig Veda, Yajur Veda, Sama Veda and Atharva Veda.

He also consolidated the 18 Puranas into written form, and was therefore a spiritual historian of sorts. The Puranas, far from being random anecdotes, are supposed to further elucidate the spiritual and religious history of ancient times to lay people, and provide living examples of the virtues, as well as warnings, mentioned in the Vedas. Lord Sathya Sai Baba recently confirmed that most of what is in the Puranas is true, even if they sometimes appear stranger than fiction. Given the amount of time Vyas spent on writing down the Puranas, it is clear he believed in the power of spiritual and divine stories in transforming individuals.

Many Avatars have been master storytellers. The use of parables, anecdotes, and also more complex and long tales and epics, are all found in the spiritual lore of mankind. Jesus, Buddha, Krishna, and the two Sai Babas have all used them.

And of course Vyasa also did great service by compiling many details of Krishna's life when he wrote the Mahabharata, the great epic. He thus provided the world with an eye witness account of this Avatar's life. These two Beings, at the dawn of the present age of darkness (Kali Yuga) provided Hindus with a rudder and a foundation that continues to serve the religion to this day. The delineation of duties between them creates the need for a cluster of beings to appear with an Avatar in order to assist with the overall Mission of the Avatar...Vyasa is the lunar counterpart of the Krishna Avatar. Krishna's brother Balarama, is another vital member of this Cluster as was Radha.

The Avatar clearly approved of the Puranas being written down or it quite simply, would not have occurred during His lifetime...There are 18 main Puranas, and they had also survived largely through the oral tradition... The Puranas span a very wide range of divine events, revelations, and struggles, including the eternal tussle between the forces of ignorance and the forces of light, with many shades in between. But they mostly center round the Hindu triumvirate, Brahma, Vishnu, and Shiva. There are also Puranas dedicated to the primordial Avatars of Vishnu. And there are several minor Puranas, some dedicated to various demi-gods.

The Puranas have also resurfaced in recent times and some of them are more known now than they were perhaps a hundred years ago. One point to note is that the Puranas are not idealized portrayals of Divine Beings but in fact also point out their limitations and even describe the constraints these Beings have to work under...

And so, while the scriptural and devotional sides of Hinduism received a boost with the lives of Krishna and Vyas, interestingly, the gradual emergence of the "spiritual intellect" also began to be felt on earth. The growth of non-theistic doctrines continued side by side with the growth of theistic doctrines. For example, Vedanta, increasingly became a force. Perhaps as a forerunner to all this, Krishna sought to preempt the future from becoming totally godless. And even though He set the tone for the devotional side of spirituality as being the easier path in the age of Darkness, this did not prevent other more difficult paths from emerging or continuing to exist. In fact "Krishnaism" (better called Vaishnavism) began to wane and for some centuries was even superseded by other doctrines such as Vedanta (which receive a boost following the more widespread dissemination of the Upanishads), Buddhism, and Jainism. However during the last 400 years, Vaishnavism has bounced back noticeably, and such a rebound has the Grace of Lord Vishnu written all over it. Krishna and Lord Datta have come together to integrate everything, and more will be said about this in future chapters.

The world of today is unrecognizable from the world of Krishna's time...and yet the name Krishna has resurfaced all over the world in the 20th century. The Bhagavad Gita is now being discussed in study groups all over the world, and new temples to Krishna are being built. These temples, especially those built by the ISKCON and other Krishna centered movements, are full of the fervor and devotion that existed in centuries gone by. The

Indian Movie and TV industries have also given a lot of attention to the legends and teachings of Krishna during the last 2 or 3 decades, and this has led to a renewal of Krishna rituals and satsangs (spiritual gatherings) all over India. Hymns and prayers to Krishna have also resurfaced.

During peace and war, during mundane times and monumental, in village meadows and palaces, in times harsh and joyful, The Same Krishna Danced.

Omnipresent and Hidden, Peace loving and Valorous in Conflict, Blessing Devotees and Destroying Demons, the same Krishna danced...

Here is a hymn sung by Sathya Sai Baba:

Govindeti Sadaa Snaanam   Govindeti Sadaa Japam

Govindeti Sadaa Dhyaanam   Sada Govinda Keertanam

(Immerse yourself in the name of Krishna or Govinda, chant His name frequently, meditate on Him perennially, and never stop singing His praises).

Chapter Twelve

The Integral Practice of Patanjali Yoga

> When you are inspired by some great purpose, by an extraordinary project, all your thoughts break their bonds. Your mind transcends limitations, and your consciousness expands in every direction---***Patanjali.***

Yoga is the child of Samkhya and Tantra. The Tantrics had over millennia developed a complex picture of the body as made up of channels through which energy flowed and also looked upon the body as a potent reservoir of intelligence that needed to be tapped, but needing more than one approach to fully bring it to fruition... Yoga was also a way of making Tantra more accessible to laypeople and right-handed practitioners. The beginnings of Yoga lay in the practices of people who believed in spiritual regimen, or practice on a regular basis...and yet something that could be practiced in less formal settings, such as one's own backyard or home. Yoga's origins in Tantra almost automatically led to hybrids coming into existence, such as Mantra Yoga and Kundalini Yoga. The last-mentioned is an intermediary practice between Yoga and Tantra...

Yoga was in some ways the first spiritual science of the body/mind complex. But it was also a way of combining penance with prayer or meditation. Sages especially would sit (or stand) in one pose for a long time and while holding the pose perform their (usually silent) prayers, sometimes as an atonement for their transgressions. Holding a yogic pose for a long time was considered restricting one's freedom and therefore was a penance in its own right, and besides, many of them were powerful poses with benefits for the practitioner.

The earliest yoga poses, found in Shiva Tantras, were all mostly static sitting poses. For example, the Lotus Pose is extolled as a very therapeutic pose in the Shiva Samhita, especially if done on a regular basis. The "4 most important poses" given in this Samhita are all various ways of just sitting...They were sometimes combined with Mudras, or hand gestures, in both Tantra and Yoga. The practice of sitting facilitated the practice of breathing exercises (or Pranayama). In the final analysis however the objective of sitting was to practice Pratyahara, considered one of the most important aspects of Yoga, and involving withdrawing of the senses. It was thus a way of mind control or an "escape from Prakriti" for a while, and to create an empty and silent stage for Purusha so to speak.

Since I have placed this chapter after the one on Krishna, it shouldn't be concluded that Yoga mostly flourished after His tenure on earth. Yoga predates Krishna by thousands of years.

The practice of physical stillness for a significant duration inevitably brings about a need for stretching and movement, especially in lay practitioners... Thus dynamic exercises were also created and became part of the corpus of Yoga. Most yoga exercises however were practiced in a "reined" manner, with emphasis on holding the final pose for some time, and not in a "loose" or uninhibited manner. The use of deep breathing as a means of relaxing and yet rejuvenating the body were soon discovered, and in some schools of Yoga it was considered highly useful to relax between yoga poses...

The symmetric structure and suppleness of babies and young children provided clues to the yogis for the need to make the body supple rather than strong, internally harmonious rather than annealed, and pure rather than impervious to disease. All the secondary attributes, such as strength and immunity, would automatically follow...In an indirect manner, Yoga is an integrator of masculine and feminine energies in the body, just like its predecessor Tantra was.

For some, diet became an integral part of their yoga...food that had a minimum of processing done to it and a minimum of spices was considered the healthiest. Such a diet became known as a Saattvic diet. The term Saattvic diet refers to food that generates a feeling of calmness and sobriety in the body/mind complex. It is food that is fresh and pure, and vegetarian without being vegan. In fact, ghee has been considered a health food in yoga and Ayurveda for the longest time...Over a period of time, such a diet it was felt, would lead to a steadier mind.

At the higher level, a saattvic person is one who is spiritual and contented. He or she doesn't seek to actively compete or indulge in manipulative behavior. Also, a saattvic person is a somewhat integrated person, whose mind, speech, and actions coincide. In other words, he/she is a pleasant asset to everyone around. A Saattvic person is said to possess the Saattva Guna (or Saattva Quality). And there are two other broad Qualities: Rajas (the quality of active worldliness) and Tamas (the quality of dullness and ignorance, often accompanied by sloth). These 3 Principles were noticed by Kapila and were stated by Him to be found in all of Nature.

However, it must be said that none of the above Principles is the ultimate aim of Hindu spirituality. Rather it is to go "beyond the three Gunas". And that is the state of non-duality, and/or the state seen in a polymath (a multi-faceted person) who can adapt to changing circumstances: He can display Saattvic qualities one day, Rajasic qualities on another occasion, and even Tamasic qualities at times, given the circumstances. And yet he is detached from all of these...He becomes a Gunathitha (free from Gunas).

The existence or non-existence of a connection between Dattatreya and Patanjali is a matter of some controversy, and in all probability they did not live in the same era...Instead the legacy left behind by Dattatreya reached Patanjali many centuries later through the oral tradition...

So when did Patanjali live? Was he also a pre-Ice Age being like his teacher Dattatreya? Yoga is very ancient, and Patanjali was merely a chronicler and compiler of Yogic texts. Perhaps it matters little when exactly he lived. The more important fact is that his Yoga Sutras have influenced the whole practice of Yoga down to this day....though the very nature of Yoga makes it quite open-ended and amenable to various modifications and embellishments.

Lord Shiva is said to be the first Yogi and the first Tantrik. In the Nath tradition, He, both as Himself and in the person of Dattatreya, set the wheel of Yoga into motion...And He is the ultimate practitioner of what He preached...He was after all the loin-cloth-clad resident of the Himalayan peak, Mount Kailash, where there are three types of weather: Cold, Very Cold, and Extremely Cold. For a Yogi of His Cosmic magnitude though, it doesn't matter very much what season it is...

In the Shiva Sutras, yoga is of the spiritual kind and there are said to be 3 types of such yoga. The first is focusing on external objects with a view to improving concentration. It is called Kriya Yoga. While breathing and exercises are indeed practiced in this tradition, the focus is more to improve mental powers of concentration, using techniques like looking for a long time at an object without developing any feelings for or against it. Instead the practitioner "merely" stares intently at it for a long time...Usually an object like a pebble or a large rock is used, and later even a situation or idea. It is particularly suited for people who are emotionally extroverted but lack things like analytical ability, discriminatory powers and detachment. But this Yoga is only a first step for such practitioners. It is recommended they move on to the second type when they are ready...

The next type of Yoga in the Shiva Sutras is a type that could be called Wakefulness (or Mindfulness) Yoga, using one's Shakti or intrinsic energy rather than effort... Here, the practitioner is given techniques to transcend duality by becoming very mindful and aware of what is going on, especially inside him or her. The person becomes mindful of his thoughts and even his breath, and all this as he is going about his daily life, and not necessarily while sitting in meditation.

The third and final type of Yoga in the Shiva tradition is the Yoga of immersion in the Divine or Shiva. There is neither practice nor discipline involved here, but rather the growth of wisdom by learning from Shiva (through the Shiva Sutras and other texts). The whole canvas of Life is shown in stages to such a person...As one grows in understanding one is irresistibly drawn to the Lord and one seeks to merge in Him and His Love for humanity. For, He resides in the hearts of all creatures…and also pervades the world. In this Yoga, Shiva becomes synonymous with the Ultimate Reality (or Brahman as called by the Hindus). This type of Yogi begins by saying Om Namah Shivaya (I bow down to Lord Shiva) and at some point graduates to saying Shivoham, Shivoham (I am Shiva, I am Shiva).

The three types are designed to progressively lead the practitioner to the ultimate objective of liberation from the cycle of birth and death. These three Yogas form the essence of what has come to be known as Kashmir Shaivism.

The power and teachings of an Avatar are such that He can take us straight to the third stage…of immersion and merging with the Divine. Neither the practice of Yoga poses, nor Yogic meditation, is needed. And nor is the need for mindfulness per se, though mindfulness is needed by default because *mindlessness* is spiritually counter-productive…

Rather, on making a commitment to an Avatar, the first two stages (of concentration and mindfulness) begin to happen effortlessly, though they may not always occur with high intensity in all devotees of the Avatar. This is one of the reasons why there is often great diversity among the devotees of an Avatar. On the one hand, we have highly evolved souls taking birth at the same time as the Avatar. Then we have advanced beings that are drawn to Him and become His close disciples. Then we have a circle of devotees, then somewhat more casual devotees, and finally the ignorant public that have had no contact with the Avatar…

Let us hark back to Patanjali. His Yoga Sutras are divided into 4 parts:

1. Samadhi Pada (being absorbed in spirit).

2. Sadhana Pada (spiritual practices)

3. Vibhuti Pada (the development of Siddhis, or supernatural abilities)

4. Kaivalya Pada (the attainment of liberation).

It is believed by some that Patanjali was a polymath, but others have refuted such claims and instead called him a very good propagator of Yoga instead. Be that as it may, these Yoga Sutras have resurfaced in the 20th century and greatly influenced teachers of Yoga all over the world. Patanjali describes Yoga as being Eight-fold in Nature (I am using phonetic spellings below).

1. <u>Yama</u>: These are restraints on behavior…They include non-violence, truthfulness, and non-stealing.

2. <u>Niyama</u>: These are spiritual observances like purity and contentment. Today, we may wish to include forgiveness and gratitude as powerful ways of setting our inner house in order.

3. <u>Aasanaas</u>: Practice of yogic postures or exercises.

4. <u>Praanaayaama</u>: Increasing vital energy through control of breath.

5. <u>Pratyaahaara</u>: Withdrawal of the senses from the external world…

6. <u>Dhaaranaa</u>: Concentration, leading to the next stage of meditation.

7. <u>Dhyaana</u>: Meditation to achieve great tranquility.

8. <u>Samaadhi</u>: Complete absorption on the Infinite Absolute.

The first four in the list fall under the rubric of Saadhanaa or practices to purify and prepare the body. The next three are for the development of the mind and the gaining of self-knowledge and abandonment of ego. They reduce the fluctuations of the mind, leading to a more tranquil state.

But Patanjali doesn't consider Yoga to be a non-theistic doctrine…rather he also emphasizes Svaadhyaaya (or the study of the scriptures) as *one of the Niyamas*, (see #2 above) and then to the path of bhakti (devotion) by the practices of chanting of the names of God, the chanting of mantras, all finally leading to surrender (Pranidhaana). For God is, in his words, the unexcelled seed of all knowledge.

Patanjali uses the word *Shraddha* to denote faith with firm conviction. The word Shraddha was used a lot by Avatar Shirdi Sai Baba. Why does Patanjali go on to suggest the study of the scriptures and surrender to God? In his view, these will only serve to further increase the practitioner's knowledge and wisdom. Such a person becomes a true Yogi.

Patanjali then provides the ultimate aim of all yoga: It is to resolve the apparent dichotomy between Purusha (called Mahat by him) and Prakriti, and to achieve a state of oneness with both. This finally leads to the non-dual state of Self-Realization, or the attainment of Brahman, the Causeless Cause of both Purusha and Prakriti. Thus Patanjali's yoga is an early attempt at integrating the various practices and philosophies that were already in existence within Hinduism. More specifically, we find the teachings of Kapila and Lord Shiva coming together in Patanjali's Yoga. Patanjali echoes Kapila's view of man being composed of the 5 elements: earth, water, fire, air, and ether…

An interesting term that appears to have been coined by Patanjali is Kaivalya, which is his version of liberation. The meaning of Kaivalya is somewhat different from words like Moksha and Samadhi. While Moksha implies liberation from the cycle of birth and death, and Samadhi implies a passive and highly transcendental state free from all worldly concerns and stimuli, Kaivalya implies an *active* state of liberation even as one continues to function in the world, where the yogi becomes immune to the influences of the world…This term was later also used by Rishabha, the great founder of Jainism.

In keeping with the state of Kaivalya, a term Amanaskatva is sometimes used, which is the opposite of an empty mind…rather it is a full state of mind that integrates all of spirituality into a harmonious whole…it is mental clarity because of little or no personal desires. In terms such as Amanaskatva one senses the influence of Lord Datta.

A question that can arise in the minds of some seekers is: How spiritually "necessary" are things like Yoga, Tai Chi, or Chi Gong, etc.? So many saints and seers appear to have got along quite well without any of these... Also, yoga doesn't feature significantly in the teachings of any of the Avatars. Instead one finds an emphasis on the paths of devotion and surrender.

Not all souls appear to need Yoga or other system of initiation. Some people take naturally to the path of devotion and appear to be drawn almost by instinct to a spiritual teacher or guru, who then takes them to higher levels, often without the use of physical regimens.

Other seekers seem endowed with the intelligence and inner resources to take to the spiritual path almost on their own, and needing a teacher only occasionally to prod them along in the right direction. Again, there's little need for a system such as Yoga. But of course, there are many who find Yoga or Tai Chi to be very grounding and useful indeed. Some like the idea that the body is taken care of and "out of the way".

Whether Patanjali was an Avatar or not, his contribution to humanity has been immense. As mentioned before, he was a great integrator, but for some reason he did not develop a large fan-following either during his life or later. He does not appear to have had any typical Avataric powers, even though he spoke about them in his Sutras. His chief role in the spiritual history of mankind appears to have been as a great chela of Lord Shiva. While playing this role, he ended up influencing not only lay persons but also accomplished sages like Sage Agastya another great devotee of Lord Shiva, who was one of the founders of Dravidian Shaivism and a benefactor of Lord Rama. Agastya is said to have received knowledge of holistic Siddha medicine from Lord Sanat Kumara as we have seen before. Apparently, Lord Shiva's son was a great healer too, like His father. More recently Ayurveda has somewhat superseded the Siddha system though the latter is still very much with us.

Chapter Thirteen

The Masters of the Ancient Middle East

If you are Abraham's children, do the deeds of Abraham---
Jesus Christ.

Around 1800 BC, we had on earth a major figure of the Old Testament, Abraham, whose spiritual experiences were mainly His direct interactions with a God of both Sustenance and Destruction. We have encountered Abraham before in the chapter on the parents of the Avatars. This Old Testament Figure is mentioned several times in the New Testament also and is known for His surrender and obedience to God. However, His teachers Enoch and Noah who preceded Him are also held in great esteem as beings that had direct interactions with Divinity...

Abraham was asked by the Lord to move away from his native land of Haran in Mesopotamia and in return Abraham was promised much, and indeed the name of Abraham is revered by 3 religions today. He is one of the mysteries of the Bible, since so little is known about his early life and his previous lives, though there are some who view him as the reappearance of Adam's third son Seth, the Virtuous One, who by all accounts was a blessed figure himself. These people believe that Seth, Noah, and Abraham are the same soul...When one hears of Abraham's deeds he already appears an old soul, sensitive to the will of God...One therefore has little doubt that he lived before in other bodies, and more than likely lived virtuous lives for him to be so blessed in this one...

Of course, he was also tested and evidently passed all of those tests... In him the Lord found the father of countless generations. The gospel doesn't begin with Jesus Christ....it starts with Abraham if not earlier...And in the Koran, there is a chapter entitled Ibrahim (Abraham) where He is referred to as the Upright One, a frequent worshipper (not just for his gain but also for others), and a Fulfiller of Commandments.

In the Koran (we find the following: [2:131] When his Lord said to him, "Submit," he said, "I submit to the Lord of the universe."

[2:132] Abraham also exhorted his children to do the same, and so did Jacob: "O my children, GOD has pointed out the religion for you; do not die except as submitters."

In Genesis 13 we find God addressing Abraham: *I will make your descendants as the dust of the earth; so that if a man could number the dust of the earth, then your descendants also could be numbered.*

Even if there is a controversy about this, it appears that Abraham did leave a teaching for humanity (or at least was the initiator of): The Book of Formation (also called the Letters of Abraham). This teaching emphasizes there is only one God who however has chosen to manifest Himself in myriad forms. The Book of Formation is abstruse enough to remain a mystery to this day... However, certain features do stand out, and suggest a link with ancient Hinduism:

In passage 5, Abraham speaks of how the world has the opposites contained within it, and how the Lord is however One and is above the opposites...and the opposites are ultimately subservient to Him...for after all, He created the opposites as a way of balancing the forces of the Universe...This is akin to the non-dualism of Kashmiri Shaivism for example, where since ancient times, Lord Shiva has been interpreted as the Lord of Opposites, since He contains all the opposites within Him. A Shaivite might say, "Non-dualism is for the intellect and for the Higher Consciousness of man, while devotion towards the Lord is for the heart" and the Shaivite might add: This is the way to salvation. Abraham, even if indirectly, suggests the same in His Letters.

Abraham also speaks of Universal Spirit in this Book of Formation. The Universe emerges out of Spirit and in the form of Air (or Space), Water, and Fire (or Energy). Air came first, followed by Water and then Fire, and all substances come out from emptiness and are formed from the mere utterance of a word

(His Name)...This is akin to the 5 Elements (or Panchabhutas) of Hinduism, the only difference being there is a fifth Element in Hindu scripture which is Earth (or Matter). But Abraham also includes the 5th element by saying that "Mud and Mire" came from the Water Element...

These Elements are not to be taken literally because they are actually Principles, manifesting into myriad forms...Also, interconnectedness between them is important...There are no closed systems in Nature...everything influences other things and so ultimately, "Everything is connected".

The Kabbalah is a great symbol of Jewish mysticism and Abraham is said to be the "first Kabbalist". The Kabbalah has been developed over many centuries and is abstract enough to need an expert to fully decipher it...This writer considers it to be somewhat out of the scope of this book.

One of the most spiritual beings of the Old Testament is Melchizedek, who blessed Abraham once and offered Him bread and wine. Melchizedek was a high priest and highly regarded as being endowed with a divinely graced birth, which is one reason why Abraham visited Him while returning from a military campaign. The other reason is that sometimes highly evolved souls will be attracted to each other's presence, without their conscious minds being aware of what is really happening...Such meetings are sometimes fully appreciated only later by the people involved...

The Ancient Brotherhood mentioned earlier, which was founded by Lord Sanat Kumara, was initially called the *Order of Melchizedek*. Thus the connection with Ascended Masters is strong enough so that when one hears that Melchizedek was Jesus Christ Himself in a previous incarnation, it appears more than plausible...Scripts discovered at Nag Hammadi in 1945 also state that Melchizedek is Christ... Christ once said, "Before Abraham was, I AM."

This God of Abraham promised Him a name in posterity, and many descendants, even while destroying the twin cities of Sodom and Gomorrah. I do resonate with Gene Matlock when he says that Ishwara or "Yishwara" (i.e. Lord Shiva) is the original God who was worshipped in the area where Judaism was later born…The worship of the Shiva Lingam (or Shiva Pillar) is probably the oldest kind of worship in the world, and as we saw in the chapter on Lord Rama, was already well-established more than 20,000 years ago. The lingam (or short stone pillar) represents the formless God, who later became YHWH…

One of the names of God in the Jewish religion is El Shadhai (the Destroyer) while in Hindu terminology, Sada-shiva is one of the names of Lord Shiva. However, we also know there are some substantial differences between Hinduism and the Abrahamic religions: Judaism, Christianity, and Islam. How did these differences come about? For example, the concept of Trinity exists in both Hinduism and Christianity. But while Trinity in Hinduism refers usually to Creator, Preserver, and "Destroyer", in Christianity it is Father, Son, and Holy Ghost. How and when did this "Trinity Transformation" so to speak, take place?

As mentioned before, there is one important distinguishing factor about Lord Shiva. While other deities (major and minor) chose not to live on earth but rather in more ethereal lokas (or higher planes), Lord Shiva decided to make the earth His home. This is one of the reasons the Lord has been involved in some way or the other with almost every Avataric Descent…This gracing of the earth with His permanent presence happened long before Sanat Kumara moved to Earth…

In other words, in the now-famous Trinity of "Father, Son, and the Holy Ghost", one possible interpretation is as follows: When taken in their pre-Biblical "Original Meanings", the Father is Shiva and the Son is Subramanya or Sanat Kumara. The Holy Ghost is simply Universal Spirit, and Universal Spirit does feature prominently in the Teachings of Lord Shiva, who after all, is the Originator of several Tantras (or tantric texts if you will) and also the Shiva Sutras. Incidentally, to equate Sanat Kumara with Lucifer is simply an error as was also pointed out by Madame Blavatsky. Quite the contrary, Sanat Kumara who has had to take His fair share of rejection by the orthodoxy, is a benefactor of humanity par excellence.

Abraham was clearly a devout worshipper and a builder of altars to the Lord. At one point He prayed to the Lord to spare Sodom and Gomorrah but was met with a rejoinder: If Abraham could spot 10 good people in Sodom, the city would be spared. Abraham tried but did not succeed. A little later the city was razed to the ground...The spiritual lesson here seems to be: *Collective evil will invariably be stamped out, sooner or later.* As for individual evil, the law of karma is more likely to be followed for that ... Collective evil has never survived for long in the world...whether it was the Kauravas of the Mahabharata, or the Mongols, the Huns, or the Nazis... they all met inglorious ends.

Avatar Krishna made specific comments about this during His physical sojourn on earth. He insisted that if large scale evil reared its head on earth, He would come down to sort things out. It is said that He even "took care of" His own clansmen, the Yadavas, who He felt were unusually aggressive, brutish, and more than capable of inflicting suffering on others...

Abraham recognized Enoch as his teacher, and Enoch is one of the spiritual giants of old, and lived a few generations before Abraham. Enoch is said to have had regular contact with Archangels such as Michael, Gabriel, and Raphael. We observe that the angels' names usually end in "el" and that signifies their devotion and service to God. These great Archangels have done yeoman service to humanity over the millennia. Even though we don't worship angels, they of course deserve the highest adoration. Angels continue to be channeled by Lightworkers and continue to appear at spiritual gatherings...

Enoch used expressions such as "the Lord of the Spirits" and "the Ancient of Days" to refer to His God. He described many of His past spiritual experiences and also made predictions, and is considered a pioneering prophet. One of Lord Sanat Kumara's names is indeed "Ancient of Days"...

While in Hindu lore such great souls are called sages, in the Abrahamic religions they are called prophets. Admittedly, there are some differences between the two: There was an emphasis on "ashram living" in the case of ancient sages, while prophets tended to be perhaps more mobile. Hindu sages did a lot of meditation and fire ceremonies since they were heavily influenced by the Vedas, while prophets spoke inspiringly to people in an effort to "light a fire in their bellies". They both had spiritual experiences and they both kept pointing heavenwards...

The ancient Zoroastrians also performed fire ceremonies but such ceremonies are apparently absent from the Old Testament...but on closer examination we find that fire indeed had a role to play in the early history of the Abrahamic religions and more than not indicated the presence of God. Thus we have the burning bush of Moses and fire also appears as a sign of God's anger. In Exodus 13:21 we find reference to the Lord appearing as a pillar of fire to light the way at night to allow His people to travel both by day and night. As seen before, a pillar of fire is exactly the original interpretation of the Shiva Lingam, but either ignorant and/or naïve or even mischievous elements chose to interpret the lingam as a phallic symbol and even built stories around it, such as Lord Shiva being cursed by some other powerful being that He will only be worshipped in this form. These stories are lacking in credibility, because they completely ignore the grandeur and potency of Lord Shiva...

Another reference to Lord Shiva is when Jacob slept using a pillar as a head rest and that night had a vision wherein he saw a huge ladder (thereafter known as Jacob's Ladder) extending up to Heaven and he saw angels ascending and descending it...later when he awoke he set the pillar vertically on the ground and poured oil on it...this again is one of the ways Shiva lingams are worshipped to this day.

In Exodus 19:18 we hear that "Mount Sinai was covered with smoke because the Lord descended on it as fire, and the whole mountain shook and shuddered." I'm reminded of the Puranic story of Ravana the demonic king trying to dislodge Mount Kailash as an arrogant act of defiance towards Lord Shiva, who merely presses down on the mountain with His foot, and the whole mountain shudders and descends, nearly crushes Ravana, who immediately submits to Him and becomes His devotee instead.

Enoch revealed the early history of the earth, wherein some fallen angels had descended and united with human women, unleashing some undesirable giant sized elements onto the earth...Enoch even named many of the fallen angels. Skeletons of giants have been unearthed in the 20th century. Hindu mythology also speaks of giants roaming the earth at one time and Rama, who we have seen, was also born a giant to take care of such giants...

Thus not all descents are holy or happen with the best of intentions...these undesirable elements came to be also called Shaitans (Hindu term for "Evil Ones") and later satans with *"The Satan"* as their chief. For some time, their collective evil was unleashed on earth...but after a while they too were overpowered. A similar scenario appears in the Puranas wherein Asuras (or evil giants) descended on earth and created havoc, and had to be taken care of by Lord Shiva and/or Lord Vishnu. Sometimes Durga (the consort of Shiva) joined in the battle and sometimes His son Subramanya (Sanat Kumara) also stepped in.

Fortunately for us, these undesirable elements do not have anywhere near the continuity of the holy archangels and angels. While angelic beings have immortality, the evil and fallen ones do not. Besides, the law of karma has also taken care of the remaining satans and greatly diluted their presence on earth... Repeated rebirth interspersed with periods of Purgatory has quite simply neutralized them. Thus, as Sai Baba has recently reminded us, "there is much more good than bad in the world today." In the current age of cynicism and negatively biased media that we live in, this is an important point that has the potential to change our perspective and the face of modern spirituality.

The broader implication of all this is that dualistic doctrines are not the need of the hour. What we need instead is a movement towards non-dualism and the doctrine of Oneness, while being ever-grateful to the Avatars. And this was the aim of Lord Shiva and later of Lord Vishnu. Lord Dattatreya is also working towards Oneness. Sai Baba advised His devotees: Pick one Deity and pick a Guru (Avatar) and become devoted and faithful to them.

In those ancient times, Enoch also hinted at karma when he insisted that evil doers would be punished and the good rewarded...Some other revelations of Enoch came from his ancestor Noah (the well-known Noah of the Biblical flood). Enoch taught that Nature was a reflection of God's Powers and Wisdom. The Lord granted a vision to Enoch and assured Him that the unholy elements would be taken care of and that He should not worry. What was begun by Lord Sanat Kumara was later completed by Lord Shiva in the destruction of Sodom and Gomorrah.

Enoch made several trips to the astral plane as some people do to this day, and insisted that the Archangels took Him to vantage points from where they could watch the spirits of those who had once inhabited the earth... Among them Enoch said He saw the spirit of Abel, who had been slain by Cain. Then follow a host of revelations by Enoch on the nature of heaven, earth, and nature. It is no wonder that He attracted disciples, one of them being Abraham. Abraham in turn had many spiritual experiences and some of His interactions with Divinity are spelled out in the Old Testament.

Abraham was followed about 500 years later by Moses (or Moshe). He is the best-known figure of the Old Testament, having received the Ten Commandments directly from the Lord, and also led the Israelites to freedom after making the Red Sea part. Moses is also mentioned many times in the Koran. And of course He is considered the most important prophet in Judaism. The Lord revealed His name YHWH to Moses. Later Moses would declare: My God YHWH is One. This teaching is also found in the Shiva Sutras which go on to say: *Everything is God.*

Skeptics of course will abound who even doubt that Moses ever lived, but events like the Transfiguration reveal that both Moses and Elijah were indeed prophets who later Ascended. One indication of their ascendance is that they held their final forms, instead of being reborn in other bodies. When a Master ascends He can retain His most recent form if He wishes...

In the 9th century BC, there lived another spiritual force in the area we now call Israel. He was Elijah who later came to be called Prophet Elijah. He was beloved to Jesus Christ, and during a well-known event called the Transfiguration which happened at the top of a mountain, Jesus took some apostles of His and upon reaching some height, the apostles saw that Jesus was emitting a wonderful light...He then made Elijah and Moses appear by His side, and began talking to them. After a while they departed just as quickly as they had appeared...

This event is seen as much a eulogy and honoring of Christ as something that Christ performed for His apostles. Christ later told the witnesses present to not divulge this incident to anyone, at least until His resurrection. He did this perhaps because a secret had in a sense been revealed...the Ascent of Moses and Elijah as well as their eternal proximity to God. Both Elijah and Moses now belong to a select group of Masters.

Elijah appears to have been sent down to earth because of the proliferation of demi-gods and dubious religious symbols, causing fragmentation of the population and furthering tribalism.... He performed significant miracles that convinced on-lookers He represented the true God. Because He had to constantly confront His detractors from other faiths and paths, Elijah had to be careful and also needed guidance and protection from above, and these according to some accounts were provided in good measure so that His mission was successful, but not without His fair share of trials...

Because of His ability to foretell the future, He became known as a prophet. Even though Elijah and Moses were separated by at least 400 years, He considered himself a younger sibling of Moses.

Chapter Fourteen

Mind over Everything---Buddha and Mahavira

There is nothing as disobedient as an undisciplined mind, and there is nothing as obedient as a disciplined mind---**_Buddha_**

To say that the Buddha was endowed with an incredible sensitivity would be to put it quite mildly. Countless souls have beheld old people, diseased people, corpses, hard-pressed individuals, etc., and yet no appreciable change occurs in us…The Buddha on the other hand, became transformed very quickly on seeing such sights even for the very first time (at least in His last life on earth)…and despite having lived a very sheltered life where He was constantly given royal luxuries, power, and sensory pleasures…

His birth was auspicious, and both His enlightenment and His departure from the body also took place on the same day as His birth. All these three events took place on Wesak (or Vaisakha) Day, which was already considered an auspicious day, a day of blessing that occurred on a full moon day…In the Hindu tradition the month called Vaisakha is considered sacred after it was thus described by Sage Narada, who claimed this was the best month for worshipping Vishnu… this day became the most important day of the year for Buddhists.

According to the Lucis Trust, a 20th century spiritual school established by Alice Bailey in the USA, the Buddha returns in His light form every year on Wesak Day to a remote valley in the Tibetan Himalayas and blesses the great beings gathered there for the occasion, as well as blesses the earth itself…and He does so at great personal sacrifice. He has also appeared in recent times to blessed souls such as Jiddu Krishnamurti, Connie Shaw, and others. He has been channeled by some (actually several) gifted and blessed people. Please understand that many of the Divine personages covered in this book are still very available to humanity…in fact, that has been a great motivator for me to publish this work.

This writer was born on Wesak Day in 1959. Throughout his life he has felt protected and guided by an unseen hand...things really came to light only when the Guru appeared in the form of the most recent Avatar.

When the Buddha was born, Vedic astrologers were consulted as was the norm...Quite unanimously they said to the king, "Your son is bound to become a Universal monarch or one of the greatest sages the world has ever seen." This in some ways was quite a cryptic statement. The contrast is striking of course. The life of a monarch is so different from the life of a sage. The bottom line ultimately was: This baby was going to be one of a kind, and would end up being very famous. And that did happen. The Buddha is more venerated and well-known than any monarch that has ever ruled anywhere in the world. And His influence in the world even today is far greater than what any monarch of old has ever achieved. The Buddha is reported to have said: All the wealth and power of kings is a drop of oil on my foot...

We also have the well-known anecdote of the sage Asita visiting the palace a few days after the birth of Gautama, and weeping at the sight of the baby...The sage had come down from the Himalayas and hadn't been seen for a long time in those parts... When asked why he wept at such a joyous occasion as the birth of a royal baby, he said it was because he would soon have to leave his body and would miss listening to the enlightened teachings of this divine being who would one day become a great sage and teach the world...Sage Asita was one step ahead of the astrologers.

If astrology appears metaphysical to some of us, prescience and clairvoyance are far more powerful and subtle phenomena. Vedic Astrology and other similar systems are far from binding on an individual, with other factors such as karma and past lives also playing a part...Also, when one is working with a Master such as an Avatar, one's horoscope is even less binding, since it can be altered by the Avatar...for example, the Avatar may choose to hasten the karmic repayments of the individual and that may in turn lead to an increase in the trials and tribulations in that individual's life.

There is some controversy today, whether the Buddha was born in the 5th century BC or the 7th century BC. It matters little perhaps, because Gautama Buddha is indeed a historically documented Avatar...perhaps the first. However, He is considered a contemporary of another great soul, Mahavira, who is said to have lived from 540 BC to 468 BC...thus making it more likely that the Buddha (or Sakyamuni) also lived in the 5th century BC. Besides, the Buddha is said to be a contemporary of King Bimbisara, who was a great benefactor of the Buddha and His Order and Bimbisara is said to have lived from 558 BC to 491 BC...

It is said that immediately after seeing the now famous "Four Sights" (a sick man, an old man, a corpse, and a hermit), the Buddha (Prince Siddhartha at that time) approached His father and asked that he be allowed to retreat to the forest and seek the truth behind the transitory life...His father was of course aghast at the very idea. He exclaimed, "O my son, it is not the time for you to take up such a life. They say that the practice of religion is full of evils in the first period of life when the mind is still fickle."

The Buddha then uttered these famous words, "If you can promise me that I will never fall sick, or grow old, or die, only then will I not go into the forest." His father was rendered speechless by this. The Buddha then said, "If this is impossible, then this course of mine is not to be hindered; it is not right to lay hold of one who would escape from a house that is on fire."

Most people are aware of the self-deprivation that the Buddha subjected Himself to...and He has confirmed in a recent channeling session that He did not do this to invite suffering into His life. Rather, He did it to invite simplicity and joy...

The Buddha's style of speaking and presenting His perceptions, all those centuries ago, were spell-binding according to reports by eye witnesses. Effortlessly, He drew the crowds to Himself, and their numbers only increased as time went on. The Buddha's mission lasted 45 years, and during that time, He walked 100s of miles, and took His message directly to thousands. He was a charismatic speaker who held His audiences in rapt attention. Word soon got around that He slept only for an hour every day, and ate only once a day. And that He could brave the most severe weather conditions and often slept in the open, wearing only a thin robe. He always exuded love and compassion. Quite naturally, the Buddha became a legend in His own lifetime. For here was a mendicant who looked like a prince, and spoke like a god.

The Buddha taught the 6 Perfections: *generosity, morality, patience, energy, meditation, and wisdom.* The first 3 were preparatory for the spiritual life and would bring about the second three...The philosophy of the Buddha was based on the notion that the human mind is not inherently strong but rather inherently weak and easily conditioned. We learn unsound things as easily as we learn sound things...and so we have to "tread with care" in order to not be "swept away" by the various stimuli in the environment...The Buddha taught that luxury, intoxicants and a fondness of entertainment all led to a weakening of the mind, thus leading to a state of vulnerability...Another focus of the Buddha was the avoidance of negative karma...thus serious practitioners of His teachings should not accept money from anyone and never "help themselves to something that is not given."

Instead, the Buddha said, "Make haste and do what is good." The bottom line: *"Give more than you take, if you know your law of karma."* By teaching karma the Buddha was of course also endorsing the whole idea of retribution which usually occurs in a future life and not the present one...Masters like Buddha and Jesus have preferred to speak of reincarnation indirectly rather than in a direct manner...

As outlined by the clairvoyant Theosophist Charles Leadbeater in his book *The Lives of Alcyone,* J. Krishnamurti was a contemporary of Gautama Buddha in a previous life and also a student of Gautama... Krishnamurti's spiritual name is Alcyone per Leadbeater. Almost throughout his life, Krishnamurti spoke of the Buddha and His Visitations...saying that he felt the Buddha's presence at times and actually saw Him at other times. Krishnamurti said this quite overtly during the early part of his life, and somewhat less after he parted ways with the Theosophists in 1929…

The Buddha is in some ways a Hermetic, when He says: All is Mind…and Mind is the basis for everything and the predominant force in the Universe…Mind is taken here in its largest sense (the Species sense), and not in the individual and limited sense. The Buddha preferred not to speak of soul or Atma. In doing so, He was avoiding that part of the individual as largely inaccessible to lay people since it is not within reach and belongs to the Universe…

Since the teachings of the Buddha do not include the notion of Avatar, it appears to be a more earthy teaching rather than a Cosmic Teaching…until we realize that Mindfulness (one of the king-pins of the Buddha's teaching) is also a vertical force…However, it is a force that man apparently has to muster all by oneself (The Buddha said: Be a light unto your own life).

And therein lies a difficulty: In the present age of over-stimulation of the senses, it becomes very difficult, if not almost impossible… Life needs to be understood in terms of these Vertical and Horizontal forces in our lives. Karma, for example is a horizontal force…born of the limitations of Mind, which is also mostly horizontal. Human desires and actions based on these desires are horizontal forces. The great Masters have always warned humanity of the dangers of horizontal forces… And the most dangerous horizontal calamity of all is the human ego. This earth has become an immense clash of horizontal forces…

But as this book contends, an Avatar is a "Vertical Force" that literally can 'bore a hole through' and greatly reduce the potency of the horizontal force of the human mind, by transforming the human and also by His sheer Presence. An Avatar also has the power and the grace to exert a "Vertical Force" and literally lift His devotee up, and away from the quagmire of mundane existence…In other words, He can give us liberation from rebirth…and send us to the Highest Heaven if He so wishes…

As mentioned above, Divine Grace and Human Mindfulness are Vertical Forces and these are indeed divine forces. The soul that serves as a Witness within us is also operating like a Vertical Force because it is content with witnessing...and is therefore Divine, and The Voice of Conscience is a also a vertical force that warns us within not to succumb to horizontal temptations...Factors that increase or enhance the Vertical Forces are:

- Objective examination: The Search for Truth (any form of it), is also a vertical force, even when it is trying to understand horizontal forces...Thus Science is supposedly a vertical search for truth, but unfortunately, the way it is practiced has caused it to become a social (and political) activity and so Science has degenerated into something less vertical, with its inherent rivalries, and even dubious practices, etc.
- Being attentive/alert and watching oneself (Many teachers have asked us to watch our words, actions, thoughts, and our character itself).
- Inner Silence and Creative Endeavors without expectation of reward...or even public display.
- Seeing Avatars as standing on mountains and therefore having a much larger span of view than a human who is standing on level ground.
- Surrender (this means acceptance of all world events and circumstances) as being ultimately the Will (active or passive) of the Avatar or God. And thus, being immersed in God Consciousness and offering whatever one does to God. This is said to neutralize karma itself.

One of the causes of human confusion is a mixing up in our minds between the vertical and horizontal... For example, we feel God should satisfy our horizontal needs or earthly needs, and we even hear some people say, I can't believe there's a God, look at all the chaos and suffering in the world...We want God to fix these horizontal problems and we forget that Avatars and God are vertical forces. Sai Baba advised His devotees many times not to waste His Presence among them by asking for worldly gains...

But there is one force that began as Vertical but was poured out so lavishly and selflessly that it later became horizontal also, and that is LOVE. The Avatars descend out of their Vertical Love and then distribute it horizontally to their Devotees...even if in a "vertical manner", and by that I mean the love is camouflaged sometimes in trials and struggles.

Much can be said about the presence of horizontal and vertical forces in our lives. For example, the chakras taken collectively represent a vertical force, but when taken individually, are horizontal...

The "Everything is Consciousness" view (somewhat confusingly called the "Everything is Mind" view by some) owes its existence at least partly to the Yogacara School which was developed apparently under the auspices of Maitreya (the Buddha of the Future, who was mentioned by Gautama Buddha a few times). Maitreya is said to have revealed his teachings to Asanga, a renowned Buddhist monk who became a teacher of Mahayana, and who spent many years in meditation. He later insisted that a particular stratum of heaven, called the Tushita Heaven, was accessible to deep meditators and that he had been taught there by Maitreya Himself and that Lord Maitreya had fully endorsed the Mahayana philosophy...

Many centuries later, following in the manner of ancient Buddhist sages, Jiddu Krishnamurti would ponder greatly on the whole subject of internal order in the mind, even while accepting that the mind is fragmented (which can well happen if the mind is a continuum). Krishnamurti also hails from the lineage of Ascended Masters, though he did "break away" from that in 1929. The popular version is that he broke away from the Theosophical Society...but the situation appears more complex than that. Did Krishnamurti ultimately give way, like Ascended Masters are prone to doing, to the presence of the Lord on earth...We will discuss this further shortly.

The Buddha is said to be the great preceptor of the Buddha Dharma (or the Code of Right Living). And in that sense, appears to represent the Vishnu Principle of Stability and Consolidation...

However, when one considers the way His life unfolded, and the way He broke away from tradition, embracing transcendence and austerity, as well as promoting human evolution, He equally (if not more) embodies the Shiva Principle of Transcendence, Evolution, Mindfulness, and Blissful Centeredness all in a minimal, spartan environment. Lord Shiva is considered to be the epitome of one-pointedness or one-minded focus (Ekagrata), as well as being the epitome of self-sufficiency and wholeness. The Buddha therefore, embodies the Shiva Principle more than the Vishnu Principle...

In fact, Shaivism is more closely related to Buddhism than Vaishnavism is. For example, the Shiva Tantras later influenced the Buddhist tantras... In fact, some Buddhist tantras can be considered as almost identical with the older Hindu tantras...

However, things don't appear to quite fall in place as yet. For the Buddha was distinctly non-theistic in His approach. As mentioned before, there is a third great source of Celestial Beings on earth. Let us now consider what that might be.

In a book by Mary Lutyens about J. Krishnamurti, the 20th century teacher, there is a vivid description of one of Krishnamurti's experiences while still a minor, and being raised by the Theosophists to become a World Teacher, after being introduced to the Ascended Masters, by Annie Besant and C. W. Leadbeater. Krishnamurti is said to have traveled several times in the astral plane to be with higher beings. In one such episode, Krishnamurti speaks of meeting Sanat Kumara, who in his words "looked like a youth", and is a Guardian and Keeper of planet Earth. In that same "dream" or astral experience, the Buddha appears and pledges to serve Sanat Kumara forever...

As we are going to see later, Sanat Kumara is said to have spent a life on earth as Dipankara Buddha, and Gautama Buddha was His student then. Dipankara Buddha is said to have personally blessed Gautama (who was known as Sumedha then) and said to Sumedha that he would be born into a royal family in the clan of the Sakyas (and earn the title of Sakyamuni, or saint of the Sakya clan) and achieve enlightenment. Dipankara Buddha even went on to name some future disciples of Sakyamuni. Only a Divine Being or an Avatar can make such predictions... In some spiritual schools, Dipankara Buddha is considered to be an Avatar of Sanat Kumara. Lord Dipankara is the Buddhist equivalent of the founder of Jainism, Lord Rishabha.

It is extremely difficult to set a precise date for the Dipankara Avatar, and it isn't surprising that hardly anyone has attempted this. Even the assertion that there have been about 24 Buddhas between Dipankara and Gautama is not very helpful...It is most likely that Dipankara Buddha lived in the period between the life of Rama and that of Rishabh Dev. Ram Rajya had been established through the grand example of Lord Rama...this inspired the people in India to live lives of courage and ethics, however, it also led to a stagnation of sorts. There was an increasing reliance on traditional ways of doing things, generation after generation...The caste system also took strong root and led quite naturally to perceived injustices...

What could be done to advance the evolution of mankind? Enter Lord Subramanya (or Sanat Kumara), the son of Lord Shiva...The Lord had said in the Avadhuta Gita that the desire for non-duality arises by the grace of God...Sanat Kumara has stressed the importance of mindfulness and "working within" from the earliest times. Accordingly, the lineage of Buddhas has stressed an inner awakening based on the higher faculties in a human being, such as intellect and mindfulness. Gautama espoused mindfulness as the great liberator...This is what humanity needed to shake it out of its reverie...an enlightenment path that relied more on self-knowledge and self-sufficiency than grace from above...

Let us note here that even though Dipankara Buddha was a Descent, and therefore an Avatar, He chose to awaken and ennoble, rather than secure devotees of the Avataric kind...in other words, there was not a word about who He was or where He came from. Instead, Dipankara launched into a traveling crusade and drew students close to Him because of His charisma and wisdom. His mission was nothing less than to raise people up to a Higher Consciousness. Later in their evolution, they could be reintroduced to Deity based spirituality...I say "reintroduced" because after all, their souls were quite familiar with Deities from previous lifetimes... Dipankara, being a deity-based avatar, could monitor His students "vertically" (i.e., across lifetimes).

One major effect of the lives of Dipankara and Dattatreya was to stimulate seekers also in that direction, and Vedanta was one result of their lives, as well as the lives of other ascetics. The whole movement we call Vedanta is an old one, and Swami Shivananda claims it is as old as Lord Dattatreya Himself. However, large numbers of Vedanta adherents came much later. Vedanta gave rise to the Upanishads, which are the essence and the blooming of Hinduism....They add a wonderful dimension to Hinduism and make it a truly multi-dimensional religion.

Like Buddhism and Jainism, Vedanta is enlightenment-oriented rather than devotion-oriented. In recent times however, that has changed somewhat, and Vedanta has become more integral in its approach, especially with the advent of Ramakrishna Paramahamsa, the Great Swan in the 19th century.. Ramakrishna combined devotion to the Mother Goddess and to Vedanta in a perfect combination of heart and head, and this greatly inspired Swami Vivekananda. We will have an opportunity to see more about them later. The Vedanta Society that is present in various parts of the world owes its origin to these two great souls.

The term Bhakti-Vedanta (loosely translated as Faith-based Non-Duality, or Faith-based Oneness) has come into use and shows every likelihood of staying with us for a long time. Love can be indeed used as a ladder to Non-duality.

Our discussion of Buddhism and Jainism continue in the next chapter, but it's time to bring Lord Sanat Kumara into the stage.

Chapter Fifteen

The Great Brotherhood of Sanat Kumara

Where one realizes the indivisible unity of life, sees nothing else, hears nothing else, and knows nothing else, that then is the Infinite. Where one sees separateness...and knows separateness, that is the finite. The Infinite is beyond death, but the finite simply cannot escape death---***Sanat Kumara***

Sanat Kumara (who likes to go by the informal name Raj!) recently made some positive comments about Pope Francis and sure enough, Pope Francis' name has grown in the world and He is being seen as a unique Pope... According to Raj, this Pope has the blessings of his famous namesake St. Francis of Assisi.

Sanat Kumara has been on earth for a very long time to groom great souls for great things on earth, all for the sake of the spiritual evolution of humanity. He has thus groomed a host of Ascended Masters through many incarnations, such as Gautama, Jesus, Saint Germain, the Masters Kuthumi and El Morya, as well as the Tibetan Master Djwal Kul and others. In this illustrious group can be included the great personage known as Avatar Babaji, who was introduced to the world by Yogananda Paramahamsa.

According to some writers, no one Being has played a greater role in Earth's protection and evolution than Sanat Kumara, the son of Shiva and also known as Kartikeya. His father also is, quite predictably, known for the same two activities, consciousness and evolution. The following Commandments (among others) have been attributed to Sanat Kumara by esoteric writer Parvathi Kumar:

- *Ask yourself, "Who Am I?" and do not deviate from self-study.*
- *Function as a soul, not as a personality*
- *Love for God is one of the first steps*
- *Worship the Lord with Joy.*
- *Have the Will to be with the Lord*
- *The fire of knowledge purifies.*
- *Learn to be alone.*
- *Practice harmlessness in thought, word, and deed.*
- *Restrain from analysis and criticism of other paths.*
- *Release the mind from dualities.*
- *Remember: All is Divine.*

Several writers in the last 200 years, beginning with Madame Blavatsky, the founder of the Theosophical Society, have spoken about the Ascended Masters all of whom have lived several lives on earth and slowly ascended to truly spectacular levels of sacrifice, service, love and transcendence. This is turn has led to a great amount of power present in these Masters. The Masters form a great Brotherhood, under the leadership of Sanat Kumara as mentioned above, who is also called Kartikeya or Subramanya by the Hindus, and who is a son of Lord Shiva, and who is also a brother of Ganesha, the beloved elephant-headed God. Now, Kartikeya's teachings are needless to say, in sync with those of His father, the First Tantric and the First Yogi. Again the Shiva connection surfaces...

Sanat Kumara, who is said to have inhabited the planet Venus for a long time before migrating to Earth eons ago, (but who in recent times has made way for the Buddha to play the role of Lord of the Esoteric Seekers), is a Master of Masters…The other Avataric lineages, that of Lord Dattatreya, Lord Vishnu and Lord Shiva take precedence, since they are true Descents, not Ascents, and in that sense true Avatars.

In that vein, is Krishnamurti's backing-out of the position of World Teacher in 1929 an act of deference because of Avataric Descents (that of the Sai Babas)? The question is intriguing, especially because many years later some journalists once asked

Krishnamurti, "Why don't the Masters speak anymore", and Krishnamurti's response was: "When the Lord is there, why should the Masters speak" (!)

And so, in the Brotherhood of Sanat Kumara are two great Beings that almost all Earth-dwellers have heard of: Jesus Christ and Gautama Buddha. Both of them belonged for long (i.e., for lifetimes) in this Ultimate Spiritual School, and later entered the Great Brotherhood, sometimes called the Great White Brotherhood. Both Christ and Buddha are Ascended Masters of the highest kind who ascended early and then made a final descent with a mission…and they continue to have a presence on earth. Thus they are actually a combination of ascent and descent (or what one might call evolution and involution)…Jacob's Ladder indeed.

Sathya Sai Baba, who loved to speak glowingly about the Buddha and Jesus once said that the Buddha and Christ are "not original Avatars" and we can see why. A perfect Avatar is a Deity Quantum who descends without having evolved (or ascended) on earth over previous lives…Another point to note is that an Ascended Master hasn't displayed an "active Omnipresence" while on earth. On the other hand, Descended Avatars (especially Krishna, Shirdi Baba, and Sathya Sai Baba) have indeed displayed an active Omnipresence, coming to devotees' rescue, in times of crisis, at a few moments' notice.

The Buddha famously spoke of His previous lifetimes in various bodies… both human and animal. These make up the Jataka tales, which many Buddhists are aware of. The Buddha is said to have attained Perfect Clairvoyance, which implies perfect recall of all His past lives…Being very sensitive therefore to karma and its cumulative effect over lifetimes, the Buddha was very interested in helping individuals overcome past karma, or at least avoid negative karma in this life. He was a "Karma Neutralizer" of sorts, which is one of the roles of a Guru interested in liberating His devotee from the cycle of birth and death. Hence His exhortations to His followers: *Make haste and do good.* And: *When you see someone practicing the Way of giving, aid him joyously...*

One of the great messages of Buddhism is: Be mindful always, so that your unwholesome thoughts and temptations don't get converted into actions. Awaken and watch yourself without the ego getting involved...and thus become one with the Inner Witness. Mindfulness is what tames the mind and as Sanat Kumara also says in the Chhandogya Upanishad, "Mind is everything." *This then is the manifest great connection between the Buddha and Sanat Kumara: Their emphasis on "working on the mind."*

Connected with this is the exhortation to "go it alone" (i.e., work in solitude). In a rather well-known Buddhist sutra which has come to be known as the "Rhinoceros Sutra" the Buddha extols the merit of asceticism of the solitary kind by saying: "Let the ascetic wander alone like a rhinoceros." He did temper this though to some extent when He also pointed out the importance of the Sangha (or the Buddhist community of monks). This is yet another example of the Middle Way of the Buddha. There are circumstances that warrant solitude and other circumstances that warrant (like-minded) company. This grand aloneness and self-sufficiency is referred to as Kaivalya by some, especially by Jains. However as a human trait it can be found throughout history and in all religions. It can also be found in the world of today. Not all seekers are gregarious beings, attracted to ashrams. There are many solitary seekers in this world.

From the inherent disorder of Kali Yuga (or the age of Darkness) was born Buddhism, the refuge of the weary and the stricken, the haven of those who wanted an intelligent approach to religion and spirituality. A path that awakens and edifies its adherents. A path that considers a lack of awareness synonymous with sloth and even a form of death. A religion that put mindfulness on the spiritual map of humanity on a larger scale than the Shiva Tantras had done. For most of us are swept away by the limited worldly consciousness of humanity...

The Noble Eightfold Path of the Buddha nicely sums up the need to tread the path of Dharma (or Dhamma) which can be simply described as the Path of Righteousness.

Just like Jainism has 24 Thirthankaras, Buddhism has a list of 28 Buddhas, of whom Gautama Buddha was the last.

We now turn to what is sometimes considered a "sister religion" of Buddhism, viz. Jainism. Jainism saw a great revival during the time of the Buddha due of the life of Mahavira. We say 'revival' because Jainism has seen other great teachers in the past, and was actually given its initial impetus by the great Rishabha.

Mahavira was born into a royal family like the Buddha, and is known as the 24th Great Guru (or Tirthankara) of Jainism. The word Tirthankara has 2 components: Tirtha (which is a shallow body of water that is easily crossed) and Ankara (meaning, one who provides). Thus a Tirthankara is a metaphor for "one who provides an easy passage across the ocean of life to liberation". Mahavira spent many years in solitude after renouncing his right to his father's throne, and is said to have become a realized soul, gaining the reverence of the people around him. His bearing and style gathered like-minded Jains around Him…soon He was elevated to the rank of a Tirthankara, after showing signs of His Divinity. Mahavira taught that enlightenment is not a free ride. Right faith, Right Knowledge, and Right Conduct are essential.

The Teachings of Mahavira are found in Jain Sutras and Agamas. Mahavira openly discussed the human ego and its devastating effects on the spiritual life. He advocated the building of inner strength by renouncing worldly excesses. Even lay Jains were advised to practice lives of self-restraint and service. Far from becoming neurotic beings, as modern psychology would have us fantasize, Jains are among the most balanced and wholesome people I have met.

The following statement is attributed to Mahavira:

A living body is not merely an integration of limbs and flesh but it is the abode of the soul which potentially has perfect perception, perfect knowledge, perfect power, and perfect bliss.

This strong tendency to view the soul as something complete and inherently self-sufficient is perhaps the very essence of this "non-theistic" religion we call Jainism…And related to this is the belief among Jains that the plane (or heaven) attained by the enlightened is "preferable" to the plane inhabited by the gods...

And this is a characteristic both Buddhism and Jainism display...However, somewhat paradoxically, in their religious zeal and in the interests of attracting adherents away from Hinduism, new scriptures and even new deities (!) mysteriously appeared that made Hindu deities somehow subservient to them and also made the Hindu deities subservient to beings that have obtained Nirvana after living on earth...One must keep in mind though that the originators of the two religions did not emphasize that. Rather it their followers who are responsible for this. Throughout our spiritual and religious history there are examples of followers exaggerating and "over-extrapolating" the original teachings of a Master, and coming up with more severe, fundamentalist, and even twisted forms. Both religion and spirituality have the unfortunate ability to make humans more extreme and less Universal over time...

Deities that suddenly appear in the newer scriptures of the Dark Age have to be examined carefully. What is conveniently forgotten is that the Vedas and Shiva Sutras as well as Shiva Tantras are thousands of years older than either Buddhism or Jainism. It is also common experience that such new deities do not remain in public memory for long...

Mahavira developed a doctrine that has come to be known as *Anekantavada*, a doctrine that had an influence on Mahatma Gandhi and led to his developing ideas such as Satyagraha (passive resistance based on "truth-force" and love) and Ahimsa (or active non-violence).

Anekantavada basically says no one interpretation of truth is complete and exclusive...rather a multiplicity of viewpoints is to be respected and even encouraged. For Mohandas Gandhi, the well-known Father of Modern India, the truth of the British occupation of India was more than countered by the truth of the natives of India, who represented a different truth. And if the Indians' truth was not respected then it was time to organize for Civil Disobedience and other measures...

As a philosophical stance however, Anekantavada was opposed by Adi Shankara in his writings. Shankara saw Anekantavada as leading to a cacophony of ideas and world views, and consequently to a "tower of Babel".

Buddhism and Jainism both accept reincarnation and karma. As the Buddha acknowledged, He had lived before in various bodies. However, His immense teachings and powers appear to not be merely a product of multiple earthly existences, but also stem from the grace of Divinity. His immensely auspicious birth is one indication of the grace He received. Perhaps because of the Buddha's emphasis on gradual evolution over several previous lives, and His relative silence about His Divine origins, many of His followers began to portray Him as an Ascended Buddha only. However, some Mahayana Buddhists, when Mahayana began to take on a more deity- based approach, began looking upon the Buddha as a descent of Lord Avalokiteshwara.

While the Buddha is mostly considered a non-theistic figure and has attracted therefore a large number of agnostics throughout history, if we go by some very sincere seekers of the Higher Life, the Buddha is an eternal and metaphysical entity, who still visits the earth, and has been experienced by people even during the last 100 years, including being channeled by Lightworkers. More recently, my friend and healer Connie Shaw, had occasion to have an audience with the Buddha. Swami Vivekananda also once had a vision of Him.

Why did I begin this narrative of the Buddha in such a metaphysical vein, when He is considered one of the first Nastikas…a "soul denier"? The words of Lord Dattatreya need to be recalled here:

All non-dualistic doctrines come to this world by the grace of God.

The term non-dualistic can, with very little distortion, be extrapolated to mean also non-theistic…especially considering the times the above statement was made. In the last few centuries however they have come to be somewhat less similar paradigms…and there have also been attempts in recent times to combine theistic devotion with non-dualism, using the Power of Love...Love is the binding force that can even bring together seemingly dissimilar paradigms.

Yes, it's true the Buddha started a religion without using any name of God. Even though He did acknowledge their existence, He spoke of them only tangentially and as only slightly more exalted than man...Yes the Buddha did not even want to acknowledge the existence of the human soul. Yes, the Buddha appeared to be uninterested in Bhakti. Yes, the Buddha did not speak of Divine Love that the Avatars have for humanity. But what else other than love still keeps Him here among us? When one carefully examines Buddhism, one realizes that few religions prepare us to meet God as well as Buddhism does! It is also a religion that seeks to bring about the victory of light over darkness.

"Denying" the individual soul (the Buddha's doctrine of Anatman) does not automatically deny the existence of the Universal Self. The Buddha thus even acknowledged the presence of multiple godheads...He was well aware of the presence of Great Spirit quantums in the Universe. However, He felt it was much more useful to speak of something that was tangible rather than something that was "already complete and perfect"...Buddhism is ultimately an attempt to create a hands-on and practical spirituality. Unfortunately for it though, in this most trying age of spiritual darkness and turbulence, it has for some, the appearance of a candle in the wind relative to strongly charged theistic paths. And so Buddhism has been described by some as a "lame religion."

So why did He not make His teaching more God-centered? In some ways, He was a product of the times in which He lived. He was a keen observer and after quickly appraising the situation decided to teach the way He did...There are indications He chose to be a "step-down" avatar. A "step-down" avatar, like a step-down transformer, doesn't reveal His full potency to the masses. *He doesn't even reveal all that He knows.* Instead He focuses on what He considers vital and important... The Buddha had a formidable environment to overcome, a very traditional and orthodox Hindu dominated environment that had begun to decay, a rigid caste system, a growing materialism, and a diminishing spirituality. He came to awaken, and He carried out an amazing mission. Buddhism led a charmed life for the next 1000 years, spreading into the deep corners of Asia.

He fully endorsed Meditation (especially the watching of one's breath) and Mindfulness, or the Awareness of everything, internal and external. If I can watch the body, I am not the body. If I can watch a thought…?

It is not surprising that Buddhism later developed in a spiritual direction with the advent of Vajrayana Buddhism. Spiritual Service unto humanity (personified by the Bodhisattva who puts off his own salvation in favor of being reincarnated on earth to help sentient beings see the light) became the high standard by which a monk was judged.

One of the greatest contributions of the Buddha was His Law of Dependent Origination. It basically presents a cause-effect chain that captures many of the phenomena we take for granted in life. The chain is circular in nature and one can begin anywhere in the chain… For example: Rebirth causes not only ageing and death, but also ignorance. This is also stated by Lord Shiva in one of the Shiva Sutras. The Lord says, "When I created life, I also created ignorance." Being alive is to be covered by a pall of ignorance. Neither do we remember our origins nor do we remember our past lives in ways that are intense enough to really impact us in this life…Instead we are over-stimulated by the world around us.

Anyway, back to the chain of Dependent Origination: Rebirth causes Ignorance. Ignorance of the great continuity of lives leads us to not realize the effects of karma, thus leading very easily to bad karmic formations. This results in imperfect consciousness of worldly stimuli, which stimulate our senses and mind, and lead to craving. We then cling to what we like and become attached. We begin to see life as a worthwhile playground and even a great experience, despite its obvious impermanence. We start competing for the scarce resources of the world too. We begin to believe in the myth of becoming something significant in the world....this in turn leads to a faith in time as a great conqueror of limitations and we end up actually desiring (or at least not minding) rebirth...and so the cycle goes on...

The light of the Buddha has blessed the world...even if Ralph Waldo Emerson referred to it as the "icy light of Buddhism". But sometimes, that is exactly what is needed...

The Holy Father of Sanat Kumara, Lord Shiva, ultimately is the invisible Father of both of the non-theistic religions, Jainism and Buddhism through Rishabha and Sanat Kumara. However, we have to keep in mind that over time, all religions diverge and become more dissimilar from each other, each developing its own lore, practices, heroes, and saints. The teachings of each religion are also subject to modification to suit changing needs and times, and thus the cognitive space between religions also increases over time. The history of Jainism therefore has been very different from that of Buddhism. So much so, it is hard to imagine that Mahavira and the Buddha were contemporaries of each other.

If the son of Shiva, Sanat Kumara, actively blessed Buddhism as the spiritual schools suggest, He could be the all-important reason Buddhism grew into a global religion while Jainism didn't...It is an intriguing phenomenon because both these religions do have things in common, and yet one became a globally-recognized religion, while the other to this day is mostly unknown outside of India. There are two possible reasons for this: Buddhism is somewhat less austere than Jainism, because the Buddha advocated the Middle Path, (i.e., an avoidance of extremes). And also the Buddha is a beloved and admired member of the Great Brotherhood of Ascended Masters...with all their energies and compassion bearing upon the world through the consciousness of Buddhists...

The Tibetans, the Chinese, and the Japanese

Entire books could of course be written about the history of Buddhism in China, Japan, Burma, Sri Lanka, Tibet, etc. The number of monks that entered the Buddhist Order in these countries boggles the mind. Sometimes, half the males in Tibet were monks... In fact, it became the norm for at least one son in every family to enter monkhood. The two great schools that sprung up in the first few centuries after the passing of the Buddha were the Mahayana (or Greater Vehicle) and the Theravada Buddhism. The term Hinayana (or Lesser Vehicle) is sometimes used for Theravada Buddhism and that is an unfortunate term that needs to be avoided...

As the centuries passed, Buddhism sparked a great search within and that triggered offshoots such as Zen in China and Japan and Vajrayana in Tibet. It is to the credit of Buddhism that it was open ended enough to beget all these forms that carried it to a new level of spiritual sophistication. Also, the immense transmissibility of Buddhism is amazing. To draw a loose comparison of sorts between Hinduism and Buddhism, one can view their equivalents thus:

Theravada----Bhakti Yoga

Mahayana----Jnana Yoga

Vajrayana----Vedanta and Tantra

Yogachara---Meditation followed by Revelation (in the Tradition of the ancient Rishis of India)

Madhyamaka---An offshoot of Mahayana wherein the practitioner is like the Mayavadis of Hinduism who embrace the impersonal Universal Spirit to the exclusion of all else (i.e., the world)

The founders of Zen in China and Tibetan Buddhism were Bodhidharma (6th century) and Padmasambhava (8th century) respectively. Though they were very different from each other, they all ended up serving the Buddhist cause, which says something about the open-endedness of Buddhism. The Buddha taught for so many years and gave so many discourses as well as private teachings to His closest devotees, that the broad base He created spawned various schools and eventually schisms as well....As I have noted elsewhere in this book, schisms and denominations have dogged virtually every religion on the face of the earth...

Some of the traveling Buddhist monks who took Buddhism to the far corners of Asia were meditators, and others were teachers, while still others preferred to write tomes. They would set up monasteries and sometimes live there for the rest of their lives. Once Bodhidharma left the shores of India, he never returned. His Mahayana guru had pointed China-wards, and that was it...He learned some Chinese on the ship that took him to that already Buddhist/Taoist land and was apparently accorded a welcome by the ruler of the place where he landed, but far from being overawed by that, Bodhidharma quietly left and melted into the interior of the Dragon...he finally ended up at the famous Shao-Lin monastery, and meditated there for nine years before he built up enough credibility to attract followers...but once he did, there was no looking back...to this day, his influence in China is evident.

Later, his school called Chan spread to Japan where it became known as Zen. Zen Buddhism has made waves in the West during the last 125 years or so thanks to the efforts of people like D.T. Suzuki and Paul Reps as well as the charismatic Alan Watts, who had a knack of making the unfamiliarity of Zen seem like comfortable terrain. Many books about Zen have been published, including the teachings of Bodhidharma. Monasteries have been set up in both America and Europe.

These prime movers inspired such great movements as to be regarded as Divine Beings in their own right, a title they would probably summarily reject, so humble and grounded were they. It is said that Padmasambhava was a tantric sage, who brought great power and talent with him to Tibet.

A Tibetan tantric religion naturally sprang up because of the teachings and initiations of Padmasambhava. He was introduced to the Tibetans by another great Buddhist pioneer Shantarakshita, a spiritual giant who was well-versed in both Hinduism and

Buddhism and had been in the faculty of Nalanda University, one of the first great spiritual Universities the world has seen.

Shantarakshita's scholarly nature had led him to being a great integrator of the teachings of various philosophies of former Buddhist greats like Nagarjuna and Asanga.. He later helped construct the first great Buddhist temple in Tibet, at Samye. During his tenure as a monk and Abbott at Nalanda, Shantarakshita had come into contact with the mystic Padmasambhava and his tantric teachings.

Haribhadra was a disciple of Padmasambhava and Saraha was a disciple of Haribhadra…According to Osho the 20th century teacher, the majority of great Buddhist tantric teachings have come from Saraha. Thus in an indirect manner the influence of Padmasambhava on Indian Buddhism is also to considered as significant, at least until the 12th century, when Buddhism began to fade in India.

As we are going to see, a major reason for this decline was the Age of Dattatreya and also the Vaishnavite Renaissance, and not just the destruction of Buddhist temples and universities by the Muslim invaders as conventional wisdom says. The plundering of temples and universities can never do permanent damage to a religion, because they can be rebuilt. But what happens in the psyche of a culture leaves a much more permanent impact…

Buddhism got its first buffeting in the hands of Adi Shankara who established major Hindu centers all over India, and later at the hands of the Shaivites of the Nath Tradition as we are going to see. There was a plethora of seers and saints that sprung up at regular intervals after 1000 AD, leading to a steady decline of Buddhism in India. As the Buddha Himself had predicted about 1500 years earlier, "My Order will not last forever."

However, Buddhism was truly a Grand Experiment of the Mind that for centuries drew millions to its tent. It is still very much alive in the Far East.

Chapter Sixteen

Lao Tzu: The Tao & Its Many Manifestations

Only he who has no use for the empire is fit to be entrusted with it---*Chuang Tzu*

Daoism (or Taoism) is an intriguing spiritual path. While most of us view it as a non-theistic and transcendental doctrine as espoused in the Tao Te Ching (written by the Master Lao Tzu) and in the works of Chuang Tzu and his followers, it later branched off into a complete cosmology, with its own metaphysics, its own revelations, and yes, even an array of spiritual beings or gods. Daoism is now seen as having a complex history, combining philosophical and spiritual insights with meditation, consciousness projection and spirit communication. There's an inherent diversity now in Taoism...

While some people may view this as a dilution or even a corruption of the original Taoism, this writer thinks of it more as a natural widening of a great ethos, which is simultaneously a religion with a spiritual beginning and also a slowly unfolding canvas of human consciousness that has branched off in many directions...for after all, the serious Taoist believes in opposing nothing...Great tolerance is the hallmark of Taoists, and a quote from Vidura, one of the wise men who lived during the time of the Mahabharata, comes to mind: *The strength of tolerance far exceeds the strength of power...*

What began as a series of terse and incisive statements from its founder Lao Tzu regarding the irony of life and of his times, and how one can go about living life in a way that was both elevating and completely in flow with Nature, later became an ornate religion, filled with its own priesthood, rituals, rites of passage, and voluminous scriptures, much like its precursor, Hinduism. So much so that the early writings about Taoism in the West denounced it as mostly magic, mesmerism, and hoopla...However, in the 20th century, following mature translations of the Tao Te Ching and the works of Chuang Tzu, Taoism has gained stature once again.

Lao Tzu lived around the same time as the Buddha and Mahavira, and centuries later Taoism was influenced by Buddhism after it arrived in China. When Lao Tzu spoke of the Dao (or the Tao), it is important to note He meant it as the Absolute as well as the Way. In other words, the Source, Destination, and Path are all "one and the same". Everything is the Dao….much like the Hindu would say, "Everything is Brahman". The spirit of this Oneness is ever present in this non-dualistic doctrine.

The spirit of Taoism is similar to that found in the Shiva Sutras of Hinduism. Lao Tzu also speaks of "Ignorance of the Tao" as one of the prime factors causing the mundane morass of mankind.

Coming back to Taoism and Lao Tzu's reasoning, the "Hierarchy of Effects" is akin to this:

Cosmic Ignorance of the Tao

leads to

Mundane and False Wisdom/Knowledge

leads to

Development of Separate Identities, Egos, Competition and Ensuing Chaos

This is not very different from the basic ethos of Hinduism. One therefore must wonder: did Lao Tzu, because he had access to a vast array of knowledge, being a librarian in one of the largest libraries of China at that time, become familiar with the philosophical underpinnings of Hinduism, especially Samkhya, and develop his philosophy from it? I say Samkhya, because Purusha and Prakriti correspond quite well to Tao and its natural manifestations. Nature has now been imbued with Intelligence and almost appears to be on an auto-pilot mode. It does not appear to have a will and yet it does all... In other words the Tao is completely obscured.

This is not to take away even a little from the genius and depth of this Master. Several people down the ages have claimed encounters with Him. And so, like the Buddha, He is a master of light, and an avatar, who will always be with us. I'm sorry to "disappoint" those who see him as an impeccable transcendentalist and a stand-alone non-theistic genius, who one day simply disappeared from our midst... He is a Divine Soul, who is now an Ascended Master and had spent other lives in the East, before He descended as Lao Tzu. He is like the Buddha but more strident...His verses are at times as strident as Lord Krishna's. And yet He says at one point, sounding like a child of the Universe:

People live in joy...I alone am listless and dim...closed and uncouth like an orphan...but I value the Universal Mother.

Just like the ten avatars of Vishnu, there are the ten appearances of Lao Tzu... Just like there are the 7 immortals of Hinduism, there are 8 immortals in Taoism. Similar to the chakras in Hinduism, we have the Dantians in Taoism. There appears therefore to be some level of influence coming from Hinduism...While it is clear how Buddhism traveled from India, it is much less clear how Hinduism traveled to China, but by all indications, Hinduism spread first to areas such as Indonesia and Cambodia before moving northward to China, where however it manifested more in spiritual and semantic terms than in religious terms.

And so, it's not surprising that Taoism branched off in many directions, just like Hinduism did before it. The very being of Lao Tzu is akin to that of a Divine facilitator, who does not discourage the development of His doctrine in any direction... After all, All is truly the Dao. If I was impressed with the Tao Te Ching so many years ago as a college student, today I am completely enamored by the spiritual richness of Taoism, which fearlessly sought to create, and then maintain its multifarious identity even when faced with the so-called cultural rivalry from the non-theistic doctrines of Confucianism, as well as Ch'an (or Zen) and mainstream Mahayana Buddhism. Even though Kublai Khan many centuries ago tried to destroy Taoism, it bounced right back, much like Hinduism has repeatedly done in the face of attacks on it. Both these religions now have such a broad base that no external power can dislodge them.

In recent times, Taoism, like all religion in China, came under siege, but it has recently bounced back and will undoubtedly in the future continue to provide both wisdom and compassion to the multitudes. Its beautiful temples, often built in sylvan garden settings, will continue to attract adherents. This is a religion with such a vast scriptural heritage that much translation and codification still remains to be done. Unlike Confucianism, which preaches order and formality in a worldly setting, and perhaps does little to stir up spiritual yearnings, Taoism is both awakening and experimental. Natural living and not following a rigid code are good ways of sensitizing one's spiritual antennas…

Taoism in fact, is a spiritual uprising like no other…a set of arrows emerging from a single source and then becoming a source of gushing springs as the arrows landed….It has the added advantage of being almost entirely historically documented, unlike Hinduism, which must bear the burden of being so ancient as to depend greatly on the oral tradition. For after all, the written word always has more credibility than the spoken word…

A Chinese Bible might well begin with the following words:

In the beginning was the Dao and the Dao was with God and the Dao was God. Everything was with the Dao and the Dao is everything.

Substitute Dao with Universal Spirit or Holy Ghost and you will see the Christian equivalent. Substitute Dao with Brahman and you have the beginnings of the Hindu Upanishads.

People like to point out that Lao Tzu begins the Tao Te Ching by saying "That which can be described is not the Tao". Our words and our languages are limited because they were developed by linguists and communicators with both feet firmly implanted on terra firma. There is a danger of "reading too much" into sentences like "That which can be described is not the Tao". Perhaps the word "Spirit" (or similar word) had not yet entered common parlance in China, nor had its attributes such as omnipresence and omnipotence, and so the Master used the word Dao, that has stuck through the centuries. He judiciously left the development of the attributes to His followers, and left them to coin new terms for those attributes that almost suggest themselves and yet leave room for elaboration so that later Taoist mystics might well feel they were the great explicators...for after all that is what a great leader does, according to the Tao Te Ching.

Almost predictably, Taoism gave birth to the three jewels: Jing, Chi, and Shen. To put it simply, Jing is the nurturing essence within nature (Prakriti), Chi is the vital energy (akin to Shakti), and Shen is Spirit or Soul (or later, God, and akin to Purusha). For example, a living creature has a body that is the result of Jing and the same Jing also causes the reproductive urge... The body has Chi coursing through it, and the body, especially with regards to involuntary actions such as heartbeat and breathing, is controlled by Shen. The simultaneous presence of all three in the body gives rise to an Internal Alchemy (Neidan) that can be studied and optimized...

If "Universal Spirit" (and spirit merely being that which is too subtle to be sensed by the senses and the mind) is accepted as the parent of all, the nurturer of all, and the inhabitor of all, then a picture emerges with infinite meaning and implications...and so it is little wonder that Taoism has such a rich fabric. In Chapter 42 of the Tao Te Ching, Lao Tzu says:

The Tao begot one. (*Universal Spirit begat Purusha?*)

One begot two (*Purusha begat Heaven & Earth?*)

Two begot three (*Jing, Chi, Shen...the last being individual God Quantums?*)

And three begot the ten thousand things (i.e., *everything?*).

The ten thousand things carry yin and embrace yang (*Yin is inherent, while Yang is desired: This implies there will always be an attraction to Love & an attempt to grow in Consciousness*). Love is manifest in Nature in subtle ways as Sai Baba teaches. Love too is omnipresent...

Now, is the Dao an involuntary source, i.e., just letting it all happen? Or does it have consciousness and a will. ...Or is it just that the gap between intention and action is non-existent? For a person imbued with the Tao, there is complete spontaneity...in other words, there is more intelligence than effort involved. Well, if the Dao has a will, it is itself too subtle and/or too vast to be known. Such a viewpoint almost paves the way for a theistic base to later develop, because that will lead more easily to the notion of a supreme yet subtle Divine Will...while at the same time allowing for an "auto-pilot mode" for Nature to operate under, that Man seeks to mar to his peril. This auto-pilot mode was also developed by some of the followers of Kapila, who sought to define in mathematical terms.

One of the great things about Taoism is that the ancients sought to apply the principle of Tao to enhance all their activities, whether it was to take care of the body through exercise, or to enjoy esthetic pleasures, or to blend in better with forces of Nature. And to pursue longevity was seen as a legitimate right, and one sign of a triumph of one's practices.

And so Taoism has given birth to Tai Chi, Chi Gong, Nei Gong, Feng Shui, and various other arts. Today we have Taoist Yoga and Taoist Meditation (such as Nei Gong which also includes breathing practices), slowly coming into prominence.

While the I Ching began before Taoism, the Taoists took to it like fish to water. And few other works in the history of mankind have had such a supreme influence on a people. For those unfamiliar with the I Ching, it is a tool that can be used like an oracle to guide humans to the auspiciousness or inauspiciousness of certain decisions or actions. In other words, it can be consulted for advice especially regarding the timing of one's responses to challenges and problems. But it is also a tool for self-cultivation and for understanding the mechanisms of Nature and the Universe. And so it can be used at many levels...Many diverse authors have sought to tap into the wisdom of the I Ching from different angles. Many of them pointed out that to merely use the I Ching as a tool for solving worldly problems and to facilitate the making of worldly decisions was a "lower form" of its use...instead it could also be a tool for spiritual development... Over the centuries a Taoist I Ching was developed and books on this have recently been published in the West.

Taoists tend to be highly attuned to Nature, as are many Zen monks and practitioners. Taoists speak of the "creative spirit" that can take over when one is painting or composing music or verse. This contact with the creative well-spring within the individual made them state confidently that Heaven and Earth intersected in Man.

Taoism and Zen both like to promote a spirit of inquiry as well as tolerance and that has led to their depth and resilience. One finds that in modern China, they are both on the upswing...Acupuncture and herbology have both descended from Taoist alchemy. Adepts in Taoism tend to be vegetarian and lead very spartan lives. Some of these adepts are coming out into the open, and assisting students with their Taoist practices. The Thai Master Mantak Chia, whose family hails from China, is an example.

It's hardly surprising, given Taoism's depth and spiritual underpinnings, that it is far more popular in the rest of the world than Confucianism, which by comparison is staid, tradition-bound, and secular rather than spiritual... Taoism may seem like a mystery religion to us, but for even the common folk of China, it has been a great source of inspiration.

Chapter Seventeen

Yeshua the Christ, Beloved of the World

His disciples said, "When will the Kingdom come?" (He replied): It will not come by waiting for it. It will not be a matter of saying here it is...*Rather the kingdom of the father is spread out upon the earth and men do not see it---**Jesus Christ: Gospel of Thomas.***

Two thousand years ago, the spiritual history of the planet was changed forever by the well-known arrival of an Avatar of great presence and potency. The religion we now call Christianity began with just a few spiritual seekers, who were inspired beyond belief by this Avatar, so much so that some even laid down their lives for Him.

As I begin this chapter on Christ, I am aware of the Christ Myth Theory that suggests He never existed, and that He was a merely a hero created by some vested interests...One of the favorite arguments of some Myth Theorists is that the life of Jesus is merely a collection of fables borrowed from the lives of Krishna and Horus, an Egyptian god. Regarding this I have the following points to make:

1. The presence of a hagiography (or even a borrowed hagiography) giving the life details of a being, does not in any way provide evidence that the being himself never existed....that would be an irrational leap of faith in itself. In other words, while over-zealous devotees and followers may have created a "spicy" bunch of fables regarding the birth, life, and crucifixion, they are more like "marketing efforts" and that certainly does not mean the product itself did not exist....

2. There are a fair number of accounts in India and Tibet of Jesus' visits to different places in those regions.

3. The Ascended Masters (especially Kuthumi) have spoken at length about the Jesus incarnation...with Kuthumi insisting that

Jesus is an incarnation of Sananda (a son of Brahma). Sananda is in turn an ecstatic devotee of the chief Kumara, Sanat Kumara.

4. Several people through the centuries have claimed visitations and visions of Jesus and His mother Mary, down to the present day.

5. Major Healings take place in Christian holy sites, down to this day.

6. To say that the Dead Sea Scrolls suggest that Jesus was not a historical figure (as some have claimed) also doesn't make sense, since the Gnostic Gospels speak of Jesus in the first or second person much more than the third person, and so sound more credible than any third person account…

7. An Avatar of great Power, Knowledge, and Compassion, Sathya Sai Baba, has confirmed that Jesus lived, taught, traveled in India and other countries, and was finally buried in Kashmir.

8. Christophanies, such as the appearance of Christ in Damascus in His light body are not restricted to the New Testament alone. They have happened several times since.

And so, this writer will now proceed to discuss a great Being, Jesus Christ, who apparently was a talented musician, and who had a sense of humor, even in the most challenging of times. A Being that was the ultimate Gnostic and could perform miracles, while still downplaying them, and claiming that others would do even greater things…

The discovery of the Nag Hammadi scrolls in December 1945 could be viewed as a "stroke of luck" or a "coincidence". But intuition suggests this discovery was hardly a coincidence…It happened just after World War II ended. The situation seemed ripe for a new beginning…The discoveries at Nag Hammadi (usually pronounced Naaj Hummaadi) have truly embellished (and some might say revived) Christianity. Gnostic Christianity (the spiritual version of Christianity), is destined to play an ever increasing role it appears…Further discoveries at Qumran have shown that Nag Hammadi was intended to be an open-ended phenomenon and not just a one-time occurrence.

Two now-famous works that were found at Nag Hammadi were the Gospel of Thomas and the Secret Book of John. Their spiritual content can make Christianity spiritually vibrant once again, and that can in turn lead to a kind of renaissance... Christ's immensely colorful and spiritually uplifting life can shine forth once again when the full extent of His life and teachings are better appreciated. His efforts to communicate with people of various backgrounds and religions in a way that was never before seen will lead many to appreciate Him in a new light.

The life of Jesus (Hebrew name Yeshua) reads stranger than fiction, and not only because of His meteoric rise to Messianic prominence and His equally speedy capture and crucifixion. Rather, His life is a great example of an Avatar that chose to both experience other lands and to make His presence felt over as much territory as possible, and an Avatar that chose to cast His spiritual net with great zeal and sincerity. Jesus says in the Gospel of Thomas, "Birds have their nest and animals have their holes. But the Son of Man has no place to lay down and to rest."

He traveled far and wide, and finally left His body in the distant land of Kashmir. Jesus traveled to India twice. The first visit occurred when He was a youth and the second happened after the crucifixion, which He survived, going on to live a long and eventful life. If, as the Master Kuthumi says, He is an incarnation of Sananda, a son of Brahma the Creator in the Hindu pantheon, then it isn't surprising that the spiritual gravitational pull of India attracted Jesus to her, and made Him linger for a long time...Some Jesus myth writers have commented that no secular literature of the time mentions Jesus...the reason for that might well be: He hardly spent much time in His homeland...instead <u>he was an intrepid wanderer, much like Adi Shankara</u> later was.

It was of course known in those days that India had two main parts, the southern portion accessible by sea, and the northern portion accessible by land. Jesus sent Thomas to South India, while He himself went to the northern half of India, encountering people of three main religions, the Jains, the Hindus, and the Buddhists. Thomas performed miracles in India and managed to convert many to the new faith. He always mentioned the name of Jesus when he spoke, and was successful in giving discourses to the multitude.

Though Jesus disagreed with some of the practices He found in India, at no stage did He seek to impose His teachings on anyone. Nor did He seek to proselytize or begin a church, unlike His apostle. This is true of most Avatars. They do not try and begin a new faith or religion. At one stage, when the priests at a temple in Puri, on the east coast of India, showed displeasure at His presence, Jesus simply moved north to the spiritually blessed city of Kasi (or Varanasi) on the banks of the Ganges River, the home of Lord Shiva. The thought of Jesus in Kasi, bathing in the river Ganga, and listening to the Shiva prayers being recited, is gratifying: A true mingling of cultures.

It is more than probable that Jesus would have encountered the Samkhya philosophy of Kapila that was firmly entrenched in India by that time. The idea of Purusha preceding Prakriti (or Consciousness preceding Matter) is echoed by Jesus in His teachings. Also the idea of God as the Indweller of all beings is something Jesus would have encountered in India as also the twin concepts of karma and reincarnation.

There are records in monasteries in India (both Tibetan and Hindu), confirming the arrival and prolonged sojourn of a Saint Issa during the time that Jesus was occupying His physical body. In trance readings Edgar Cayce also declared that Jesus Christ had traveled to India. His beloved mother Mary accompanied Him when He hurriedly left Palestine after surviving the crucifixion.

There is also little doubt that Jesus would have encountered Goddess worship in India…His later pronouncements on Sophia and Barbelo are therefore not surprising. He may not have used the names of Hindu deities in Palestine, but that is again not something to be too surprised about. After all, the majority of His audiences were Jews who were completely unfamiliar with the names of Indian deities. The names Sophia and Barbelo were however known... For the Lord, the Divine Mother takes on various forms...call Her by any name and She will respond...

Jesus speaks of Barbelo the Divine Mother at length in a work called the Secret Book of John. Jesus says about Barbelo:

Her light resembles the Father's light. She is the image of the perfect and invisible virgin Spirit...She is the first power and the glory. She became the universal womb, for she precedes everything.

He thus describes Barbelo in a way that is reminiscent of Hinduism's version of Adi Parashakti, the Primordial Mother, who gave birth to both Heavenly and Earthly Beings.

(Incidentally, in the Apocryphon of John (also called the Secret Book of John), the Apostle John (brother of James) experiences a visitation by an exalted Being, who goes on to say He is from the Highest of the High, and then proceeds to reveal a beautiful message to John).

Both Mary and Jesus have been seen in modern times by blessed souls. For instance, Anne Catherine Emmerich had visions of Jesus. She was a stigmatic, like St. Francis of Assisi. Stigmata are wounds that have appeared spontaneously on the limbs of extraordinary saints that replicate the crucifixion wounds of Christ.

Mother Mary in particular, has appeared in many places in the world...Around the year 1300, the German theologian Albertus Magnus (also called Albert the Great) claimed that Mary had appeared in front of him...The somewhat well-known Thomas Aquinas was his student.

Mary's origins as well as selection for the task of bringing Jesus into this world are both a spiritual mystery. And she was given this task around the age of 15. She was clearly an Old Soul, highly sensitive to the vibrations of the Divine Mother. The angel Gabriel appeared and informed Her of the divine assignment. Here is a spiritual hymn attributed to her, called the Magnificat (also called the Song of Mary):

My soul doth magnify the Lord.

And my spirit hath rejoiced in God my Savior

Because He hath regarded the humility of His handmaid;

For behold henceforth all generations shall call me blessed.

Because He that is mighty,

hath done great things to me;

and holy is His name.

And His mercy is from generation unto generations,

To them that fear Him He hath showed might in His arm:

He hath scattered the proud in the conceit of their heart.

He hath put down the mighty from their seat,

and hath exalted the humble.

He hath filled the hungry with good things;

and the rich He hath sent empty away....

Mary is said to have uttered the above words quite spontaneously at the home of her cousin Elizabeth. Mary's spiritual attunement comes through quite clearly in this hymn. Elizabeth later gave birth to John the Baptist, beloved of Jesus. John was declared before his birth by the Angel Gabriel to be filled with the Holy Spirit even in his mother's womb. As we know, John would later baptize Jesus. He was a being of great spiritual potency, said to be of the same lineage as Sanat Kumara.

The Avataric Descent of Jesus led to a cluster of advanced beings coming down with Him. This often happens when an

Avatar descends. For example, along with Rama, we had Hanuman, Vishwamitra, and others descending. With the Krishna Avatar we had Ved Vyas, Balarama, and Radha and the Gopis. The allegory of a comet with a tail comes to mind...

The Apostles and Mary Magdalene were part of this cluster of Old and Blessed Souls, who had reincarnated at the right time, to assist the Lord with His mission. It would be shortsighted to think of the Apostles as mere humble fishermen...for example Paul's letter to the Galatians is strikingly resonant with the light of Spirit and has had an inspirational effect ever since it was written. In Corinthians also, the faith of Paul shines forth when he says, "Hath not God made foolish the wisdom of the world?"

In the Gospel of Thomas, the spiritual sayings of Jesus are both uplifting and hard hitting at the same time. To be forewarned is to be forearmed, and so the Lord says in this Gospel: *The person who is near me is near the fire. And the person who is far from me is far from the kingdom.*

And He also says: I have cast fire on this world. And see, I am guarding it until it blazes. The Beautiful Anger of Jesus is both exciting and humbling. One is reminded of when He bore down on the money-changers and overturned their tables... 33 years is just not long enough a life for such an intense Avatar... Thank God His life was longer than that. India and other regions were the spiritual beneficiaries...

As has been pointed out before, we had turbulence such as was accompanying not just the Jesus Avatar but also other Avatars. So, does this all in any way diminish the validity of these Avatars? Far from it.....By their grace, sacrifice, renunciation, and Love, they stand vindicated. They make us realize that the crucible of life needs to be churned quite aggressively at times, or only degeneration (or at best stagnation) will result. The Avatars rock the boat with the best of intentions, to aid in the evolution of mankind to a higher consciousness.

The Avatar does not come only to soothe, reassure, and teach. He also comes to further the cause of human evolution, and often by employing Shiva Principle tactics. This is to either accentuate or sublimate the tensions that already exist both within and outside an individual, and that raises His devotees, and even humanity itself to a new consciousness. Sometimes, as we know, the only way humans will learn is the hard way…

The Avatars all gave much more than they took…in fact what they gave was infinite compared to what they exacted or took from humanity. The Avatars who descended into a chaotic world had to use their power judiciously according to the format they had chosen for themselves. Not all Avatars choose the same format or template to manifest themselves…

People who are old souls see the chaos around, and become convinced that union with God is the most worthwhile objective. Thus, the Avatars become prime movers of liberation-seeking for disillusioned people.

There has been some controversy regarding Jesus Christ's fundamental nature…Was He two separate natures (human and Divine) existing in the same body or just one fundamental nature? Was His body even real or just a mirage? From all indications, given that He traveled extensively to far off lands such as India and Persia, it is clear that He was a true Avatar, or in other words, "The Word made flesh," as the Gospel of John says. There was indeed a body, and a mind…though a mind that was overwhelmed by the potency of His Spirit…which is the basic nature of an Avatar. This was a mind that soon began to vibrate with the frequency of Spirit. And so the mind effortlessly interacted with the Pharisees even when He was only 12.

Did Jesus have former lives? Edgar Cayce insisted that Jesus did have former lives. Since these former lives, such as Adam and Melchizedek, come nowhere near the potency of Jesus, we have to infer they were mainly a preparatory exercise for the main Avatar of Jesus Christ. So now the question arises, was He an Ascended Master or a true Descent? Again, the answer appears to be: both of these. He and His father had *become* one after several lifetimes on earth. He had become Unconditional Love. And then He was sent to be among humans once again…

He was asked to help in the design of a new temple of Shiva in Kashmir and He is said to have actively participated in this... However, the sheer pull of Buddhism did have an influence, as evidenced from reports that He assisted in conducting one of the Great Buddhist Councils. Was His attraction to Buddhism an informed one....in other words, since both the Buddha and Jesus are said to belong to the same Brotherhood established by Sanat Kumara, was Jesus' ambassadorship of Buddhism a natural consequence of that?

His urge to travel came from His universality, and that is evident when one hears him say, "Whoever does the will of God is my brother, sister, and mother." Here is the passage:

And a crowd was sitting around him, and they said to him, "Your mother and your brothers are outside, seeking you." And he answered them, "Who are my mother and my brothers?" And looking about at those who sat around him, he said, "Here are my mother and my brothers! For whoever does the will of God, he is my brother and sister and mother.

The above passage reveals both His universality and his detachment at the same time. Avatars like Buddha and Krishna also displayed such a detachment.

Sai Baba said about Jesus:

He gave very important messages to the world: God is One, God is omnipotent, and don't hurt anyone. And Jesus went through three stages: First He said He was a messenger of God. Later He said He was the son of God, and finally He said, "My Father and I are One." These correspond to: I was in the Light, The Light was in Me, and finally I am the Light.

A renunciatory spirit appears in the Gospel of Thomas, like it appears in The Uddhava Gita of Krishna. Self-knowledge, and knowledge of the environment, are both important. Jesus hints at both karma and reincarnation in this beautiful gospel. The Gospel has both revelation and discussion of the true Meaning of life itself.

To bring back the Lord into the Lives of the Laymen and Laywomen was of course one of the missions of Christ. The pendulum was swinging, from the non-theistic to the theistic....for after all, Buddhism had spread into the Middle East also...However, all paths go through trials and challenges, whether they are theistic or not....thanks to the frailty of the human mind.

Christianity and Judaism have been criticized by some philosophers as being dualistic religions...However, Love is the strongest force on earth and can overpower any Duality...

In the 20th century church attendance is apparently decreasing in various parts of the world....But there is little doubt that humanity will recover from the 20th century soon, according to more than one Avatar. And so, let us be positive about the momentous discoveries at Nag Hammadi: Better late than never.

CHAPTER EIGHTEEN

GNOSTICISM AND PERSONAL SPIRITUALITY

For the Gnostics, space and time have a malevolent character and may be personified as demonic beings, separating man from God. However, within each man is an "inner man," a fallen spark of the divine substance. Since this exists in all, we have the possibility of awakening from our stupefaction--- ***Clark Emery***

Gnosticism has somewhat resurfaced, thanks to the discovery of the Nag Hammadi scrolls… Gnosticism is a stimulating development in the spiritual history of mankind, with its emphasis on direct knowing and experiencing, rather than taking the traditional path of organized religion. It is the basic philosophy that all of us have the innate potential to understand and grow in spiritual wisdom, using our higher consciousness (or High- C) as a guide, as some would say.

The very birth of Gnosticism is intriguing, given that Judaism and Christianity had a fairly strong presence along with the Greco-Roman philosophies. What else but an inner urge and inner inspiration could have led to its birth and sustenance?

A gnostic quite simply, knows. His intuition is as important as his intellect. He "knows reincarnation" or at least, the moment he hears about it from someone, he has little or no inner resistance springing up within him against it…in other words, his left brain doesn't get in the way of his spiritual attunement. For the Gnostic, there is an inner Cosmos within us that is the mirror of the outer.

Gnosticism owes its medieval sustenance to teachers like John the Baptist and the Apostle Thomas. Meditative teachers like the Buddha and mystical teachings from the East also had an indirect influence as evidenced by Gnostics like the Prophet Mani who knew much about Eastern mysticism and scriptures. There are also similarities between Hindu spirituality and Gnosticism…for example, the belief in a supreme formless entity, and the belief in Deities. An example of a Gnostic Deity is

Sophia, the Goddess of Wisdom. However, the Gnostics also believed in sages or great teachers, without actually directly believing in Avatars.

However, when he or she first hears about an Avatar, instead of moving away from that, a true Gnostic would try and find a way of knowing more about the Avatar. Similarly, there is an inherent attraction for sacred places on this planet, and perhaps even an attraction for ancient scriptures, perhaps in the hope of finding something sublime...

At about the same time that Avatar Babaji first manifested on earth, there lived a prophet in the Middle East called Mani. He lived mostly in Iran, and started what became a very strong religion in many parts of the world. It however began fading around 1000 years later... The religion was called Manichaeism, and its founder attained legendary status very quickly after his birth in 216 AD. He is said to have lived for 60 years, and written prodigiously, with most of his works of a dualistic bent, similar to the teachings of Zoroaster.

He is said to have had many mystical experiences. His writings suggest an inspired soul. He was a great devotee of Jesus Christ and considered himself an apostle of Christ. Like Christ, he was later persecuted and finally met a violent end in the hands of a ruler.

The Prophet Mani depicted the Universe as polarized between the material and the spiritual, between good and evil, etc. To this day we use the phrase "Manichean worldview" to denote a polarized view of the world that some people display, wherein life is seen as an eternal struggle if good is to survive...and people are labeled sinners all too easily... Mani's works have mostly been lost, but bits and pieces have survived due to his being quoted by other writers and thinkers. Mani insisted he was a distilled version of the teachings of Buddha and Christ...he (and some of his followers) even claimed to be the reincarnation of legendary figures such as Krishna, Buddha, Jesus, and Zoroaster. Mani asked his followers to acquaint themselves with various paths, but to eventually come back to him...

Manichaeism was preceded by another similar faith called Mandaeism. Mandaeism claimed Adam as its founder, and yet followed a more spiritual track than mainstream Judaism. The Mandaeists also followed a dualistic doctrine…believing in the struggle of light vs darkness, and called their kin the Christians of Saint John, since they accepted and revered John the Baptist and some personages from the Old Testament such as Seth, but not Abraham, Moses and Jesus. They took "baptism" and on-going purification rites very seriously, believing in frequent water ablutions throughout their lives. They even tried to settle on the banks of rivers for this purpose. They believed in a Supreme, formless entity that was Omnipresent. They also believed in individuals aspiring for liberation and merging back with their Source. They also believed in "savior spirits" who watched over individual souls and guided them in their journey through life. The Mandaeans later also came to be known as Sabians.

Gnostic paths appear to have sprung from an inherent progressiveness in certain individuals which gives such faiths their initial impetus. Later other progressives, feeling stifled perhaps by the religion they were born into, join in and preserve the faith. However, of the Gnostic religions, only Mandaeism survives. For centuries the Mandaeans were mainly in Iraq but after the 2003 war in Iraq many fled that country and now they are found in small introverted groups in other countries.

It turns out that Mandaeists have their own esoteric doctrines, carried over from their Gnostic past. The very word Mandaean means "an enlightened person" or a "knowledgeable one". *Manda* is spiritual truth and needs to be pursued. It is said to be experienced internally and is held to be a direct experience. Like other Gnostics, they believe in the whole idea of personal seeking and attaining of an enlightened state. For the Mandaeans, John the Baptist is one of their last great teachers, and they claim an even more ancient history than Christianity. Their reverence for John has led them to be also called Johannites.

According to the Mandaeic Book of John: *Our Lord, the King of Light on high, He is ONE.* In the same book there is an account where the priests of Jerusalem say to John that he should leave town because he was literally making the kind of waves that "make people and the temple of Jerusalem tremble". John refused and said, "Burn me if you will." "Bring a sword and cut me." And the priests hung down their heads and said, "No fire can touch you John because the name of life is mentioned over you, and no sword can cut you John because the son of life dwells here upon you." John was a stern teacher who believed in divine retribution. He insisted that after death "sinners would be given just punishment, including time in hell."

John said, "Praise His name, my Lord of Light - For those who love his name are not condemned". He insisted that every one of his followers give alms and participate in other acts of charity. John's path was thus quite strongly based on performing acts of service to your neighbor.

The Mandaeans believe in the "Great Mind", that is the source of all things…they also believe in a human soul. They consider themselves propagators of Divine Light. However, there is also an earthly mind and this is limited in nature, and the cause of much of mankind's travails…Within the Mandaean community, there is a group of adepts called Nasoraeans. A Nasoraean is considered to be spiritually gifted and possessing great knowledge. John the Baptist did leave disciples to continue his path.

The question arises: Why and how do such religions even arise? What made the descendants of Adam believe in a formless God if Adam was said to have had direct interactions with God and even received instructions from Him? Is it because the inner world also contains formless entities…or was it the Mandaean belief that the human soul originates outside the earth (i.e., outside the world of form) but is imprisoned now in the human body… The Mandaeans believed that the human spirit itself was bifurcated, and there is a higher/divine level and a lower spirit that had to deal with the world…they also believed their religion had no earthly founder but rather Great Teachers. They uttered long and beautiful spiritual prayers, reminiscent of Zoroastrian Gathas. And in both Gnostic religions as well as Zoroastrianism one senses the influence of Hinduism...

Incidentally, John the Baptist is also adored in Islamic poems written in the Sufi tradition. While his life was largely overshadowed by Christ's Mission, it is clear they were great admirers of each other.

Gnosticism has had more than a passing influence on the history of philosophy and psychology. The Humanists, like Carl Jung and Abraham Maslow, either directly or indirectly drew inspiration from the basic tenet of Gnosticism, which is to acknowledge the "world within" as inherently divine and not inherently morbid, like a Freudian might assume. Gnosticism has also influenced philosophers like Ralph Waldo Emerson.

CHAPTER NINETEEN

AVATAR BABAJI: ETERNAL SPIRIT OF THE HIMALAYAS

When Primordial Energy first appeared, the first mantra that She uttered from Her holy mouth was Om Namah Shivaya---*Avatar Babaji*

About a couple of centuries after the departure of Christ from His physical body, a remarkable birth took place....of Avatar Babaji, immortalized in Yogananda's book "Autobiography of a Yogi". Yogananda gave Him the title Maha-Avatar (or Great Avatar), and insisted this Maha Avatar is very much in our midst, and has been for about 1800 years. While other Avatars have "come and gone", this Avatar is still here, and so, in Yogananda's view, is fully deserving of the title Maha Avatar. Besides, He is said to have resurrected Himself from the dead more than once...There is a mention of Avatar Babaji's ability to resurrect Himself from the dead in Neale Donald Walsch's book Conversations With God (Volume 3).

However, as mentioned before, nearly all the major Avatars are still with us, so great is their love and their involvement with humanity's evolution. However, they may be more reluctant to appear before humans in their physical form than perhaps Avatar Babaji, who has apparently also taken other incarnations such as Haidakhan Baba as recently as the 20th century, even though admittedly, this incarnation is not accepted by the Self-Realization Fellowship of Yogananda. This makes Avatar Babaji similar to Lord Dattatreya, who was an Avatar and who later had other incarnations...

So, who is Avatar Babaji? He who incarnated to teach humanity techniques of mind and soul also had a guru. Babaji's guru was a great sage called Bogar or Boganathar, who was a devotee of both Lord Shiva and yes, His son Subramanya (also known as Sanat Kumara). In fact Bogar built legendary temples dedicated to Subramanya, also called Kartikeya or Muruga. One of these legendary temples is in Sri Lanka in a town called

Kataragama. Bogar is said to have lived during the 3rd and 4th century AD and was a formidable adept and polymath. Many of His writings have survived to this day. His Tantric Yoga was designed primarily for life-extension. He is said to have taught His students such as Babaji Nagaraj (now known as Avatar Babaji) advanced techniques to preserve one's body indefinitely by halting the aging process.

Bogar in turn considered Sage Kalagni to be His mentor. Kalagni was the student of another legendary sage called Thirumoolar who was greatly influenced by Sage Agastya, the father of them all.

Sage Agastya was a one-of-a-kind sage who lived in South India and is said to have manifested many powers. All of these adepts trace their origins to Lord Shiva, the Adinath (or "First Lord"). Sage Agastya moved from North India to the South, setting off a glorious tradition in South India called Dravidian Shaivism. Thus, historically we see that Lord Shiva who began His mission in the Himalayas moved both West to Asia Minor and South to Peninsular India. Lord Vishnu's influence on the other hand went eastward to the Far Eastern countries such as Cambodia and Indonesia. Many Vishnu temples are found in those countries and the legend of Lord Rama is especially well-known in those parts…

When Lord Shiva acts, so does His son Subramanya. Lord Subramanya (Sanat Kumara) has played a big role in the nurturing of Dravidian Shaivism, and for example, handed over the secrets of the *Siddhas* (which included secrets of life extension and Tantric Yoga) to Sage Agastya, who then transmitted them to his followers…To this day, Lord Subramanya (or Muruga) is worshipped widely in Tamil Nadu State in South-East India. All the Saints mentioned above became highly adept in the Siddha System of spiritual empowerment. Many of these early Siddhas are said to be still present in the hills near the town of Palani in Tamil Nadu.

According to Yogananda, Maha Avatar Babaji is in constant communion with Jesus Christ. Avatar Babaji is said to have an eternally youthful appearance. He looks like He is in His mid-twenties or so. He reveals Himself to a chosen few, works with them for a while, and then disappears. He is the ultimate " rarely seen but highly sung about" Avatar. Whether Avatar Babaji's influence will persist forever remains to be seen...Other beings such as the Old Haidakhan Baba (19th century) and the more recent Haidakhan Baba who appeared in the 1970's have claimed identity with Him. However the teachings of the "new" Haidakhan Baba do not involve such paradigms as Kriya Yoga, for which Avatar Babaji has come to be known...

Babaji is said to have given humanity the Cosmic Cobra Breath technique, a Tantric breathing technique designed to move energy up the chakras. This appears to be one the central tenets of His teachings, that too much of man's energy is trapped in the lower chakras, which are the grosser chakras, controlling things like the reproductive urge, material desires, ambitions, and so on. In other words, we have "descended too much", as mentioned before in the chapter on Tantra. One of the ways of visualizing this is that the individual descends from above and based on his past lives, his or her energy develops certain characteristics which in turn influence how the energy becomes distributed from chakra to chakra until all (or most) of the chakras are energized.

If a sincere student patiently performs the prescribed techniques, the upper chakras will become increasingly stronger and the person will begin to manifest greater compassion, greater creativity and wisdom, and greater detachment, and that will ultimately put the practitioner that much closer to liberation or Moksha. At the highest level this means union with Lord Shiva at the highest chakra.

According to a recent book "Shiva Speaks" Avatar Babaji is very active to this day...As mentioned before, Yogananda insisted that Avatar Babaji was in constant communication with Christ. Together they are sending vibrations of redemption to human beings. However we live in "the age of over stimulation". The environment throws so much at us we have become insensitive to the more subtle vibrations that are sent out by advanced Beings to the earth. We continue to be distanced from our spirit bodies. To balance this out, Avatars have become even more necessary in the modern age. And so we had several avatars of Dattatreya, including two Sai Babas (Shirdi Sai Baba and Sathya Sai Baba visit us and spend a total of more than 160 years in their physical form on the planet). And many other spiritual luminaries, such as Ramakrishna Paramahamsa, Sri Aurobindo, Meher Baba, Ramana Maharishi, and Nisargadatta Maharaj.

The Old Haidakhan Baba was present from about 1800 to 1922. In that year He announced at the town of Ashkot, near the India-Nepal border, that He would be back later for the welfare of mankind. He and some followers then set out for a trek to a sacred spot at the confluence of the Kali and Gori Ganga Rivers. There, He simply entered the water and sat in meditation and after a while became a ball of light that disappeared into the water...

The Avatar Babaji lineage and legacy includes the stern master Yukteswar, who was the guru of Yogananda. Yogananda considered Yukteswar a *Jnana Avatar* (Jnana is sometimes pronounced *Gyana* for ease of saying) . This is an interesting term that means avatar of knowledge...The student was clearly overawed by his guru's knowledge and intuitive understanding of various religions and paths, something that was quite rare in those days...Most gurus were adepts only in their own religion or path....and so the question arises, where did this knowledge and intuition of Yukteswar come from...did it come from within or without.... and also, is there such a thing as an inner guru? Sai Baba of Puttaparthi has answered this question in the affirmative...Baba once said, "The Inner and Outer guru are One." There is only One Guru...operating at many levels.

The inner guru can also operate in the realm of intuition and higher consciousness but often only in the realm of silence... Techniques such as Kriya Yoga can also improve one's spiritual intuition. Is this spiritual intuition also something that increases over lifetimes in some individuals? Does a Wall Street broker or a Business Executive or a Doctor also use intuition but at another level? Does the voice of Conscience belong to the Inner Guru? I leave the reader to ponder these...

Yukteswar spent much of his life speaking about the unity of religions, especially Hinduism and Christianity. A work by him called *The Holy Science* is devoted to this. Yukteswar stated this book was written at the behest of Avatar Babaji, who appeared to Yukteswar one day and said He was pleased that Yukteswar was an East/West person (interested in comparative religion) and familiar with both ancient scriptures and modern ways of thinking. Babaji encouraged him to write a book that would bring East and West together and show the similarities between Hinduism and Christianity. Babaji also said there were many advanced souls (or potential saints) in the West, and that one day He would send Yukteswar the kind of disciple that would move to the West, and awaken many...And of course, that disciple turned out to be Yogananda, who made a big impact in the United States and other countries.

Yukteswar promptly set out to write the book and it remains a popular work to this day. Among the surprises of this book is its emphasis on Bhakti Yoga (the Yoga of Love and Devotion to God) rather than the Kriya Yoga that he had been trained in. Yukteswar makes it clear what he means by liberation: It is Union with God. In some ways, the book portends what the Krishna cults of the 20th and 21st centuries are saying, as well as what the two Sai Babas have been saying: In this age, there is no better and easier liberation (or Nirvanic state) than to be one with the Lord. Even for someone who seeks Oneness with the impersonal God (Brahman or Holy Spirit), the answer still lies in seeking the help of Deity or Avatar... To use an analogy: If you and I are 25 miles from Universal Spirit, Krishna or Sai Baba are only *25 feet* from Universal Spirit. One push from Them (metaphorically speaking) and the devotee can merge with Universal Spirit...

Yogananda was in India when his guru left his physical body in 1936. He presided over the burial of the guru. However, in his *Autobiography of a Yogi*, Yogananda states that Sri Yukteswar appeared a few weeks later in Bombay in his hotel room, and blessed him. Yogananda calls it the Resurrection of Yukteswar. At that time Yukteswar stated He had been chosen to work in an astral plane called Hiranyaloka to assist spiritually advanced souls after they left their physical bodies. In other words, he was a celestial guru now.

Yukteswar insisted there are astral planets where there are many astral beings. The astral Universe is also much larger than the physical one. It is beautiful and pure, (reminiscent of the Pure Land, called Sukhavati, of Pure Land Buddhism). Yukteswar described a land of bliss and plenty, accompanied by ease of living. For example, He related to Yogananda how astral beings ate luminous ray-like vegetables that abounded, and drank nectar flowing in astral brooks and rivers. This is perhaps the first instance of such graphic details being given by what Yogananda called a Resurrected Being. .

Yukteswar went on to describe the Causal Plane. Even more subtle than the astral plane is the causal plane, and there are even more advanced beings there in their causal bodies. They are truly spirit quantums and have an aversion for both the physical and astral forms of existence. They can make things happen by merely thinking about it...Even this plane is not the ultimate...a causal being can choose to give up its boundaries completely and completely merge into the Universal Spirit, a truly free soul.

Yukteswar's guru, Lahiri Mahasaya, was Avatar Babaji's chosen student. He was hand-picked by Avatar Babaji to spread the doctrine of Kriya Yoga amongst the lay public. No longer would Kriya Yoga be practiced only by adepts and yogis. Lahiri Mahasaya once said, "Everything is possible when one does Kriya properly. Prana (breath) is God, and so concentrate on this all your life." This was a natural statement to make, considering that his Mahaguru, Avatar Babaji had made an even more emphatic statement regarding Kriya Yoga. Babaji had said, "Nobody can be called a Swami or a Sannyasi just based on name or attire. It requires attaining a state of mind attained through the practice of Kriya.

But Lahiri Mahasaya also sincerely believed that every man has to go through serious inner struggles and he felt that Kriya Yoga was the most effective way to deal with one's inner conflict...Lahiri Mahasaya directly received initiation from

Avatar Babaji and five years later Mahasaya himself had an enlightenment experience. Thereafter, he insisted, "Babaji and I are one. I am omnipresent like Him." He went on to say that Jiva Lahiri had become Brahma Lahiri. Thereafter He no longer mentioned Avatar Babaji in public...

Lahiri Mahasaya did not advocate renunciation to his followers. Instead he encouraged them to lead the life of a householder while practicing meditation and Kriya Yoga. Here are some quotes from Lahiri Mahasaya:

Settlement in the advaita (non-dual) state removes the difference between God and the devotee.

The state in which knower, known, and knowledge become one, that state alone is true science. And that is also true devotion and the true knowledge.

Always remember you belong to no one, and no one belongs to you. Reflect that, one day, you will suddenly have to leave everything in this world, so make your acquaintance with God now.

Attune yourself to the active inner Guidance; the Divine Voice has the answer to every dilemma of life. Though man's ingenuity for getting himself into trouble is endless, the Infinite Succor is no less resourceful.

The stamp of Krishna is seen in this entire lineage, whether in the constant meditations of Avatar Babaji on Krishna, or the Gita discourses given by Lahiri Mahasaya, or the primacy given to Krishna by Yogananda. And yet, as we have seen, Avatar Babaji comes from the Dravidian Shaivite lineage that acknowledges Lord Shiva as the Originator of all Tantric Yoga and Knowledge. This again is a wonderful example of the Age of Integration, or the Age of Dattatreya that is now prevailing on the planet and that we will revisit in detail later. Hereafter the combined force of Lord Vishnu (Krishna) and Lord Shiva will bless the human race forever.

When I look at these four, Avatar Babaji, Lahiri Mahasaya, Yukteswar, and Yogananda, I'm reminded of a huge spiritual voltage gradually being stepped-down, in the fashion of a step-down transformer. For example, if the Voltage at the place of generation (Avatar Babaji) is something like 800 Volts, it is reduced in stages to 400, then 200, and then 100 Volts, so to speak. However, the *current* is correspondingly increasing from say 1 Amp to 2 A, then 4 A and finally about 8 A. That happens in an electrical transformer because the product of Voltage and Current (V x C) is the Power in the electrical circuit, and must remain constant...

The Voltage represents the state of spiritual advancement of the Being while the current represents intensity of the overt manifestation on earth, or *concretization* of the Being. With each generation of student, this overt manifestation (or current) increases, until finally we have Yogananda who travels all the way to the West and puts everything in a form that is palatable and tangible to the masses worldwide. Entering temples run by the Self-Realization Fellowship of Yogananda and meditating there, one feels the energy of the lineage...

However, it takes someone like Avatar Babaji's Voltage (another term for Voltage is Potential Difference) i.e., His vastly higher state of Power and Presence vis a vis the rest of us, to set the ball rolling and to provide that initial impetus.

If at the worldly level Yogananda had the biggest impact, at the spiritual level (or the cosmic level) it is Avatar Babaji that set the ball rolling in a way that can scarcely be duplicated. This analogy can be extended to Avatars and human beings. Avatars have incredibly high voltage....while humans might well be very efficient creatures on earth, efficient at wealth generation, efficient at becoming highly educated, etc. (in other words, pack a good current).

Lord Shiva's Descents are many and complex... We will now encounter Adi Shankara, another of the Lord's emanations.

CHAPTER TWENTY

ADI SHANKARA---FATHER OF MODERN HINDUISM

The Soul appears to be finite because of ignorance. When ignorance is destroyed, the Self which does not admit of any multiplicity, truly reveals itself by itself---*Adi Shankara*

Adi Shankaracharya's life was truly short and intense like a Spiritual Comet…and His was perhaps one of the shortest of all Great Descents. I use the term Great Descent to denote very advanced spiritual beings that fall just short of being Poorna Avatars (or Full Descents). What do we mean by this? An Avatar like Krishna comes under the auspices of a supreme Deity such as Vishnu, shows superhuman powers, and is a Full Descent. Adi Shankara also showed signs of being a Descent of a Major Deity (Lord Shiva), but with less material/physical powers…However, what He lacked in terms of powers He more than made up with His spiritually driven accomplishments.

So far and wide was His influence, He was given the title of Jagadguru (or Teacher of the World) and was the first to be honored with this title in the annals of Hinduism. A Jagadguru is considered to be a "safe bet" by the population, a teacher whose credibility is beyond question. This title has been bestowed to only a handful of people in the history of Hinduism. At the last count there have been less than 6 Jagadgurus.

During His youth, Adi Shankara was already recognized as both a genius and a hard-working student, and later a formidable debater and Master, well-versed in almost every extant philosophy…How He packed everything into such a short life is a mystery that can only be rationalized by resorting to Divine support of this great Descent. His knowledge of many paths and religions proved to be very useful when He debated against great masters who were perhaps not as well-read and open minded as Shankara.

The energy that He brought into play into the physical plane too is something to marvel at. This avatar was never at one place for more than a few weeks at a time during His mission. Once He left His guru's abode, Shankara was always on the move, and thought nothing of combing the length and breadth of India while searching for ideal places to cast roots... His intrepid feet carried Him to the remotest corners of the sub-continent, and it is possible that the sheer physical demands made on them took their toll and that led to a premature departure from the body... Or, His work was simply "over" and there was no need to stay any longer... We will never know why Adi Shankara lived only 32 years. However He did more than almost any other human being ever has...He opened several missions (called Maths, but pronounced more like Mutts) as well as temples all over India, took part in debates, wrote books and translated what He thought were important scriptures.

He was the perfect synthesizer of various doctrines and practices. He was a Unifier and Integrator, greatly committed to bringing the Shaivites and Vaishnavites together. He advocated equal adoration of both Lord Shiva and Lord Vishnu (at a time when it was a rarity), as well as Shakti (the Goddess Principle), Lord Ganesha (the elephant-headed son of Shiva and Shakti), and Lord Surya (the "god of the Sun").

Not only did He establish great spiritual centers and temples that exist to this day, but He also set up *Akharas*, or Martial Arts centers. By "being a Dattatreya" Himself, He paved the way for the Age of Dattatreya that began in the Middle Ages and continues to this day...

Speaking of the martial arts, it is commonly believed that the Chinese were the first purveyors of the martial arts, but there is evidence that the practice of a martial art-form called Kalaripayattu from the area now known as the state of Kerala, predates any other form of martial arts in the world. Adi Shankara hailed from Kerala, and He quickly saw the corporeal as well as psychological advantages of the intense physical training that went on in the Kalaripayattu schools of His homeland...He went on to set up such schools in many places. Another great teacher who was also influenced by Kalaripayattu is Bodhidharma, the South Indian prince from the neighboring state of Tamilnadu, the founder of Chan (or Zen) Buddhism in China. When Buddhist monks traveled over land from India to China and other countries, the martial arts were their only defense during an arduous journey that could easily be sabotaged by robbers, etc. Carrying arms was not an option for the monks…

Adi Shankara's famous debates with scholars who were usually of a more dualistic bent than Him are legendary, and Shankara always prevailed in such debates. The same Shankara when He was with lay people, in the villages that He passed through, was a great devotee of Shiva, Shakti, and Vishnu, and composed hymns in their praise.

He was that rare combination of head and heart, and His contribution to the Indian spiritual ethos stands undisputed to this day. The fact that He worked in remote parts of the sub-continent speaks of the importance He gave to the basic underlying unity of the religion of the entire sub-continent. Kashmir and Kasi were as dear to Him as Kaladi, His birthplace in Kerala.

The importance He gave to faith in the Deities resulted in His warning people of the inherent limitations of non-theistic doctrines. This included debating with Buddhist scholars and these debates almost invariably ended with Shankara being the victor. I would not go to the extent of saying He was responsible for the decline of Buddhism in India…that privilege belongs to the Muslim conquerors of India more than anyone else, but curiously enough, after the life of Shankara, Buddhism slowly began to wane in India, even while it grew stronger in the Far East.

Here was a Guru who was attuned to both the Male and Female Aspects of Divinity and who wrote moving hymns to the Goddess. His hymn called *Soundarya Lahari* (Waves of Beauty) stands out as a great attempt to impress upon the people the importance of Goddess worship. The Soundarya Lahari is comprised of 100 verses explaining the process of Goddess adoration and worship. It is considered a Tantric text. It provides instructions on how to worship the Goddess, using yantras (mystical diagrams) that have been used for meditation and symbolic worship.

In some ways, Adi Shankara was a right-handed Tantric in the way that He went about things...He was proactive (which is one manifestation of the Rajas Principle, as thought of in the Samkhya Philosophy that we encountered in an earlier chapter on Sage Kapila) while also being non-dualistic (the Sattva Principle)...Shankara was a hard-nosed debater (the Rajas Principle) while being a humble devotee (the Sattva Principle). What He absolutely was not is Tamasic. And here's where there could be some confusion in the minds of some who consider Lord Shiva to represent Tamas (or inertia). The so-called inertia of Lord Shiva is a blessing in disguise and extends the effective life of Earth, or it could get destroyed after a shorter time-frame...Let's keep in mind that Lord Shiva has all the opposites within Him...if He is Tamasic, He is also the great Dancer and Divine Sculptor...If He is "inactive" He is also the Great Transformer who aids the spiritual evolution of mankind...

The legend goes that He received 100 verses from Lord Shiva Himself when Shankara made a trip to Mount Kailas to worship the Lord. However, on His way back He encountered Nandi (the Lord's Vehicle, a bull) and there ensued a big argument between them. Nandi being far too strong for Shankara, took the document, tore into two pieces and gave only one to Shankara, who immediately went back to the Lord to weep on His shoulder. Lord Shiva said to Shankara, "Go ahead and write the remaining verses yourself." (considered a subtle revelation of their oneness). So the first 41 verses are Lord Shiva's and the remaining 59 are attributed to Shankara. It is little wonder that Shankara and Shiva are considered as one by many...

His debates with other scholars and sages were often about the fundamental nature of the Universe and of humans. He could don the garb of a devotee as easily as the garb of a mystic. He is best known however for His revival of Advaita Vedanta, the philosophy of non-duality and oneness. His famous statement,

"*The individual is identical with Brahman* (Universal Spirit)", echoes through the spiritual annals of mankind. Everything has come from One Source...Apparently Shankara did not say this from Day One. Instead there was an evolution in His thinking.

With the passing of years, His pronouncements changed somewhat. Let's look at their progression from Dualism to Non-Dualism:
- I am floating in Brahman!
- Brahman is in me.
- I am Brahman.

Statement 1 is the most dualistic of all while Statement 3 is non-dualistic in its essence...Incidentally, Dualism is called Dwaita while Non-Dualism is called Advaita. Statement 2 amounts to a "qualified non–dualism" (called Vishishta Advaita). All these three are established movements within Hinduism, which led it to become very open-ended...The term Advaita Vedanta has been coined to represent the highest essence of Hinduism.

By reviving Advaita Vedanta (the highest philosophical stratum within Hinduism, He revived in a sense, Hinduism itself. It is against Advaita's very nature to take sides, and so, even though it had historically closer ties with Shaivism, the Advaitins advocated equal worship and adoration of both Shiva and Vishnu, with Shankara going beyond that and also including Shakti or the Goddess Principle, and Ganesha the son of Shiva and Shakti, who is considered to be the seat of both earthly knowledge as well as all spiritual wisdom. The surprise inclusion is Surya the Sun God and that is a throwback to Vedic times, when Surya was worshipped extensively...

This book is not delving into the details of the controversy as to when exactly He lived. Some of the ashrams He founded claim that He lived in the 8th century AD and others even say He was born nearly a thousand years earlier and was a contemporary of the Buddha! The latter possibility is however, highly unlikely given other details of His life. Most of the major scholars, after examining other clues and indicators, now accept 8th century AD as the time of Shankara.

There was something unabashed and strident about Adi Shankara. He charged "full-steam ahead" almost as if He knew His physical tenure on earth was going to be short. Books keep being written about Him and His teachings. The Internet has to some extent led to a Shankara renaissance, and yet we must try and see Him in a historic context...

As mentioned before, it is said that in Kali Yuga (the Age of Spiritual Darkness), theistic doctrines and devotion are the quickest and safest paths. And so there is some confusion regarding the true meaning of His life. He too appeared to advocate a judicious combination of non-dualism as well as devotion towards the highest deities, as mentioned above, and importantly, *these deities are in turn seen as transcendental and non-dualistic.*

Adi Shankara wrote extensively and while some feel He was unduly harsh on the Buddhists and the Jains, He did not spare Hindu schools like Sankhya and others either. Any philosophy that attempted to create categories (even if it were only two categories Purusha and Prakriti) drew His criticism. He was determined to resurrect the doctrine of non-dualism (Advaita Vedanta) in India, a la Lord Dattatreya.

He had His share of mishaps and close calls too, and that was perhaps to be expected as He traveled through the jungles and villages of India. But the benefit to India was the wide net He spread both with His philosophy and His presence. Many sects and cults now feel obligated to Him and consider Him their inspiration. Also, hundreds and thousands of ascetics accept Shankara as their supreme master and original inspiration. To Him is attributed the Ten Names Sect of renunciates. These are the various last names of Swamis, Gurus and Masters in India. The Ten Names of such teachers are:

Saraswati, Thirtha, Aranya, Bharati, Asrama, Giri, Parvata, Sagara, Vana, Puri.

Every math or ashram He established became a lighthouse in its own right, and a chain of ashram chiefs (called Shankaracharyas) was established. These ashram leaders in turn were given very high credibility in the surrounding countryside, the people convinced that the very position of Shankaracharya was divinely ordained.

Fortunately for us, He had a close group of disciples who clung to His every word and fulfilled His every request. And thus we have a fantastically large output and a large bibliography of works emerging from Shankara. He must have been continuously working or speaking or traveling to have been so prolific. One wonders if He ever paid much attention to His body's upkeep.

When I think of Shankara I am reminded of a spiritual lighthouse that was ever emitting light into the surrounding countryside. He became famous even in His lifetime for His original and memorable assertions such as:

> *God alone is real, the world is unreal, and the individual is none other than God.*

CHAPTER TWENTY-ONE

THE GREAT JESUS AMBASSADORS

If the only prayer you say in your entire life is "Thank You", it will be enough---***Meister Eckhart***

There have been innumerable mystics in every part of the world since the beginning of civilization...Needless to say a single book like this can hardly even approach an exhaustive treatment of the various saints, seers, and sages of humanity. In this section, I'm restricting myself to some who stand out for their unabashed spirituality and inspiring devotion. Many of them were influenced by the "Theologia Mystica" of Dionysius, who declared in the 5th century that God was the ground of the soul and that every human could therefore seek God through an "inward way". Personal experience was therefore everything. Even though the ultimate reality was inexpressible, it could be experienced... It appears this early work of Dionysius influenced mystics from more than one faith...

We shall speak here of Saint Augustine, the redoubtable Saint Francis of Assisi, Hildegard of Bingen, Teresa of Avila, and Anne Catherine Emmerich. We will conclude this section with a look at Emmanuel Swedenborg. These were legends even in their lifetime. We are not considering the Apostles here of course, and needless to say, Apostles like Paul, Peter, and Thomas and contemporaries like John the Baptist were the first and greatest ambassadors of Christ, and as is said by some Avatars themselves, you don't get to walk side by side with an Avatar so easily...you should have accumulated a lot of merit in previous lives to qualify. To descend as part of an Avataric Cluster is truly a special privilege.

St. Augustine of Hippo lived from 354 to 430 AD and was a prolific writer and teacher who taught about salvation and divine grace even while being enamored about non-duality. He was therefore quite an integrated personality and a man before his time...

He was a convert from Manichaeism to Christianity and went on to provide a great boost to the aura around Christ. He was influenced by Neo-Platonism, or the teachings of Plotinus the ancient mystic who had spoken so convincingly of the One and the Soul and who had in turn been influenced by Persian and Indian philosophy. This resulted in Plotinus having a very transcendental and non-dualistic of the One, very similar to the Hindu (Vedantic) view of Brahman. Plotinus had also spoken of the True, the Good, and the Beautiful (In Sanskrit Satyam, Shivam, Sundaram) as attributes of the One, who was behind everything and the very Source of the Universe. It was by recognizing the Good or the Beautiful that one came closer to the Divine. And if the One was like the Sun, the Soul was the Moon, reflecting the light of the One. In Plotinus' philosophy, the Soul yearned for an ecstatic union with the One. All this evidently had a profound effect on the young Augustine as well as many others through history, including Ralph Waldo Emerson the great New England transcendentalist of the 19th century.

It is said that on hearing of the life of St. Anthony of the Desert, a monk who had lived in the Egyptian desert and practiced monasticism, Augustine converted to Christianity. And his awe and enthrallment with both Jesus and Mary grew rapidly after that. A well-known assertion of Jesus: "Before Abraham was, I am," convinced Augustine that God exists outside of time and in the "eternal present". He gave over 350 sermons and these have come down to us. He ended one of his books with the prayer: "Let me remember You, understand You, and love You. Increase these things in me until You reform me completely"

Bob Dylan during the sixties sang:

I dreamed I saw St. Augustine

Alive with fiery breath

And I dreamed I was amongst the ones

That put him out to death

Oh, I awoke in anger So alone and terrified

I put my fingers against the glass

And bowed my head and cried

Francis of Assisi

St. Francis is of course one of the best known saints of humanity. He was a spiritual giant who strode among us with such assuredness and devotion to the Lord. And his humility was exemplary. He once famously said: I have been all things unholy. If God can work through me, he can work through anyone.

What mattered to Him were the direct words and life of Jesus, and not the way the Church was organized or had been organized in the past. This intense focus on Christ quite naturally led Him to gladly accept simplicity and even poverty. For had not His master extolled renunciation as a gateway to the eternal life.

His energy was so contagious He ended up starting a new order of monks. They wandered barefoot from place to place, begging for their food. They did not preach to rulers and the high and mighty but rather to the poor and marginalized. Something within Him made Francis aspire for perfection itself...and holy martyrdom. During a trip to Egypt He was captured by some soldiers who took Him to their ruler. When Francis got a chance to speak, He spoke so eloquently of God that the ruler was taken aback. He tried to tempt the saint with gifts but soon realized they had no effect of Him whatsoever.

At His core, St. Francis was a spiritual non-conformist, who came up with His own rules and yet He was humble about it and sought approval from the Pope. Explicit rules were laid down for the Franciscan Friars to follow. For example, the friars were forbidden to accept money in any form. This and other injunctions such as to wear only the humblest of clothes and not to indulge in idle conversation with the opposite gender, remind us of the Buddha's rules for His monks.

His lunar counterpart was Clare of Assisi, who was one of His first devotees and started an Order of Poor Ladies even though she had been born to nobility and had been raised in an atmosphere of relative luxury. As a child she had been devoted to prayer. Her sister and other women joined her Order and they lived in seclusion, doing manual labor and praying. They lived in the most humble of circumstances, did not eat meat, and observed almost complete silence. She once said, "They say that we are poor, but can a heart which possesses the infinite God be truly called poor?"

The Order of Poor Ladies came to be called the Poor Clares later and today there are Poor Clare communities in many countries.

Saint Francis described Himself as a "spouse of the Holy Spirit", and lived His message. The way He cared for the poor, and adored Nature, and spoke of Divinity, all convinced people of His innate divinity. He urged His followers to focus on the beauty, graciousness, and compassion of Jesus Christ.

He was the first recorded saint to display stigmata, also called the Holy Wounds of Christ. In other words, He was the first whose stigmata were witnessed and written about by others.

Speaking of stigmata, if St. Francis was the first, Padre Pio of the 20th century was the most recent. A unique figure in Italy, he began showing stigmata soon after the end of the First World War. He also showed other divine traits such as bilocation, prophecy making and miracles. There have been several other stigmatics in Christianity, including Paul the Apostle, John of God (16th century) and Anne Catherine Emmerich.

Hildegard of Bingen

She was a rare saint who lived in the 12th century and is said to have experienced profound mystical states, according to writers like Pandit Gopi Krishna, the 20th century Yogi and mystic whose autobiography is entitled *Kundalini, the Evolutionary Energy in Man*.

According to him, Hildegard probably had her Kundalini awakened and so experienced a state of bliss, love and psychic awakening. Such a state of mind has been gifted to others throughout history and may also be accompanied by visions, fire or flames, and the darshan of one's chosen Avatar. Darshan refers to the opportunity some devotees get to see their Master who may grant visions and not just face to face but also through dreams, visits to the astral plane, etc. In some rare cases the Avatar may be invisible to others who are also present and be visible only to the devotee.

Gopi Krishna's work finds a parallel in the book *Cosmic Consciousness* by Richard Maurice Bucke. Bucke speaks of the prevalence of Cosmic Consciousness in some fairly well-known people throughout history, a state of mind beyond that acknowledged by any school of Psychology. He himself was a certified and practicing psychologist in the 19th century. His openness to states of mind not normally explored in conventional circles of his time is quite noteworthy. However his listing of beings that experienced such a state in their lifetimes leaves something to be desired.

According to Bucke, the following people could be said to have attained this profound state of clarity and oneness with everything:
Gautama Buddha, Jesus Christ, Paul the Apostle, Plotinus, Muhammad, Dante, Las Casas, John Yepes, Francis Bacon, Jacob Behmen, William Blake, Honore de Balzac, Walt Whitman, and Edward Carpenter.

Then follows a longer list of people possessing what Bucke calls a "less perfect" state of consciousness, including such beings as Moses, Socrates, Swedenborg, Emerson, Thoreau, Ramakrishna Paramahamsa, and many others. Perhaps because of the nature of the times when this book was first published (1901), not a single woman makes the list...If this same book had appeared in the last 50 years or so, it would have probably contained names such as Hildegard of Bingen, Teresa of Avila, and Joan of Arc.

The prospect of there being some gifted souls that can live in their bliss sheath (Sheaths or Koshas are discussed in an Appendix) almost permanently, is a fascinating one, and there is every possibility they could do that. Anandmayi Ma, who was a saint in Bengal and left her body in 1982, is one who was, according to her devotees, in a "perpetual state of bliss". This kind of bliss appears to be most likely when it is accompanied by extreme devotion towards an Avatar or Deity, such as the one Meera experienced. Sometimes the devotion has already been expressed in a past life and the devotee is blessed with visions in this life.

Hildegard was blessed with visions even from her childhood. She later wrote that she would sometimes see immense visions of light that would cover a huge portion of the sky. She was a fountain of creativity and composed some memorable music. Music for her was the soul longing for God.

She wrote much about her visions. Here is a sample:

....when I was forty-two years and seven months old, Heaven was opened and a fiery light of exceeding brilliance came and permeated my whole brain, and inflamed my whole heart and my whole breast, not like a burning, but like a warming flame, as the sun warms anything its rays touch.

Her first book *Scivias* attracted a fair amount of attention and at one point she was investigated by the Pope...She came to be seen as authentic. This bride of Christ thereafter was not shy to express herself and the world is richer for that.

Teresa of Avila

At the peak of her devotional and contemplative life, Teresa's body would spontaneously levitate. But she was against the display of miracles in public and would ask her sister-nuns to sit on her so her body wouldn't float away...she however did state that she experienced levitation during moments of rapture. A witness to one of her levitations said that it lasted about half an hour.

Many instances of levitation have been recorded in various religions of the world. Simon Magus in the first century was one of the early ones. Milarepa a Tibetan yogi and master who lived in the 13th century was reported to levitate for hours at a time and even carried on activities like eating while doing so...Joseph of Cupertino was another and he lived in the 17th century. Levitation appears to happen as a sequel to more than one type of "cause". If bliss and rapture lead to levitation in some, intense concentration or the use of yogic techniques can lead to it in others...A recent example of levitations would be the advanced TM (Transcendental Meditation) practitioners who have been through a program called TM Siddhi developed by Maharishi Mahesh Yogi.

Teresa, who was born in Spain, drew as much attention during her life as after she became a legend and was canonized. She became a symbol of a step-by-step transformation from somewhat ordinary beginnings to a stellar life when she became both an example and a teacher to others. Born in 16th century Spain she showed a strong devotion even early in her life. After she lost her mother at an early age, Teresa spontaneously embraced Mother Mary as her mother. She later would say that none of her prayers to her Divine Mother went ever unheard...

She would speak directly to Jesus and claimed to have felt His presence many times in Her life, even if at the energy level rather than the visible level. Teresa's claims would sometimes generate idle gossip and accusations that she was possessed by the devil, but her severe penances and sincere pronouncements ultimately made her prevail over her detractors. She became known for her progressive states of devotion culminating in divinely inspired ecstasy. She reminded people of Hildegard of Bingen with her prolific writings and her poetic zeal.

Anne Catherine Emmerich

We have encountered this soul before and I'm mentioning Her again now more in the spirit of reiterating this uniquely gifted soul's piety and both inner and outer visions. She could see into the past and also was blessed with visions of both Christ and Mother Mary. The unknown details of the New Testament were for her an open book that she could read whenever she desired and from any page...

But her great gifts did come at a price. She had a hyper-sensitive body that often fell ill. She was bed-ridden for many years. But she clung to her cross, like Meera clung to a statue of Lord Krishna for many years. How much of the Divine Mother was in her is hard to tell...but sacrifice was her lot and not a life of privilege.

I would like to conclude this section with the mention of two unique mystic-scholars, Meister Eckhart and Emmanuel Swedenborg. Their influence is felt down to this day. Many New Age spiritualists have made reference to them. Meister Eckhart (1260 to 1328) was a prophet before his time. He exhibited a profound understanding of spirit and mind. He spoke of the "Power of Now" probably before any other Western mystic. He insisted that God lives within each of us. Eckhart apparently inspired a present-day author and mystic-scholar Ulrich Tolle to change his name to Eckhart Tolle.

Emmanuel Swedenborg has inspired the formation of Churches that exist day. He once declared, "man was so created by the Lord as to be able to speak with spirits and angels, as in fact was done in the most ancient times...". Several metaphysical and spiritual experiences in his life cause Swedenborg to change direction significantly and become an ardent votary of the Life Divine. He quit his job to devote many years to writing prolifically, including working on a spiritual version of the Bible, wherein he sought to interpret each verse of the Bible with a spiritual eye. He also claimed he had received revelations from Christ Himself, and insisted that all his writings were divinely inspired.

The name of Swedenborg resurfaced in the 19th century in the writings of *Andrew Jackson Davis* who according to various accounts was a great psychic and clairvoyant who claimed he was blessed with a super consciousness that permitted him to contact the dead. Andrew Davis insisted that while in a semi-trance state he had come into contact with Swedenborg who had left his body in 1772, at least 50 years earlier. Andrew Davis is one of the great psychics and clairvoyants of the 19th century.

Chapter Twenty-Two

A Revelation Called Islam

To overcome evil with good is good, to resist evil by evil is evil---
Muhammad

Lord Sai Baba appeared in my dream one night and made me sit beside Him. He was sitting cross-legged and I was like a child looking up at Him. He said in very clear and precise words: *Read the Koran also.* And soon after that He was gone. He had once said in a discourse: *Interest yourself in understanding the practices and beliefs of others...this cleanses your mind.*

He well knew that in my eclecticism I had mostly ignored one faith, and that was Islam. I promptly read the Koran, and found that it too was the word of God. In the world of the spiritualist, there is no conflict between one's past exposures and the present one...only one more path up the mountain. This helps us know the mountain better...but it takes an Avatar to actually clarify that it actually cleanses the mind.

The Holy Koran for some readers has a very clear and precise meaning, and for others there are mysteries hidden in it...For this latter group, the Koran has a few levels of meaning. According to Shams Tabrizi, a well-known Sufi Poet and Teacher:

...Every reader comprehends the Holy Qur'an on a different level, according to the depth of his understanding. There are four levels of insight: The first level is the outer meaning and it is the one that the majority of the people are content with. Next is the Batin – the inner level. Third, there is the inner of the inner. And the fourth level is so deep it cannot be put into words and is therefore bound to remain indescribable.

The Prophet Muhammad, after receiving a starting boost by the angel Gabriel, who appeared to Him and said, "Recite!", went on to recite what became one of the most influential teachings and revelations in the world, the Koran...Muslims believe that the Koran has the solutions to all problems that beset humans, no matter how complex...

As we know, the angel Gabriel is revered by all the Abrahamic religions, and appears to have been the chief messenger of good tidings for many very prominent people in the spiritual history of mankind. He is mentioned in both the Old and New Testaments and is famous for appearing to Mary and delivering the news of the imminent births of John the Baptist and Jesus Christ. He is considered an Archangel by some and as a saint by others...He is of course one of many Archangels.

Muhammad was first visited by the angel Gabriel around the year 610. Muhammad was terrified by that first experience that took place in a mountain cave, and quickly retreated to His home and wanted to hide...Later when He calmed down and related His experience, Khadijah said, "You have been chosen because of your wonderful nature...you always help the poor and the needy, and you are honest." Khadijah then consulted a relative of hers who was known to be a saintly man, and quite well versed in the revelations and the scriptures...That man confirmed that Muhammad had been visited by the angel Gabriel and that Muhammad was going to be a Prophet. When Khadijah heard this, she quickly became Muhammad's first devotee...

The other sayings and practices of Muhammad were put down in a separate text called the Hadith. Both the Koran and the life of Muhammad need to be considered keeping in mind the environment of that time, a milieu of tribalism and inter-tribal rivalries. And so it's not surprising this Prophet had to wear many hats, including being a military commander.

In the Koran, monotheism is the key message and according to it, the supremacy and omniscience of the one God is beyond question. God is the Creator of everything and all humans are completely dependent on Him. Thus He is the Sustainer, especially of the faithful. But an almost equally emphasized message is that the day of Destruction (or the Final Hour) is imminent and is also referred to as Judgment Day when "Each human and God shall meet". A complete cataclysm is believed to then occur, which will lead to the earth being virtually annihilated...but humans will be resurrected by God. Thus God is also going to be the final Destroyer.

As we can see, both the Vishnu and Shiva Principles appear in the Koran. Shirdi Sai Baba was raised by a Muslim family in India and was equally at home in a Hindu temple or a mosque....Needless to say, He attracted many devotees from Islam as well as Hinduism...The message from Shirdi Sai Baba was clear: It was indeed possible for both religions to respect each other. He would often exclaim: "Allah Malik!" and at other times would say: "Dattatreya Malik!"

Sathya Sai Baba has also attracted Muslim devotees including some from Saudi Arabia. Known for making stunningly accurate predictions, Baba predicted that one day, even the Muslims who believe in a formless God will one day accept His form and realize that the formless God can do anything...

In the Koran, Muhammad states that the Kaaba, the most sacred spot in the world for Muslims, was built by Abraham and His son. If that's the case, it has had a rich history of being a temple for many centuries before the birth of Muhammad. What sort of deities were there? Some claim, based on a hymn or poem written by Muhammad's uncle in praise of Lord Shiva, that the Kaaba was associated with Lord Shiva in the past...We have also seen how some writers have associated Abraham with Lord Shiva.

Faith, voluntary service, and charity are strongly encouraged in the Koran. Charity is considered a means of purifying oneself. Fasting during the month of Ramadan, and praying 5 times a day are ways of enhancing one's spiritual growth. The Koran is also a source of Islamic Law (Sharia).

Incidentally, all religions extol fasting as good for one's spiritual growth and fasting is considered useful in developing self-control. In Judaism, Christianity, and Islam, the practice of fasting has existed for centuries. In Judaism, fasting has been undertaken as a penance for sin, and also the propitiation of divine anger since Biblical times. Fasting is said to arouse the compassion of God. As the *Lenten Triodion* of the Orthodox Christians says:

Let us set out with joy upon the season of the Fast, and prepare ourselves for spiritual combat. Let us purify our soul and cleanse our flesh; and as we fast from food, let us abstain also from every passion.

In Buddhism and Hinduism too, fasting is considered most appropriate for spiritual aspirants as a means of practicing self-control. Buddhist monks and priests consider fasting to be a process of internal invigoration, as long as one doesn't carry it to extremes (i.e. keep on the Middle Path while fasting). Muhammad also warned His followers to avoid extremes, whether they were fasting or praying or reading the Koran.

Do all the Abrahamic Religions have a common thread that has served humanity? The message of the three religions appears to be: Create a structure to overcome our disorganized and random lives...i.e., the movement is away from tribalism to a God-centered and more inclusive society with a clergy, and also a movement away from less education to more education, and a movement away from random acts of individual prayer to more structured and consistent collective prayer.

The benefits of prayer are well-documented, and the benefits of mass prayers are even more pronounced and widespread. All this has allowed Western civilization to grow and advance. With increased education came discovery, innovations, and a greater sense of esthetics and all these combined to later create the Renaissance in Europe. While it does seem like a long time had to elapse after the physical departure of Christ for the Renaissance to occur, we see in this, and other examples, that "Divinity is not in a hurry"... It is said: *A year on earth is but a day in heaven*...Besides, for true evolution to occur, the momentum needs to come from humanity and not from Above, no matter how long it takes...

The 3 religions all trace their roots to Abraham except that Jews and Christians consider themselves to have descended from Abraham's son Isaac, while Muslims trace their lineage to Abraham's son Ishmael. All three religions rightly consider themselves to be the recipients of Divine Grace and Revelation.

Speaking of the inner meaning of the Koran, the Sufis were greatly inspired by the inner meaning and some of the Sufi poets would regularly quote from it. Islam and Sufism also have produced many saints, like all the other religions have.

Let's now spend some time looking at this mystical and ecstatic path of Sufism that has inspired people in all corners of the world.

CHAPTER TWENTY-THREE

SUFISM AND THE BLISS OF DIVINE LOVE

"Dear One: what has he found who has lost God? And what has he lost who has found God?"
— *Ibn 'Ata' Allah Al-Iskandari*

Sufism has been described as the mystical side of Islam, with its emphasis on resonating with Divine Love, and seeking knowledge through a direct experiencing of the Divine. It's quite understandable that many people associate Sufism with Islam....however the spirit of Sufism existed before the birth of the Prophet Muhammad. In fact, the revered Prophet is said to have had utmost regard for the spiritual sanctity of the Sufis. According to a Sufi scholar, Idries Shah, the Prophet is quoted to have said: "Anyone who upon hearing the voice of a Sufi does not say aamin (amen) would be considered a heedless person". Out of respect, prominent Sufis were sometimes called Shaykhs (or Sheikhs), a term normally used only for royalty...Sufism reached its zenith between the 10th and 12th centuries. And it still has a presence in the world, thanks to people like Inayat Khan, who did much to revive Sufism. He left his body in 1927.

If Sufism existed long before Islam came into this world, how does one explain the origins of Sufism? They remind us of the Gnostics, with their regard for direct knowing. The Gnostics several centuries earlier had also sought a direct knowing and a direct experiencing of the Divine, so if the Gnostics influenced the Sufis, is there a difference between them?

The difference appears to be: While the Gnostics were more "Knowing oriented" (or intellect oriented), the Sufis were more "Faith and Devotion Oriented (or heart-oriented). Even the way each group viewed *wisdom* is somewhat different...while the Gnostic might gauge wisdom according to how spiritually independent a person is, for a Sufi wisdom came in the form of increasing connection with the Divine...and subsequent immersion in the Divine...a certain god-intoxication...often revealed quite overtly as in the great Sufi poets. To a Sufi, such an exalted state automatically leads to surrender and subsequent receiving of direct messages from the Divine. And that in turn leads to self (or ego) annihilation.

For example, in the middle of his travels in the Middle East, Sufi Saint Moinuddin Chisti suddenly decided to move to India after having a dream where Prophet Muhammad bade him to travel to India and work there... Moinuddin Chisti settled in Rajastan and became a legend in the area we now call Pakistan as well as its contiguous region of India. He ended up attracting both Muslims and Hindus to his fold.

Having said the above, there is also a more conservative view that Sufism began only in the second century after the advent of Islam. Most Sufis took great pride in tracing their lineage back to one or more apostles of the Prophet Mohammad or the Prophet Himself. For example the Chishti order traces its lineage back to Ali, the cousin of the Prophet.

The Sufis themselves came in different shades of conservative and liberal, and the personality of an individual seeker probably determined which group he might more closely identify with...We need to appreciate that by about 200 AD there were several paths, cults, and religions in the public domain. Hinduism and Buddhism, though born a fair distance away, had made inroads into the Middle East. It is known for example that the uncle of the Prophet Muhammad was a devotee of Lord Shiva, and wrote poems in praise of the Lord...India was considered a spiritual land where one could seek salvation. We also had Zoroastrianism, the teachings of the prophet Mani, and other cults such as Mandaeism. And then of course we also had the Gnostic cults. In this diverse spiritual arena, an independent seeker almost had the same range of choices that were present, say, in the 19th century...I will not go as far as saying "20th century"...that would be an exaggeration because of the significant increase in the number of spiritual paths and teachings in the last 100 years...

The more well-known Sufis appear to have been highly God-immersed beings…and were spiritual poets and dreamers. For them God is the one and only Beloved, before whom everything else pales. This almost effortlessly brought about a certain detachment from worldly affairs, and so a transcendence…A Sufi is like a lotus and it seems to matter little what kind of water he or she is in…As one Sufi put it: *In the face of one's belief in the Unity, there exists no old or new; all is naught, naught; God alone is.*

A Buddhist monk might well the same thing speaking however from a different framework or Gestalt. The greatest Sufis were often known to possess an eclectic outlook and open-mindedness, highly inclined to look upon *all* spirituality with unbiased vision no matter where it sprang from, and they continue this tradition to this day. They are said to have reached their apex in the 11th and 12th centuries… however, their spirit lives on, and not just in Islamic regions. Rather than relying upon the soil of organized religion or the practice of traditional customs, they were and are spiritually open to old and new voices…the Sufis are to a great extent, spiritual mavericks that have adorned the world.

One has to perhaps distinguish between the earthy Sufism of a Nasrullah and the ethereal Sufism of a Rumi…the former was a regaling speaker with a biting sense of humor, while the latter was an enlightened and endearing poet, lost in reverie… Predictably perhaps, they were rivals of sorts, having taken birth around the same time and in the same part of the world, Turkey.

Add to them the whirling dervishes, and Sufi music and prayers, and we have a wide canvas indeed. And so it is not surprising that Sufism spread all over the medieval world in some form or the other.

The legendary Sufi, Rumi (13th century), once said that language was completely inadequate in expressing the ultimate Divine essence…and He went on to say that Love was an adequate remedy for this inadequacy. He believed in the supremacy of love over reason. The poet Rumi is considered by many to have been an enlightened soul who displayed the heights of humility. He claimed he could not have done what he did if not for the inspiration of two other Sufi luminaries, Attar of Nishapur (in Iran), and Hakim Sanai who hailed from Afghanistan. Rumi was also an admirer of the legendary Sufi Bayazid Bastam who lived about 400 years before Rumi and was an ascetic and a God intoxicated man according to Rumi.

Attar of Nishapur was a mystical poet who embraced pantheism at one point in his life. He is known for his "Seven Valleys of Spirituality" depicting the evolution of a typical seeker. They are:

The Valley of Quest, the Valley of Love, the Valley of Understanding, the Valley of Independence and Detachment, the Valley of Unity, the Valley of Astonishment and Bewilderment, and finally, the Valley of Deprivation and Death.

Why the overarching notion of "Valley"? It's as if one has to begin one's search in the thick of life on terra firma so to speak, and not in some lofty and remote peak...all lessons and growth are also on terra firma. Everything happens to the Sufi while living and not in a place or state removed from reality. This is to be contrasted with the Hindus' ancient attraction to the mountains (such as the Himalayas) in search of salvation, for the "Valley" is Maya to a spiritually aspiring Hindu...If renunciation needs to begin internally rather than externally, the Sufi's stance is quite understandable.

Search, for Attar, leads to the awakening of the heart to the love of the Lord and this happens prior to the awakening of the intellect...what results later in the mature seeker is a sense of detachment from worldly affairs coupled with a certain solitude. Later, things become unified and integrated and the seeker is open to other spiritual paths also. The whole thing leads into the realization that spirituality is an ocean of great beauty and insights and progressive realizations (called "minor enlightenments" by the Zen Buddhists), but (and here the inevitable poignancy inherent in the Sufi emerges) it all finally has to dissolve in aging and death and after all death is a kind of renunciation. Again to contrast things with Hinduism, for the Hindu, death is a transition rather than a renunciation...

Rumi was not the only spiritual giant to be influenced by Attar. Many centuries later, Bahaullah (the founder of the Baha'i faith) was also inspired by the Sufi. He also used the Seven Valleys framework in his writings.

As mentioned above Rumi also expressed his gratitude to another source for his inspiration: Hakim Sanai. Sanai was a prolific writer of mystical verse, and according to Osho Rajneesh, there has been no one like Sanai when it comes to sheer depth of expression. Once on a trip to India with the king Bahram Shah, Sanai chanced upon a Sufi saint called Lai-khur. Even after a short interaction with Lai-khur, who was a God-intoxicated soul, Sanai decided to renounce the worldly life, in spite of being offered a lot of wealth when he got back to his homeland. The king even offered his daughter in marriage to Sanai but the latter was unmoved.

Sanai in his Hadiqa (The Enclosed Garden of Truth) says of the Lord: *In comparison with His existence eternity began but the day before yesterday.* Another quote from him: *Love's conqueror is he who is conquered by love.* Rumi, Attar, and Sanai are the three musketeers of Sufism.

Many of us have heard of the Rubaiyat of Omar Khayyam, but perhaps not so many of us are aware that Omar Khayyam was an admirer of the Sufis, even if he was himself more of a pragmatist and a critic of the world around him. He wrote: *"For a lover of God, intuition is guide, not discursive thought."* Omar Khayyam was a man of many parts, and wrote a book on Algebra, and also wrote on science and music. His Rubaiyat has been admired for centuries for its pithy and poignant verses.

Some prominent Sufis were: Abdul Qadir Jilani, Al Ghazali, Ibn Al Arabi, Rumi, Nasruddin, and Idries Shah.

Saadi Shirazi a traveler and chronicler, whose teacher was a Sufi and who met several Sufis during his travels, said:

Human beings are members of a whole

Creation of one essence and soul…

This well-known verse of Saadi's is displayed at the entrance of the United Nations in New York.

In the 14th century, the Valley of Kashmir was blessed with the birth of a great Sufi, Sheikh Noor-ud-din Wali, revered to this day by both Muslims and Hindus. Wali was greatly influenced by the Shaivite woman saint, Lalleshwari whose mystical verse greatly influenced Wali. In one of his verses he requested God to grant him the same grace He had bestowed on Lalleshwari. The latter's pronouncements have convinced many that she attained enlightenment. She was a contemporary of Wali.

The Mughal Emperor Akbar and his great grandson Dara Shikoh were two prominent personages who were influenced by Sufism. The Emperor Akbar, despite wielding great political power, was a mystic steeped in spirituality. According to one New Age writer, he was the reincarnation of a great saint. He was also a lover of knowledge and the arts.

Believing strongly in spiritual oneness, Akbar even began a new "religion" for those who were interested in integrating the best aspects of Sufism and devotional (or Bhakti-oriented) Hinduism. The path was called Din-i-llahi, and combined aspects of not only the above two religions but also Christianity, Jainism, and Zoroastrianism. The new religion encouraged the self-purification of the soul by yearning for God…

On becoming familiar with the works of some Jain sages, Akbar even embraced vegetarianism. He also famously journeyed incognito to the place where Meera (the most well-known of modern day women saints in India) was performing, to see her sing and speak of her Lord Krishna. It is not surprising that this Emperor who had been influenced by Sufis traveling through his kingdom, found Meera's God-intoxication very similar to that of his Sufi heroes… He and a companion Tansen sat silently in the audience. However, as the legend goes, He was recognized by Meera who expressed her gratitude and said, "If you only had given the word, I would have come to you instead."

Much has been said about saint Meera, and suffice it to say here that she is considered an institution in her own right, especially by the people of Western India. She is considered by some as the reappearance of Radha, Krishna's beloved companion in His younger days, until He left the place of His birth and moved to Dwarka in Gujarat.

Emperor Akbar also built a House of Worship called the Ibaadat Khaanaa which was ultimately thrown open to people of all religions. It was also a place where inter-religious exchanges and debates took place. Even atheists were allowed to speak at these debates...

The life of Akbar was not all smooth sailing however. His religion was not accepted by the multitudes and never really took root. Some orthodox Muslims were repelled by his pronouncements and methods. And secular and worldly concerns were always tugging at his feet and making him appear more mundane than he wished... He however was a cut above the other Mughal emperors when it came to displaying a higher consciousness in the way he carried out the affairs of his kingdom. He married Hindu women with as much acceptance as Muslim women, and did much to promote inter-religious harmony. While the fact that he had many wives may appear somewhat jarring, he lived at a time when marriages were often conducted for political ends rather than involving any significant attraction between groom and bride...

Dara Shikoh (or Shukoh) is another example of a Mughal prince who turned out to be innately spiritual from a young age. The eldest son of Shah Jahan (who built the Taj Mahal), Dara too had a dream of bringing Muslims and Hindus together. Even though he was born into privilege and power, he had other ideas. He would spend a lot of time in libraries reading Muslim sacred texts as well as the Upanishads. He was convinced of their inherent and underlying connection....(A Mingling of Two Oceans).

At one point in his life, Dara met the Sufi mystic Sarmad Kashani who had wandered into India after becoming a Sufi following his being raised in a Jewish family. He qualifies to be regarded as a Sufi maverick whose way of "telling the truth like it is" endeared him to Dara. The latter accepted Sarmad as his guru. Sarmad later became highly attracted to Hindu mysticism also. However they both ultimately met untimely ends at the hands of Aurangzeb, the 6th and most fanatic Mughal emperor.

Al-Ghazali, a Sufi, and Saadia Gaon (a Jewish genius) have given us philosophies that have influenced thinkers to this day. For example, the Kalaam Cosmological Argument which was formulated in 1979 by William Craig was based on Al-Ghazali's views. The KC Argument says in brief:

Everything that comes to exist has a Cause. The Universe came to exist. The Universe therefore has a Cause. If this argument is taken backwards, ultimately a Cause is encountered that has to itself be Uncaused. This Uncaused Cause is what people call God.

Thus William Craig was trying to establish a base for his theism. In this he took inspiration from the ancient Sufis, especially Al-Ghazali. Al-Ghazali was an Integrator, who tried to bring the factions in Islam together. He is considered by some to be the second most important personage in Islam, and the first of course was Prophet Mohammad Himself. This was as implied earlier, quite appropriate to the age. Shankara the great Integrator had come and gone…Also, the new Age of Datta was to come and that too is a harbinger of Integration as we're going to see.

Chapter Twenty-Four

The Count and Master, Saint Germain

*Saint Germain is a man who knows everything and never dies---**Voltaire***

Saint Germain is one of the most remarkable Masters to walk this planet. He is still with us ethereally, and has donned a physical body a few times. He continues to speak to us through mediums.

We know that channeling through mediums will always be a controversial issue... Some of us have sat through channeling sessions perhaps. Others have watched videos of channeling sessions. Unfortunately a few mediums have abused their privilege or even been somewhat dishonest about it. Basically, channeling a spirit refers to the use of a human known as a medium to transmit messages from the spirit to an audience. The medium usually goes into a trance-like state but not always.

In his book *Channeling Zone*, anthropologist Michael Brown takes great pains to examine the world of the channels or mediums. The very fact that an anthropologist thought it worth his time to move far from his usual track and pursue studying this phenomenon says a thing or two about the prevalence of channeling today, which has indeed come a long way from the early days of J. Z. Knight and Ramtha, an old soul from Atlantis.

Saint Germain is, and was in His last incarnation, an alchemist and a polymath, who effortlessly manifested a great knowledge of history, esthetics, the arts, and the various languages of Europe. He reportedly could convert base materials into gold using His knowledge of alchemy.

One of his most recent chelas (or protégés) was Godfre Ray King (the pen-name for Guy Ballard), who has written extensively about his physical and metaphysical interactions with his Master. King came from an extensive background in

Theosophy. Saint Germain introduced King to his previous incarnations and also the locations of these, which included exotic lands such as Luxor and the Sahara when it was a bustling and green place, harboring civilizations in it around 70,000 years ago.

Saint Germain also revealed that in ancient times, people could travel about in airships of various sizes, and it is most intriguing that in recent times, remnants of ancient airships have been excavated, one of them being in Afghanistan. Ancient Indian scriptures and epics speak of such airships in several places. In particular, in the legend of Lord Rama, both Rama and His arch-rival Ravana travel in airships, albeit smaller not large…

Mankind is mostly ignorant of what happened before the most recent Ice Age… Giants walked the earth it is said. Why did they become extinct? Is it because evolutionarily speaking "they did not have what it takes", just like the dinosaurs? The ending of the dinosaurs itself should not be looked upon as a coincidence or a freak of biological calamity. Dinosaurs, with a small brain to spine ratio, and a large surface area that was difficult to keep warm, and also with the potential to do much harm, could just as easily have been allowed to perish…

The meetings between King and Saint Germain took place around 1930, in the Mount Shasta area in Northern California, a place considered by many to exude spiritual vibrations… Later his assistant Pearl Dorris lived there in the 1970s and this lady is said to have experienced and exuded the Divine Presence so much that her home became a magnet for spiritual seekers. They set up the I AM movement in California and Illinois.

Another place that comes to mind in this regard is Ojai, in Southern California. Sathya Sai Baba once referred to Ojai as a spiritual place… It was also one of Krishnamurti's favorite haunts, and houses the Krotona School of Theosophy, with a well-stocked library. Ojai is the home to various meditation groups. It's also the home of *Meher Mount*, a retreat and spiritual center established by Meher Baba in the 1950s.

Are there similar places on planet Earth that are spiritual vortices attracting sensitive souls? Sedona in Arizona and Machu

Picchu in South America, appear to be two note-worthy spiritual vortices. There are many centers along the Nile Valley that were once places of great spiritual vibrations, but in the modern age, have diminished somewhat...The Gobi Desert in Mongolia and some places in Tibet like Shigatse with its many monasteries also come to mind. Shigatse and Lhasa have apparently become large cities after the Chinese take-over and so have lost some of their mystique...

There are many vortices in India and that is one reason the spiritual history of India is very long. Among them are Rishikesh, Kasi (or Varanasi), and Jagannath Puri, as well as Vrindavana, near Mathura, where Krishna spent His youth. Mount Kailash in Tibet, with Lake Manasarovar near it, is probably one of the most spiritually potent places on earth, followed by Amarnath in Kashmir where every winter there manifests a huge natural formation of an Ice Lingam of Lord Shiva. In South India, we have Arunachala Hill where the ashram of Ramana Maharishi is located, as also a famous Shiva temple. Besides, there are many temples and cathedrals all over the world where the vibrations are truly magnificent.

Saint Germain along with a group of evolved beings called Ascended Masters play a great role in the evolution of mankind, however by definition they have ascended over lifetimes rather than descended... Sometimes they do take on human bodies, but often end up being incognito avatars. They may participate in secret societies or even encourage the formation of one, but they tend to avoid the limelight...Benjamin Crème who has done much to publicize the presence of Maitreya (or at least his version of Maitreya) and other Masters on earth has provided us with examples of their maintaining a low profile, and even appearing in public incognito...

The Ascended Masters can certainly help in bringing down the light and they continue doing so to this day. Publications of the teachings of Saint Germain continue to inspire us. Also, Lightworkers have channeled His teachings. Saint Germain's teachings are held in very high esteem among other Ascended

Masters and also by Sanat Kumara, who is of course one of the great mysterious figures in the spiritual history of Planet Earth.

In particular, Saint Germain's discourses on the "I AM Presence" are considered His most important messages to humanity. Here are some statements attributed to Saint Germain:

Life, in all Its Activities everywhere manifest, is God in Action; and it is only through lack of the understanding of applied thought and feeling that mankind is constantly interrupting the pure flow of that Perfect Essence of Life which would, without interference, naturally express Its Perfection everywhere.

When you say and feel "I AM," you release the spring of Eternal, Everlasting Life to flow on Its way unmolested. "I AM" is the Full Activity of God.

Through long centuries of willful misunderstanding, humanity has charged the very atmosphere about them with falsehood and unreality…

People of the Baha'i Faith (who I discuss in a future chapter) have open-heartedly accepted the teachings of Saint Germain…The above passages remind us of the mission of Adi Shankara who famously said, "The individual is Brahman" (i.e., the individual is a part of Universal Spirit). The phrase Aham Brahmasmi later came to be used by His followers, and it means "I am Brahman or Universal Spirit".

Saint Germain works in conjunction with other Ascended Masters such as Kuthumi Lal Singh, El Morya and Djwal Kul who sometimes appear for short periods of time in physical bodies and then disappear without a trace…They have become known for their "Cameo Appearances" with a focused objective each time they appear. Their love and commitment to humanity is obvious from their messages. The renowned Theosophist Madame Blavatsky in the 19th century claimed to have seen all three Ascended Masters at various times in her life, and a similar claim was also made by Annie Besant.

Speaking of Theosophy, the question arises, why has Theosophy not flourished as one might perhaps expect it to? Perhaps the turbulence of the 20th century, with two world wars and a host of other conflicts, economic depressions, and other human tribulations, has taken a large toll on this and other 19th century spiritual movements. Some Theosophists like to point to the departure of J. Krishnamurti in 1929 for their lack of presence in the spiritual map of the 20th century, though that appears to have been only one of the factors…

One needs to acknowledge the spiritual energy of Madame Blavatsky sooner or later in a work such as this. She and Colonel Olcott did have some achievements to their credit, one of them being they almost single-handedly revived Buddhism in Sri Lanka, after it had languished for several centuries under the onslaught of foreign rule… On visiting the bookstore at a Sri Lankan Buddhist Center in Washington DC, I found a huge portrait of Colonel Olcott there, and for good reason… Convinced that Sri Lanka was destined to become a Buddhist nation once again, the pair worked tirelessly to resurrect some of the old monasteries of Sri Lanka (then called Ceylon).

Saint Germain often said during his discourses that every sincere seeker should frequently remind himself or herself of the great I AM presence that is everywhere. The Omnipresence of God and the influence of God in our daily lives would make the seeker transcend the demands and pulls of earthly life.

Saint Germain's interactions with Godfre King in the 1930s received a setback of sorts with the onset of World War II in the late 30s… Humanity went into crisis mode so to speak. And yet, people did take things in their stride, and soon after the war ended, things began looking up again. If anything, people became more interested than ever in forging a new, 20th century spirituality. Thus, the presence of Yogananda, Sri Aurobindo, Meher Baba, Ramana Maharishi, and several other teachers was once again acknowledged by a hungry public, tired of the ravages of wars.

I'd like to take the opportunity to now turn towards 20th century spirituality. There have been a plethora of gurus, both Eastern and Western that have made an impact on the world scene. Western gurus such as Ram Dass, Andrew Cohen and pandits like Ken Wilber have done significant work.

There has been an attempt to "bring it all together" so to speak, with some success. For example, there have been distinct attempts to bring science and religion together through international conferences and the like. SAND (Science and Non-Duality) is gradually becoming a significant movement in California, with an interesting logo: $Om=mc^2$. The group regularly holds conferences in Northern California where scientists who are open to the mystique of the Universe meet to discuss things without promoting any type of dogma.

Clearly, there are today scientists who are spiritually open-minded…for example there are even scientists who are spiritual aspirants under a guru or Master. Sai Baba has personally interacted with many scientists, some of whom have gone on to become staunch devotees.

There still appears to be an East-West divide however, despite the best efforts of great writers like Wayne Dyer and Deepak Chopra. The full impact of Ancient and Modern Spirituality has yet to manifest itself in the world of the media and of science even if significant beginnings have been made.

As should be expected in the Age of Dattatreya, which we will be seeing more of shortly, there have been serious efforts at Integration of Spiritual Paradigms, even if we also find examples of simplified and "instant" spirituality in the world (an example of that would be TM). Also, the Nichiren Buddhists have been accused of promoting an over-simplified form of Buddhism, even if its founder Nichiren (who lived in Japan in the 13th century) was himself an erudite and prolific writer and interpreter of ancient Buddhist Sutras (or teachings). In his view, the Lotus Sutra of the Buddha was the ultimate teaching and deserved special reverence. Nichiren ended up distilling the practice of the Buddhist canon to just one mantra, "Nam Myoho Renge Kyo" which translates to: I devote myself to the Mystic Law (of the Lotus Sutra). Nichiren in some ways transformed Buddhism from a silent interior practice to an overt chanting of this mantra. He went through his share of persecution in Japan but ultimately ended up starting a movement which exists to this day.

In the world of Buddhism, some thinkers and monks have tried to rejuvenate the deeply spiritual aspects of Vajrayana and Zen in the West. One remembers as a youth reading Zen Flesh Zen Bones by Paul Reps, an excellent exposition of the basics of Zen, showing also its possible relationship with (and possible descent from) the Shiva Tantras…It is a fact that several Buddhist Tantras have originated from the Shiva Tantras.

The growth of various schools of psychology in the 20th century, such as Freudianism, Behaviorism, and Archetypal Psychology have all made an impact on us, though as one might expect, non-theistic doctrines such as Freudianism and Behaviorism don't have the influence today they once had. Having said that, there is always room in secular sections of society for such doctrines to find a niche…

Two movements that come to mind are Maharishi Mahesh Yogi's Transcendental Meditation (TM) movement and the ISKCON (The International Society for Krishna Consciousness) movement. The Hare Krishnas as they are sometimes called are of course, a very different movement from TM. The faith and fervor of the Hare Krishnas have made them a worldwide movement blessed by Divine Grace no less. Its Founder, Srila Prabhupada, who came to the US with something like $10 in his pocket, went on, despite fragile health, to create a huge international organization. He stated many times that He was asked by Lord Krishna to take birth one more time for the sake of publishing books on Krishna and setting up Krishna centers in the West.

TM on the other hand has mostly branched off to other forms, such as Vedic Universities and Ayurvedic Healing. Transcendental Meditation itself, which at one time attracted the attention of both commoners and celebrities, appears to have petered out as a practice, though one important consequence of the movement started by Mahesh Yogi is the arrival of Deepak Chopra on the scene and Dr. Chopra has certainly made a great impact…Dr. Chopra began his spiritual life with Mahesh Yogi but of course later branched off to do some pioneering work.

I have to mention the highly experimental spirituality of Osho Rajneesh which began in the 1960s in India and later spread to other parts of the world and especially the USA. A township came up in Oregon and became known as Rajneeshpuram, which has since become defunct…the Osho group continues to have a fairly strong presence in Pune, India, however. The Pune Ashram still displays an air of unconventionality that characterized its early days…On a visit there I noticed the continuing importance being given to a hands-on approach to spirituality and of course that does appeal to some…We know for example there are Visual Learners, Auditory Learners, and Kinesthetic Learners and the last group are those who prefer to "learn by doing"…Rajneesh introduced techniques such as Dynamic and Kundalini Meditation as well as other partially modified Tantric techniques to literally create a technology of enlightenment.

Many teachers appeared in the 20th century who can be described as "non-theistic but spiritual". Five masters in particular come to mind: Meher Baba, Nisargadatta Maharaj, Ramana Maharishi, J. Krishnamurti, and Osho Rajneesh.

CHAPTER TWENTY-FIVE

A NEW AGE OF AVATARS BEGINS

> There is no nobler quality in the world than love. It is wisdom, it is righteousness, it is wealth and it is Truth. Let us light the lamp of love within---***Sai Baba***

A long drought of Avatars ended in the 14th century, with the arrival of Sreepada Sree Vallabha, approximately in the year 1320. This extremely benevolent Being did not enjoy much exposure and publicity, nor did He seek these. As Sai Baba once said, "Each Avatar has His own format". Sreepada left His mark on a relatively small area of India. A spiritual text from that period called the Guru Charitra covers in some detail two Avatars: Sreepada Sree Vallabha and Narasimha Saraswati. The latter lived in the 15th century. They are both considered manifestations of Dattatreya, who as we have seen before, embodies both the Vishnu and Shiva Principles.

Why did Sreepada lead such a quiet and largely unnoticed life? The answer perhaps lies in the conditions in India at that time....By the 14th century, invaders from the Middle East had fanned out over much of India and displayed a mostly intolerant and aggressive presence. Buddhism had all but disappeared under their onslaught. Buddhist monks were put to death by the hundreds. Nalanda, a renowned Buddhist University, was razed to the ground. The Buddhists were targeted even more than the Hindus were. Perhaps the invasions of the Middle East by Möngke Khan and Hulagu Khan, both predominantly Buddhist rulers from China, were still fresh in the memory of the invaders...or again perhaps Buddhism was seen as an atheistic religion, and therefore even more infidel than Hinduism...

The conflicts between India/China on the one hand and the Middle Eastern empires on the other shows a (karmic) pattern wherein the tables kept turning from one side to the other, down from ancient times to the present. For example, around the time of Alexander, India was at the receiving end...Later, King

Vikramaditya's empire stretched all the way up to Arabia. Then, after the time of Mohammad, Islamic hordes once again occupied India. Still later, the Chinese made serious inroads into the Middle East and at one point virtually destroyed the city of Baghdad. The forays of Islamic hordes westward into Europe later resulted in the Crusades, etc. Observing such cyclic patterns, the historian Toynbee was once prompted to say that nations and peoples have karma too, just like individuals…

Sreepada Sree Vallabha earned His name because He was born with auspicious and rare markings on his feet (Pada). He never needed formal education…He finished studying of the Vedas and the scriptures by the age of 7. Early in life, when pressured to get married, He claimed to be married to only one woman, *dispassion*, and also claimed to like this divine woman, and so He came to be also called Sree Vallabha, the "beloved of a divine woman".

His birth was marked by several metaphysical events. Immediately after birth, He chanted the primal mantra Om. After just a month He could walk. Within a few years He could converse in Sanskrit. By the age of 7, He knew the Vedas, Mimamsa (inquiry and investigation into the Vedas), and Thark (or Logic). Effortless were His ways…

When He was approaching his 16th birthday, the parents began looking for a bride for Him. But He refused, saying His life was meant to be lived like that of an Avadhoota. It is said that before He left home, He healed His brother who was blind, and gave him back his eyes. He also cured another brother, who was born lame, and made him walk normally…He then left home.

He would later say His incarnation was merely a physical re-embodiment of a form He had used many times before and for hundreds of years to give darshan to His devotees and saints who meditated on Lord Datta…

Sreepada wandered northwards, first to Banaras, or Varanasi, once called the Center of the Planet by Jack Kerouac, which is the city of Shiva, and then on to Badrinath/Kedarnath in the Himalayas. According to legend, He also visited the ethereal city of Shambala, which is said to be the site where the Kalki Avatar will be born many thousands of years from now. He was only sixteen years of age…It is said that throughout His life He never lost His youthful appearance, and resembled a boy of sixteen.

He then came back to South India and lived in a place called Gokarna on the west coast of India for some years. Gokarna is known for its Shiva Temple, one of the 12 main Shiva Temples (called Jyotirlingas) in India. The Shiva Linga here is called Mahabaleshwar. In the Guru Charitra, Gokarna is praised as a place of extreme spiritual potency. Sreepada is said to have lived here for 3 years, all the time keeping a low profile…All His life He would advocate doing penance to Lord Shiva.

He finally ended up living at Kuruvapur, an island on the river Krishna. A beautiful temple was built later, to commemorate His days there. In a biography written by one of His contemporaries, Shankar Bhatt, many of His miracles are described. People were moved by the way He spoke most respectfully to all souls. He would use terms like Amma and Ayya (mother and father) when speaking with older women and men.

Dattatreya Avatars display a remarkable characteristic: They have the ability to look at someone and know their previous lives. Sripada displayed such abilities in ample measure. He once scrupulously avoided a particular man who had been a dangerous criminal in his previous life. But when the man came and fell at His feet, Sreepada forgave him, and even blessed him.

Sathya Sai Baba also displayed this characteristic and perhaps to an even greater extent. He also foretold people's future lives and not just past lives. He did this especially for His close devotees. When looking at a person, Baba immediately could tell what was on the person's mind. A well-known newspaper's editor interviewed Baba in 1976, and later wrote:

Before I began asking each question, Sathya Sai Baba would begin to answer it. In the end, I did not ask even a single question, but I had enough material for this report.

Related to this ability of knowing previous lives is the ever-willingness of a Datta Avatar to assist a devotee in burning up karma. Sreepada did this by conducting fire ceremonies called Agni Yagnas. He would ask the devotee to bring particular kinds of vegetables like eggplant, gourds, etc., and burn them in the fire while chanting special mantras. The karma of the person would become infused in the vegetables, which would then be cooked and eaten by all the guests.

One day, a woman who was ostracized for having given birth to a retarded child and was living in extreme poverty, approached the river and was going to commit suicide when Sreepada stopped her and said that if she did so, that would lead to even more suffering in the next life…instead she should worship Lord Shiva all her life and the Lord would finally deliver her.

It has been said by others too that the karmic consequences of suicide are apparently quite severe… Looked at from the vantage point of Spirit, suicide is considered a capitulation of mind, and a refusal to accept one's conditions because of weakness in the mind…because we all have to ultimately evolve enough to be able to put up with the rigors of worldly existence, such a person's future lives will be filled with more than average trials and tribulations…

This Avatar rarely showed His power, but when He did, He left no doubt in people's minds of His Divinity…Walking on water frequently is one such. Everyday this Avatar would be observed worshipping the Goddess Gayatri. Just like his predecessor Lord Datta did many thousands of years prior, Sreepada extolled the Goddess Principle. Before He left the physical body, He made several assurances and promises to His devotees, stating that He would come to the rescue of any of His devotees until the end of time…He said His very nature was Supreme Love, and that it was a far cry from the love displayed by human beings. His was the Love that was the basis for all things…it was Oneness Itself.

An Avatar can greatly bless humanity with just His presence…He said He appeared in response to the prayers of many devotees, demoralized by the opposition to Hinduism and other indigenous religions, like Jainism and Buddhism. The hordes of Mahmud of Ghazni and Taimurlane had plundered and terrorized India. It seemed as if India had no protection from any quarter…It would take many centuries for India to finally achieve independence, but Indians have been fortunate that great souls appeared at frequent intervals and sustained the spirit of Hinduism, even while still not castigating any alien culture, and allowing other religions and paths to co-exist. Some of these great souls are the Avatars of Datta covered in this chapter and also Vaishnavite heroes such as Chaitanya Mahaprabhu, as well as Meera. They greatly assisted in reviving the Krishna culture in Hinduism, and will be covered in another chapter.

Like Dattatreya, Sreepada Sree Vallabha is referred to as a Digambara. Sreepada later stated that He was the reappearance of Dattatreya. He was the herald of a new age of Avatars that eventually led to the two great modern Avatars, Shirdi Sai Baba and Sathya Sai Baba. Sreepada literally began a Datta Marg or The Way of Datta… By definition, Datta Avatars will display signs of both consolidation and transformation/evolution. Some features of consolidating Avatars would be following the path of Dharma (or Righteousness) and a deep sense of Personal Responsibility, in addition to a life of Discipline and Service. As for evolutionary Avatars, they tend to focus on personal transformation and transcendence.

Not long after Sreepada left His physical body, there arose another great Avatar, Narasimha Saraswati. Narasimha Saraswati is also said to be a manifestation of Dattatreya and He lived in the 15th century. During His sojourn on earth He too showed extreme precociousness, exhibiting marvelous abilities and talents, including showing mastery of the Vedas at an early age…

Leaving home at an early age, He proceeded first to Badrinath via Kasi, just like His predecessor had done. Later He would claim to be a reappearance of Sreepada. His devotees would sometimes get His darshan (or visual manifestation, usually done to reward a particularly pious devotee) and sometimes Sreepada's darshan.

His teachings and pronouncements could be viewed as chauvinistic in this day and age…for example He would exhort women devotees to look upon their husbands as embodiments of Lord Shiva and serve their husbands. He would also say things like, "Women cannot hope to win over this worldly sea without the help of their husbands."

He finally ended up at Ganagapur on the banks of the Bhima River, after traveling far and wide, and performing many acts of transformation of devotees and also miracles that included bringing back people from the dead. His name spread far and wide, and an ashram was built for Him at Ganagapur. Even during His lifetime He was regarded a manifestation of Dattatreya.

One day, two Brahmins who were well-versed in the Vedas insisted that Narasimha Saraswati enter into a debate with them. The Avatar explained He was a sannyasi and did not believe in such things, but the Brahmins would not listen and accused Him of cowardice.

In order to teach them a lesson, Saraswati hailed a passerby who was just a simple peasant and barely knew any scriptures at all. The passerby was dressed extremely humbly and had the look of a laborer. Saraswati then drew 7 parallel lines on the ground and asked the man to cross them one by one. At each step, Saraswati would sprinkle holy ash on him and say to him, "Now tell me who you are." The man first began by saying he was an uneducated peasant. On crossing the next line he claimed to be a worshipper of Shiva. After the next step he described himself as a spiritual seeker…and so on.

By the time he crossed the 7th line, he insisted he was a Brahmin, well-versed in all the Vedas, and a teacher in his own right. Narasimha Saraswati then said to the man, "These two would like to debate with you." When the two Brahmins saw all this, they were terrified and fell at the feet of Narasimha Saraswati and begged for His forgiveness.

Narasimha Saraswati was the first Avatar who gave importance to sacred ash (or Bhasma, or Vibhuti), and said that it possessed immense spiritual power. He related that Lord Shiva taught that anyone who wished to do penance should apply sacred ash over his/her entire body and worship the Lord thus…however the ash had to come from a Guru…

Later the two Sai Babas would be famously associated with sacred ash. Both had the ability to make sacred ash appear on pictures and statues anywhere in the world they chose to…Holy ash and nectar still appear on their pictures and statues all over the world. Sometimes the ash appears between the photo and the sheet of glass or plastic covering it, i.e., inside the frame of the photo and out of contact of people's prying hands…Baba has said that the ash that appears randomly on His pictures is not for human consumption…

Narasimha Saraswati was a systematic and thorough teacher of the correct way (i.e., the Vedic way) to worship, perform penance, rituals and the like. At a time when such knowledge had become rare and scarce, this Avatar revived the knowledge of the ancient ways…He greatly extolled the Guru Gita of Lord Shiva as one of the ultimate guides for a serious spiritual aspirant…

In the traditions of Jesus and other Avatars, He performed several miracles including once helping a poor Brahmin who had barely enough resources to cook for 3 people, but ultimately fed hundreds of visitors on the same day. The food simply kept multiplying and even after everyone ate, there was food still left over. A similar miracle was performed more than once by Sathya Sai Baba in Puttaparthi in His youth. And like Sai Baba, Narasimha Saraswati could appear at multiple places simultaneously as He once did when He appeared at the homes of 7 devotees who lived some distance away, during an important function at His ashram, while remaining in full view of the ashram dwellers…

These two Avatars of Dattatreya, Sreepada Sree Vallabha and Narasimha Saraswati, are described at length in a work called Sri Guru Charitra, which was originally 7000 verses long, but was, apparently under the instruction of Lord Datta Himself, shortened to 2000 verses. While they were both Avatars of the same Integral Being, they were just a little apart in terms of format used, with Sreepada manifesting more the Shiva Principle and Narasimha Saraswati manifesting more the Vishnu Principle...the former emphasizing more the life of the Avadhoota, while the latter emphasizing more the Vedic Path. Narasimha Saraswati beautifully brought together the path of Knowledge, the Path of Action, and the Path of Devotion, just like a Datta Avatar would be expected to do, i.e., teach an integral path.

The Guru Charitra reasserts the whole concept of Universal Spirit as being the Primary Phenomenon, and the visible Universe as being a child of Universal Spirit, and also relates the great cycles of existence when the Universe is subject to repeated cycles of creation and dissolution, with life being introduced in each cycle, to undergo a slow process of Evolution and perfection in the material plane... Mind, which is a necessary layer between Matter and Spirit in order to allow the body to consolidate and sustain itself in any environment, quite naturally relates more to the visible body rather than the invisible Spirit, because of the influence of the senses, and the task before mind therefore is to become more dedicated to the infinite rather than the finite and ephemeral...Awareness and mindfulness are needed for this, but when these are also buttressed by faith in a Guru or Deity and by the teachings of the Guru, the mind is usually transformed. However, the old tendencies will sometimes emerge and it is important not to be disturbed but stay calm and continue on one's way...

This integration and harmony of mind and spirit is greatly thwarted by us because of a sense of separation from the Universe, which is the distortion of ego, and ego is therefore the biggest calamity of life. However, to our rescue come Divine Love, and Avataric Love, to act as a binding force to prevent things from falling apart...

Discipline and Devotion to the principles of Evolution, and also Integration of Mind and Spirit are needed by the spiritual aspirant. This leads to the mind surrendering itself to the call of the Universal Spirit, or The Universal Guru. Lord Dattatreya, who is a complete and perennial symbol of Universal Guru, since He carries the energies of all three Gurus, Brahma, Vishnu, and Shiva, and who manifested to His fullest extent in the twin Avatars of Shirdi Sai and Sathya Sai Baba, is always present to help the whole process of the evolution of mankind along.

The strengthening and solidification of this evolution is vital in order to make it really robust, and therefore aspirants are subject to testing…True spirituality is far from a free ride…it needs to withstand the test of time. The testing reaches a maximum during Kali Yuga since this is when the entropy or disorder seems to be at its maximum. But at the end of it all, a more resilient and wonderful integration occurs.

In this process all religions are playing a part. It is an act of great short-sightedness therefore, to insist that one's own religion is the best. The great religions of the world all have a role to play in evoking the Devotion and Discipline needed. In order to spiritualize the whole thing, in order for wisdom and faith to grow, we need the presence of a teacher, and who better than an Avatar, a direct descent of God into the world.

There is a delightful sequel to the story of Avatar Narasimha Saraswati. When He left His physical body in 1458, He is said to have retired into an anthill, or perhaps an anthill grew around Him as He was lost in meditation. This went on for more than 300 years… One day in the 19th century the anthill was sought to be cleared by a woodcutter wielding an axe…the woodcutter was shocked to see blood on the axe and immediately stopped what he was doing and carefully moved the anthill out of the way. Out emerged a being who consoled the woodcutter, saying the whole thing was planned because it was time for Him to emerge from His meditation and take Avatar once more….This new being came to be called Swami Samarth. He later moved around a bit and ended up in a place called Akkalkot. He came to be known as Akkalkot Maharaj.

I do not wish to dwell at length on this particular incarnation, except to say that He once granted a vision to a lady by giving her the darshan of Dattatreya… Soon His fame spread, and people of all religions, Hindus, Zoroastrians, Muslims, and Christians came to Him for solace and healing.

Now, Shirdi Sai Baba, the Avatar of the current Age, acknowledged that Akkalkot Maharaj was also an Avatar of Dattatreya like He himself was. Thus, we truly have an "Age of Dattatreya" that began in 1320 and *continues to this day*, with the recent advent of the two Sai Babas and the oft repeated prophecy of one more Sai Baba to appear before the year 2030...This Avatar will be called Prema Sai Baba.

All of the above goes to suggest that a being like Dattatreya can resurface (or multiply, if that's a better word) and literally take on many Avataric forms... a truly remarkable and significant event in the spiritual history of humanity. The Spirit Quantum called Dattatreya is a formidable one indeed. Every part of Him is also All of Him.

In the 15th century, Lord Dattatreya gave a darshan to Saint Eknath, a great devotee of Lord Krishna. Saint Eknath had many spiritual experiences, including coming into contact with Saint Jnaneshwar in a remote forest, more than 300 years after Saint Jnaneshwar had been considered dead... Jnaneshwar welcomed Eknath and asked him to re-edit his famous work Jnaneshwari (a commentary on the Bhagvad Gita) because it had been corrupted by others...Eknath dutifully did this. Eknath famously said, "The Lord and His devotees are like the ocean and its waves." Eknath left his body in 1606.

Chapter Twenty-Six

The Love and Surrender of the Modern Era

*Faith is an oasis in the heart which can never be reached by the two caravans of thinking and doing---**Kahlil Gibran***

In this chapter, we will look at various developments in the Middle Ages and also in more recent times in different parts of the world.

A special era occurred in India even as she was being slowly overrun and dominated by foreign powers. After the latter half of the Middle-Ages (1000 AD to 1500 AD) ended, the Modern Era is said to have begun. Just like there was a Renaissance in Europe, there was a lesser-known spiritual renaissance in India, punctuated by attempts to bring people together, whether followers of Shiva and Vishnu, or Hindus and Muslims. Such instances cannot be ignored simply by using such arguments that they were "few and far between" or "superficial". The fact that they even occurred is a miracle, or rather, a series of miracles...

I have already spoken of Akbar and Dara Shikoh. They were the spiritual ambassadors of the Mughals, and a refreshing change from the rest of the Mughal rulers. If Dara Shikoh had become emperor instead of Aurangzeb, the subsequent history of India might well have been quite different... Aurangzeb alienated so many people that all he ultimately ended up doing was to bring a premature end to the Mughal Empire. In fact there came a time when no one wanted to ally with the Mughals.

But in the middle of all this tumult, and perhaps because of it, there was a renewed upsurge of devotional spirituality among people. When one looks for the source of all Devotional Spiritual Movements in India however, one must inevitably end up looking at Ramanuja as one of the sources...Even though Ramanuja had illustrious teachers in Nathamuni and Yamunacharya, it is

Ramanuja that is considered the most significant personage when it comes to the origins of the Bhakti (or Devotional) Movement.

Ramanuja was a great Master who lived from approximately 1017 to 1137. He ended up influencing many other great teachers and therefore can appropriately be called a Guru's Guru.

His movement has been described as Qualified Non-dualism...and while it's perhaps intellectually less appealing than Non-Dualism, it has an energizing by-product: Looking upon the Lord as one's ultimate goal, and looking at devotion and surrender as the pathways to liberation... This basic tenet has influenced so many spiritual movements in India that Ramanuja's contribution is almost impossible to quantify...

What is Qualified Non-Dualism (QND)? Rather than saying "All is One" (i.e., accepting the complete oneness of the Universe since everything emanated from the same Universal Spirit) these QND adherents look at human aspirants as "small souls" compared to Lord Vishnu who is the Great Soul and the goal of aspirants. At the end of the Universe, when all merges back into the Lord, then and only then is all One. Until then all is not One.

Ramanuja influenced Ramananda who in turn influenced Kabir, a stellar figure in the Bhakti Revolution that swept India in the Middle Ages. Ramanuja also had a long-term influence on other Bhakti movements such as the Swaminarayan Sect, known for their exquisite temples in various parts of the world, including Europe and North America.

And of course, the energy of Sripada Sri Vallabha (1320 to 1350) was still around and so was the presence of Narasimha Saraswati (1378 to 1459), both appearances of Dattatreya.

As discussed before, the Age of Dattatreya began in earnest with Sripada Sri Vallabha, with Adi Shankara having paved the way about 5 centuries earlier...Adi Shankara had insisted that Vaishnavites and Shaivites needed to come together, and not emphasize the divisions between them. In effect He wanted Hindus to integrate the two sides of the same spiritual coin...

However, centuries of bias cannot be got rid of so easily, and this bias continues to this day.

Few saints in the spiritual history of mankind have captured the imagination of followers like Saint Kabir (c. 1440 to c. 1518). This Being is reminiscent of Shirdi Sai Baba because of His nebulous early life (to this day people are not sure if He was born in a Hindu family or a Muslim family) and there is little doubt that Divinity willed it that way… Kabir ultimately took up a Muslim name, but called His God Rama. He also called God Krishna and Allah. He openly embraced concepts such as Parabrahman, karma and reincarnation. He also mentioned the Hindu concept of "atman" in His discourses. But as might be expected from a Muslim Saint, He spoke about the One God, and was against idol worship as a way to salvation…Later, Shirdi Sai Baba would say He had the soul of Kabir within Him...

Was Kabir therefore a hitherto unrecognized avatar? His numerous followers certainly think so...and there is indeed a certain hagiography surrounding His life. However, He famously became the disciple of another great soul Ramananda who in turn was the protégé of Ramanuja, who we just met. Ramananda was a devotee of Lord Rama and this clearly rubbed off a lot on the young Kabir. A true Avatar is His own guru, self-sufficient and complete...and so we have to stop short of calling Kabir a Super Avatar...But what is interesting is that He ended up being quoted by two Super Avatars, Shirdi Baba and Sathya Sai Baba who have both declared Their love for Kabir.

Kabir's fondness for Banaras, the city of Lord Shiva, is obvious because He spent almost His entire life in that area...His satirical confrontations with the orthodox Brahmins there is also known.

There is a remarkable similarity between Christ, Shankara, Kabir, and the Sai Babas....they combine the highest non-dualistic thinking with love and devotion. Jesus Christ said, "When thine eye be single, thy whole body is filled with light," a clear reference to oneness and non-dualistic perception of the

Universe...all is God and naught else. Shankara also taught basically the same thing....and so did Kabir.

Kabir insisted God is formless and without beginning or end and that God is pure and omnipresent. He was an effortless and prolific poet. To this day His poetry captures the imagination of many. Many of His couplets and verses appear in the Guru Granth Sahib, the holy scripture of the Sikhs.

Kabir is often praised in songs sung by celebrities in India to this day. With the life of Kabir, the Bhakti movement in India got a major boost. There are Kabir devotees all over the world and they have built temples. They are called Kabir Panthis. The poet Robert Bly is one of many completely enamored by the mystical bliss of Kabir the poet, the teacher, and paragon of simplicity and humility.

The 16th century saint Meera Bai (1498 to 1547) considered a saint called Raidass (or Ravidass) as Her guru. Saint Ravidass was an eclectic teacher and was known by both Hindus and Sikhs. Some of his writings have been included in the Guru Granth Sahib, the main scripture of the Sikhs. He was a contemporary of Saint Kabir and was born around 1450..

Ravidass was so adored by some that after his death his popularity showed no signs of diminishing. He is one of the giants of 15th century Devotion (or Bhakti) based religion, along with others like Chaitanya Mahaprabhu. He taught the oneness, omnipotence, and omnipresence of God. He claimed perhaps before anyone else that an individual is a "particle of God". He also used the analogy of individuals being waves in an ocean...

Saint Ravidass continues to attract so many followers that a new cult was born recently, called the Ravidassia religion. The Ravidassias insist their path is distinct from Sikhism, even if some of their doctrines resemble Sikhism. The Saint taught about freeing the mind from duality which in His view was essential to merge with the Supreme.

Another towering figure of this time is Chaitanya Mahaprabhu. He was a contemporary of Meera Bai and lived from 1486 to 1534. He became known for His total devotion to Lord Krishna. He went into a state of ecstasy on seeing the Lord in any form and once fainted at a Krishna temple when He saw the Deity. He spent His whole life singing and dancing in the streets of His village in Bengal. This period in India can be seen as the Great Krishna Revival period, given that two legendary devotees of Krishna were present at the same time. These two towering saints, Meera and Mahaprabhu, ushered in a Lord Vishnu Renaissance.

The ISKCON movement during the last 50 years has heavily borrowed from the charismatic life of Chaitanya Mahaprabhu to further its mission in the world. And it did not stop there. Many other personalities have been raised to a pedestal by the ISKCON devotees, thus perhaps creating confusion in the minds of the lay public...it's interesting that the apparent center of it all, Lord Krishna, is only one of the nodes now...

Ramananda (the teacher of Kabir) so energized the Devotion movement in India that His legacy continues...One of the biggest lights to be born into this legacy is Tulsi Das, the "ultimate ambassador" of Lord Rama, at least in the modern era. Like Shankara before Him, Tulsi Das tried to bridge the gap between Lords Vishnu and Shiva and this He did by making them both devotees of each other...He was one of those who sought to reconcile non-dualistic thinking with bhakti (or devotion) by saying that the impersonal Parabrahman (or the Divine Absolute, or Holy Spirit) would, in response to the repeated requests of devotees, take form and descend as an Avatar or even in a subtle body...This whole idea of a "responsive and not passive Holy Spirit" in the Universe is an idea underlying other faiths and paths as well. Human Consciousness can indeed interact with Divine Consciousness even if in humble ways.

He advocated taking the name of Rama as much as possible as the way to liberation in the Kali Yuga or "Dark Age" we are in. Whereas in previous ages meditation and rituals had been effective they were no longer so...For Tulsi Das, the formless God or Impersonal God resides in the heart while the God with form resides in the eyes...Visualizing Rama while chanting His name or mantra is both natural and advisable to Tulsi Das, who has drawn a lot of encomiums from both Indian and Western writers. Few poets in history have had such a widespread influence on their countrymen.

The Indian Paradox

Most historians would inform us that India has literally been laid siege for at least the last ten centuries, and that her wealth and culture and even dignity have been stolen from under her nose…Many Indians today hold the view that invaders from the Middle East and later from Europe greatly affected the Indian ethos and way of life…

However, a spiritual history of India for the last ten centuries reveals quite something else…Great spiritual luminaries and Avatars have trodden on Indian soil in the last ten centuries. This of course also implies that great Gurus have sought to share their wisdom and Divinity with their audiences. The great Swami Sivananda and others have spoken of the spiritual blessings that India will eternally continue to receive. Avatar Babaji has predicted a great revival of Hinduism and so has Sathya Sai Baba.

Let us now attempt a list of movements, reformers and spiritual gurus from this and other parts of the world:

9th century: The rise of Sufism---An example: Abu Yazid of Bestam, a 9th century Sufi mystic who saw himself as a limb of God and who is said to have exclaimed: Glory be unto me! In India, Kashmir Shaivism became resurrected, thanks to teachers like Abhinavagupta.

10th Century: Ramanuja and Matsyendranath. The last mentioned was a great yogi of the Nath tradition that traces its origin to Lord Shiva the first Yogi (also called Adinath), but more through the life of Lord Dattatreya.

11th Century: Gorakhnath (one of the greatest Nath Yogis) who was Matsyendranath's protégé and who was considered by some to be an avatar of Lord Shiva. He wrote the Gorakh Samhita, a Yoga Classic.

12th: St. Francis of Assisi, who we have seen before, and St. Hildegard of Bingen a mystic and visionary polymath, who wrote extensively on both Spirituality and Science, especially the science of healing. Basaveshwara (founder of Lingayatism, a radical form of Shaivism that was into social reform and especially wished to rid Hinduism of the caste system). He lived in South India. Among his followers at this time, almost like a counterpoint to Sufi poetry, there arose a form of spiritual poetry called Vachanas that were mostly verses ecstatically dedicated to Lord Shiva, though they could also be spiritual admonitions.

13th: Thomas Aquinas who was known for levitating in ecstasy and for his visions of Mother Mary. He was a great theologian who considered theology a science. He sought to bring together the ideas of Aristotle and Christianity and ended up becoming a very influential figure. He wrote about humans being a composite of soul and matter and considered the soul the primary principle.

Madhavacharya the Indian philosopher who was the chief proponent of the Dualistic School of Vaishnavism (Vishnu followers) and Tattva-vada meaning, a "philosophy of reality". Considered a genius and a legendary teacher who wrote prolifically. He set up ashrams and opened temples to Krishna.

14th Century: Sripada Sri Vallabha (the first Dattatreya Avatar in a long time) who we have seen.

15th Century: Narasimha Saraswati another Avatar of Lord Datta) who we also saw.

Guru Nanak the great founder of Sikhism which will be covered in the next chapter.

Narsi Mehta, the great Krishna devotee who saw or had direct experience of Lord Krishna's Presence (called darshans).

And as mentioned before, Ramananda (the founder of the Ramanandi Sect, the largest group of ascetics in India today) and Saint Kabir who did a lot to bring Muslims and Hindus together.

16th Century: Chaitanya Mahaprabhu and Saint Meera, both ecstatic in their devotion to Krishna. Chaitanya Mahaprabhu is one of the main inspirations behind the Hare Krishnas (or Krishna Consciousness movement). He and Meera led such influential lives in the spiritual sense that an entire book could be written about them.

St. Teresa of Avila makes waves in Spain: The ecstasy of Saint Teresa has been commented upon by writers…Nothing was more important to her than union with God. She was seen levitating in sacred places. She advocated mental prayer, silence, and ecstatic union with God. She also reported visions of Jesus and Mary.

Emperor Akbar seeks to begin a new religion: Din-I-Ilahi (a synthesis of Islam, Hinduism, Jainism, Zoroastrianism, & Christianity). In this religion the adherent is encouraged to indulge in Soul Contemplation and is encouraged to attain a state of purity by devotion to God.

17th Century: The formidable Zen Master Hakuin teaches in Japan. He is said to have resurrected Zen which had declined for centuries prior to that. An intense teacher who called a spade a spade.

Samarth Ramdas, a spiritual poet who was both prolific as a writer, an intense meditator, as well as extroverted in his spiritual activities which included opening several temples and spiritual centers called Maths. He was known for his intense devotion towards Rama and Hanuman.

Tukaram, a poet saint of Western India was also known for his devotional poetry. He became known for his pithy verse. An example: *I could not lie anymore so I started to call my dog "God"*. He was considered an ideal combination of Head and Heart. A Vedantist and a Devotee at the same time.

18th Century: Anne Catherine Emmerich the incredibly clairvoyant mystic who was a prolific communicator of spiritual visions following travels in the astral plane, visions of intimate details of the life of Jesus and Mary, as well as visitations by

Mother Mary and also visits from angels. Mel Gibson's movie "The Passion of the Christ" was based on the writings of Emmerich. We saw her in the chapter on Jesus Ambassadors.

Swami Narayan (born in the late 18th century and passed on in 1830) brought devotion towards Lord Vishnu to a new level among the lay population. The charisma of Swami Narayan has stirred the hearts of many and continues to do so... The exquisite temples of the Swami Narayan sect all over the world have become major tourist attractions. Many of them are one-of-a-kind temples often carved out of stone in the most compelling manner by modern age sculptors.

We will examine the last couple of centuries in another chapter. To put things in perspective one wishes to touch upon the overall scenario also...While mankind began to increase in its ability to control the forces of nature, people's lower chakras were getting stimulated too, and thus desires and ambitions grew... the horrors of the early days of the Industrial Revolution come to mind as a vivid example of that. More and more cognitive space in the World Mind was being created. Thus, even while the intellect grew, humans began drifting further and further apart... No longer was everyone doing pretty much the same thing. Specialization and narrowing of livelihoods began to take root. This led to more complex interactions between humans and the creation of more diverse societies... Life therefore began to grow more complex and that trend has continued to this day...

As if to counter that, the intensity of spiritual search and struggle has also increased in the last 200 years. The sheer number of avenues that have opened up are both a blessing and a challenge for us at this point. The time has therefore come to end spiritual specialization and to integrate things. It appears to be the right time for an eclectic Avatarism and for spirituality to blossom rather than organized religions, which have had their say and have been given enough time so to speak, without having uplifted humanity too much...

Chapter Twenty-Seven

Sikhism:
God-Centeredness with Spirituality

Not in a temple, but in spirit shalt thou pray---***Jesus Christ***
(as quoted by Master El Morya)

It isn't easy in the present age to start a religion that endures. Guru Nanak did it in the 16th century by His sheer faith, devotion, and spiritual determination. That He was filled with the grace of Spirit is evident from sayings such as:

Even Kings and emperors with heaps of wealth and vast dominion cannot compare with an ant filled with the love of God.

Alone let the devout constantly meditate in solitude on that which is salutary for his soul, for he who meditates in solitude attains supreme bliss... Thou hast a thousand eyes and yet not one eye; Thou host a thousand forms and yet not one form.

The Sikh religion that was set into motion as a result of Guru Nanak's mission reminds one of Sufism, so poetic are the Guru's words and the words in the main scripture of the Sikhs, the Guru Granth Sahib. While being to some extent influenced by Hinduism, the Sikh religion, which is sometimes incorrectly labeled a religion of warriors because of the historical context in which it was born and also due to some of the practices of the Sikhs, is as much a path for the devoted as it is for the spiritually adventurous.

He had an auspicious birth and His divine qualities were recognized even when He was a youth. The Guru was born in 1469 and His mission did not begin until the dawn of the 1500s. It lasted for about 40 years, and by the end of that period the Guru had succeeded against all odds to veer Hindus and Muslims to His fold, and inaugurated a religion that, even while having some elements of both, was also distinct from both. An important reason for the success of His mission is that it began under the most extraordinary circumstances and catapulted Him to instant fame and spiritual stature.

At the age of 30, He suddenly disappeared for a while, and when His clothes were found on the banks of a river, He was assumed dead. He reappeared about 3 days later and looked completely transformed and filled with an aura of complete calm and assurance. He described a most extraordinary event where He had been taken to the presence of the Divine, offered a cup of nectar, and told to spread the name of God. Thereafter, His words and teachings were like that of a man transformed. His exhortations always involved chanting and singing the name of God. He accepted all religions as sacred and insisted however, that since God was neither a Hindu nor a Muslim, He was going to follow neither as such.

He taught that a sincere devotee should follow spiritual role models rather than be dominated by his or her own mind and limited experience. Meditating on God's name, serving the less fortunate, and earning an honest living were the cornerstones of His path.

In the tradition of Shankara, He was an intrepid traveler and traveled to all parts of India and Afghanistan, Saudi Arabia, and far beyond... His parents were dismayed to lose Him at such a young age but He convinced them by saying the whole world was in chains and suffering because of Kali Yuga and that He was going to do His best to bring light and comfort to as many people as He could. He insisted His desire to travel the length and breadth of the land was God-directed, and finally obtained His parents' blessing to do so.

His energy and zeal were extraordinary and He traveled for almost 25 years before He finally settled down to preaching within a smaller area near where He was born. He was convinced about the freshness of His message, and that conviction ultimately proved to be very inspiring to His audiences. Ultimately the last 15 or so years of His life that were spent in the Punjab area were the most influential, because many thousands of people had sustained contact with Him, whereas He had somewhat spread

Himself quite thin during His travels... And thus the Punjab was the place where Sikhism took root.

Guru Nanak's largeness of heart and willingness to speak to people of any religion or persuasion ultimately endeared Him to many. Another indicator of His largeness of heart was the appointment of a Hindu as the Second Guru of the Sikhs rather than one of His sons. However, after Sikhism took root in the Punjab, the external trappings of the Sikhs, such as wearing a turban, and carrying a comb and dagger, and also wearing a bracelet, etc., to some extent created a disconnect in the minds of the people in those lands that He had visited. However, when they heard these turbaned folk were the disciples of Guru Nanak, they found it easy to accept the followers of this new path. And so, in that sense, Guru Nanak's travels were not in vain...

The Sikhs were encouraged to be egalitarian and were all asked to drop their original caste names and instead take up the common last name of Singh (for men) and Kaur (for women) The Sikh religion was not one to suppress women. Rather, women were treated on an equal footing and were extolled as indispensable to the welfare of humanity.

Guru Nanak gave us the Mul Mantra:

Ek ong kaar Sat Nam Karta Purkh Nirbhao Nirvair Akal Murat Adjoonee Saibhang Guru Prasaad Jap Aad Sach Jugaad Sach Haibhee Sach Nanak Hosee Bhee Sach

Which translates as:

God is One He is the Supreme Truth... God is the creator and doer. God is fearless and without ill-will. God exists in the undying form. God is unborn and Self-Creating.... God is self-illumined. It is by Guru's Grace that one attains God...Meditate on Him for He is the Truth Eternal. Nanak says now he is also eternal truth and forever will he be.

Over the next two hundred years or so, Sikhism became increasingly temporal and even somewhat militant. But the origins of this religion are spiritually impeccable and it continues to inspire people. Recently the spiritual aspects of Sikhism have made a comeback and there is a small but growing interest in the West about the Sikh religion and especially its inherent spirituality.

Many miracles have been attributed to Guru Nanak, and more than any other Sikh guru. There are fascinating anecdotes regarding the materialization of objects and various metaphysical tests of His devotees. This coupled with His humility (He would work alongside other agricultural laborers in the fields even after He was proclaimed a Guru) have ensured Him a distinguished place in the spiritual history of humanity.

Chapter Twenty-Eight

The Prophets of the Baha'is

Consort with the followers of all religions in a spirit of friendliness and fellowship---*Baha'u'llah*

I have met some Baha'is and found them to be usually very accepting and easy going folk, soft-spoken and friendly. I once had a conversation in a train with a fellow-traveler Baha'i about Mahatma Gandhi. He was reading a book about Gandhi at that time. He and his friends who were all Baha'is then sat in a circle and discussed the book...I was struck by the sincerity of the discussion...they were all from Malaysia and displayed more interest in Gandhi than I have witnessed anywhere in the India of today.

The Baha'i Faith has grown over the last 150 years and has a widespread presence today, and there are Baha'i temples all over the world. The Faith has its roots in Islam, Sufism, and also Zoroastrianism. The writings of its prophets exerted an influence over the continent of Asia first and then spread to other continents.

There are two spiritual teachers that were the original contributors to this Faith. They are the Bab and Bahaullah. The former, born S. A. M. Shirazi but later called the Bab, was actually the lunar prophet who made way for the solar prophet, Bahaullah. The word Bab means "Gate" and he is considered by Baha'is to be the forerunner of Bahaullah.

The Bab was born in Persia in the year 1819. He is thought to be of the same genre, and by some even the same being, as John the Baptist, born to be a herald of a new prophet, the teacher that the world calls Bahaullah. The Bab was however also a teacher and transformer of people in his own right, and so is also considered a prophet by the followers of this faith. He is considered to be the one who ushered in a new age, which was begun by Bahaullah just a few years after the premature passing of the Bab who was heavily persecuted and then executed for his views. 20,000 other Bab followers were also killed during that dark period for the Baha'is.

The Bab described the Divine Essence of the Universe as something indescribable, unknowable and inaccessible. He would often say the world redeemer who was coming soon would be a greater soul than him, and that the redeemer would be a direct manifestation of God and would proclaim His Glory.

One of the many thousands of people who entered this Faith was a man by the name of Mirza Husain Aly Nuri, later to be called Baha and then Bahaullah. At one stage in his life he was imprisoned, as were many other followers of the Bab. It was in prison that Baha said he had mystical experiences, the most significant being a vision of a "maiden of God". Bahaullah describes it as an angel-like figure suspended in space above his head. The maiden spoke to him and said he was a very special being and was the Beloved of the Lord and also His Divine Messenger. After his release Bahaullah proclaimed the same message to the world... Shortly after that the Bahai Faith was born. It would later spread to many corners of the earth.

The prophet Bahaullah taught about the oneness of God and the oneness of humanity as well as the common source of all religions. This unity of God and humanity was therefore a spiritual one. He taught that the Founders of all the major religions of the world were each inspired by the "same Divine Source". Every soul was journeying towards that one Source, and the evolution of the soul and of life was the main reason we are all here.

The soul animates the body which is only a vehicle for the soul's evolution. The soul grows only by Divine Intervention.

He loved nature and being outdoors, and is reported to have said, "The countryside is the world of the soul, and the city is the world of bodies." He also taught that while it was easy to have a negative view of human beings, it was vital to move towards a positive view. Humans are born inherently noble and full of all kinds of potential, and are not inherently evil, which is a view echoed by several avatars... Also, for Bahaullah, Religion and Science were to be seen as complementary and not antithetical to each other...The One God sends all kinds of Messengers to the world...but the truly Divine Messengers are few. And they are, Bahaullah acknowledged, "Manifestations of God Himself". All this of course, tallies with the notion of Avatars.

Bahaullah's teachings and miracles led to the sect's growing steadily. At one point, he began writing to several prominent leaders of nations all over the world, mostly regarding world peace and unity. The Baha'is have always believed in translating their faith into pragmatic and benevolent action.

Bahaullah passed on in 1892 and was buried in Acre, Israel. Perhaps because of its youth and its acceptance of all faiths, the adherents of this religion display open-mindedness to all. They also welcome everyone to their houses of worship.

The Baha'i Faith today has over 5 million members all over the world.

CHAPTER TWENTY-NINE

A MULTIPLICITY OF AVATARS IN THE MODERN AGE

Those who think that Baba is only in Shirdi have totally failed to know me---***Shirdi Sai Baba***

The story of Swami Samarth leads us into the 19th and 20th centuries, when a wonderful protean profusion of Dattatreya Avatars happened. How do we know this? Shirdi Sai Baba did say:

"Myself, Tajuddin (Baba), Dhuniwale-dada of Sai Kheda, Narasing Maharaj of Nasik, Swami Samartha of Akkalkot and Gajanan Maharaj of Shegaon---all of us are incarnations of Dattatreya and with mutual cooperation we are working hard for the accomplishment of a goal."

This is truly a stunning revelation. It informs us in no uncertain terms about the age we are living in. It is the Age of Dattatreya, the perfect collaboration of Lord Shiva and Lord Vishnu. Shirdi Sai Baba, who would sometimes utter "Allah Malik!" (or Allah is the Lord), would also say "Dattatreya Malik!". What He said depended usually on who His audience was. If the audience was made of non-Muslims, He would say "Allah Malik" and if the audience was Muslim, He would say, "Dattatreya Malik". One of the chief aims of this Avatar was to bring Hindus and Muslims together whenever possible...

A multiplicity of Datta Avatars like this creates such a strong field that the whole paradigm of spiritual growth and liberation has been altered. Chanting the names of guru and God, singing to Him, and following the teachings will get the solid commitment of the guru. And after that it's a fast track to liberation. No longer does liberation need to be looked upon as some glorious state of self-sufficiency. Instead, the company of the Avatars will see us through. Shirdi Sai Baba has said: *When the Lord is pleased with a devotee He gives him discrimination and detachment, and takes him safe beyond the ocean of mundane existence.*

Below is a representation of an "Infinite Datta Space" with the Shiva Principle on the Y Axis and the Vishnu Principle on the X Axis.
It is important to keep in mind that the Shiva Principle and the Vishnu Principle are not in any way opposite or antagonistic forces...they are rather somewhat orthogonal in nature i.e. they complement each other.

If we imagine the Y Axis to be the Shiva Principle and the X Axis to represent the Vishnu Principle, the graph then represents a DATTA SPACE, in which all the recent Avatars can be placed. Depending on the relative strength of each Principle in the Avatar, He can be placed somewhere in this space.

S												
H												
I												
V												
A												
					D	A	T	T	A			
P												
R						S	P	A	C	E		
I												
N												
C												
I												
P												
L												
E		V	I	S	H	N	U		P	R	I	N	C	I	P	L	E

In a sense, we are all Datta Avatars and located somewhere in this Datta Space...That's because we each carry elements of

both the Shiva and Vishnu Principles. As we can see, the possible variations among Datta Avatars are almost infinite.

Finally, this Datta Space is actually three-dimensional, with the Shakti Principle (or the Energy Principle and also called the Goddess Principle) forming the Third Dimension.

Regarding Tajuddin Baba whose last name was Aulia, not much is known. This is not surprising, given the mysterious nature of many Avatars... Sripada Sri Vallabha, the first of the modern Datta Avatars, was also one such... Tajuddin Baba was a Sufi Master and lived from 1861 to 1925.

Tajuddin Baba is known more through His well-known devotees. For example, Upasni Baba of Sakori, who received God-Realization from Shirdi Baba, frequently came to Nagpur for the darshan of Tajuddin Baba. Upasni Baba's student, the well-known Meher Baba was another who served Tajuddin Baba. Meher Baba later attracted followers from around the world, including the United States.

It is also recorded that Tajuddin Baba would send his devotees to Shirdi Sai Baba and the latter sent his devotees to Tajuddin Baba.

As for Dhuniwale Dada, he lived in the state of Madhya Pradesh in Central India. He spent a lot of time at a place called Sai Kheda and performed miracles there. He sometimes gave "Shiva Darshan" to His close disciples...His appearance became transformed into Lord Shiva's form...It might seem a little odd to the readers of this book that such great Beings are hardly known by the general populace and instead have a finite number of followers...This was exactly the point that the great Meher Baba wanted to make...that the human mind has a way of actually avoiding God as it makes its way in the world, and if it does accept a guru, the mind looks no further and immediately creates a zone of comfort around one's chosen guru... To show His disappointment, Meher Baba spent the last 50 years of His life in silence….communicating only by signs and through writings. In a sense, He was discouraging sycophancy.

Lord Dattatreya's Avatars can help us overcome this narrowness of approach and make us more open to the various manifestations of God.

Wherever Dhuniwale Baba went, He would make a fire and sit in front of it. His very name Dhuniwale can be translated as "He of the fire". He left His body in 1930.

Swami Samarth of Akkalkot was also an appearance of Dattatreya and is known for mysterious origins just like other Datta Avatars like Shirdi Sai Baba. His body was unusual in the sense He never seemed to age, and had extraordinarily long arms that reached to His knees, and also very long ear-lobes that shook every time He turned His head. His pronouncements remind us of Shirdi Sai Baba and of course that's not surprising...

Thus, in modern times a parent Deity, Dattatreya, has decided to really make His presence felt on earth by taking several forms. This strong influx of spiritual energy was needed in the dark times the earth has experienced since about the late 1800s. As we know, wars became more frequent and a climax was reached with the two World Wars of the 1900s.

These several forms of Datta set up an incredibly strong field. The effects of this field are seen in the way different streams of knowledge are coming together in the modern world. Inter-disciplinary work and a synthetic approach to "science vs religion" are also happening. There are many anecdotes relating how devotees of Shirdi Sai Baba experienced His connection with Datta. For example, a devotee once entered Baba's premises but instead of finding Him found a three-headed baby instead! This incident occurred on Lord Datta's birthday.

But perhaps the greatest synthesis of all is the coming together of Faith Doctrines and Non-Dualism. In short, Bhakti Vedanta appears to be the biggest wave of the future. This represents a great coming together of Heart and Head. It is the Alpha and Omega of Spirituality. Vishnu and Shiva are symbolic representations of Heart and Head. As Baba has said: *Love needs to enter the Intellect and the Intellect needs to enter Love.*

Chapter Thirty

The Spirituality of the last 200 years

> Time is a great preacher. Your heart is a great teacher. And God is your greatest friend. And He is also willing to be called by any Name... However, the exact time and nature of His response are not predictable. And so He asks for Faith and Patience---*Sai Baba*

As we know, a great number of spiritual pandits and gurus have appeared in the last 200 years. Many of us may wonder why the amount of chaos has also increased exponentially. For example, there were more wars in the 20th century than all previous centuries put together. A spiritualist might however say, "These teachers have come down in large numbers due to the general waning of both spirituality and interest in self-realization that we find today." In other words, to measure Avatars against worldly chaos is palpably unfair.

Let us remember the words of Beings like Jesus and Krishna who in effect said they have come to stir up things rather than create a cocoon of comfort...The good news is a Golden Age has been promised by Sai Baba and if that sounds far-fetched, Baba once said: *There is more good than bad in the world.* To those of us who are used to a steady dose of negatively-slanted reporting by the media, this too would seem far-fetched...A little contemplation will however make us realize that order and honesty and sincerity never make it to the news, and also for the most part are not noticed. Disorder, mayhem, and violence however are highly salient and also will make it to the news every time they occur.

First the 19th Century: We had Shirdi Sai Baba, Ramakrishna Paramahamsa, and Swami Samarth of Akkalkot. These are all truly awesome figures in our spiritual history. Avatar Shirdi Sai Baba stands out as a teacher and sculptor of many. He performed outstanding miracles, gave many teachings, and attracted both Muslims and Hindus in droves. His birth and life are the kind of stuff spiritual legends are made of. He assured His devotees that even after He left His body, He would continue to shower blessings on His devotees. There are innumerable instances of that happening, down to this day.

Also in the 19th century, Therese de Lisieux wrote a spiritual autobiography that made her one of the most well-known saints ever, and attracted devotees from around the world. Reading the *Imitation of Christ* by Thomas Kempis apparently had a deep effect on her, and took her into the Great Silence...This saint showed her spiritual precociousness when at the age of 14 she said she had come to Carmel to become a nun in order to save souls and pray for saints! Even though she lived only 24 years, her name is forever etched in the annals of Christianity. She left her body in 1897.

Another figure of note is Allan Kardec, the author of the *Spirits' Book*, still read as one of the pioneering books of "Spiritism" that spoke at length about séances, mediums, and the spirit world. Kardec was one of the early "parapsychologists" in the sense that he was at heart a rationalist who carefully investigated all phenomena that he wrote about.

Prabhu Jagatbandhu Sundar (a relatively unknown Vaishnavite teacher steeped in devotion to Krishna, prompting others to label him an avatar of sorts), who was born in 1871 in what is now Bangladesh still has devotees. His temples are open to this day. His followers considered him to be a reappearance of Chaitanya Mahaprabhu, whom the ISKCON devotees consider to be Krishna Himself. Sundar stressed the importance of chanting the name of God, more specifically, Krishna and Rama. He left his body in 1921.

Theophan the Recluse, for whom God is in the heart and the ego is man's greatest calamity, lived in Russia in the 19th century. An author of several books, many of which have been translated into English, he is reported to have taught his followers to *Descend with your attention into the heart, stand there before the Lord and admit nothing sinful to enter there. In this is the entire activity of inner warfare.*

In addition to Transcendentalism, a significant movement of the 19th century was Theosophy, and it was remarkable in that it quickly became a world-wide movement and an "Alternative Path" at a time when global communication was nowhere as efficient as it is today and at a time when there was hardly a "media" to speak of. Both the Transcendentalists and Theosophists ended up getting a lot of attention as the years went by. Thoreau influenced Gandhi, and Blavatsky influenced Annie Besant, and both Gandhi and Besant went on to play a role in the Indian Independence Movement. Thoreau and Emerson continue to inspire us, even if Thoreau was more spiritual than Emerson. Both were products of Harvard and in its own way that led to a networking of sorts, because before long, the Transcendentalists had their own magazine, The Dial. They were also both into Eastern Spirituality. Emerson once wrote a poem entitled Brahma dedicated to Universal Spirit. Here is the first stanza:

If the red slayer think he slays
Or if the slain think he is slain
They know not well the subtle ways
I keep, and pass, and turn again

Emerson also wrote a poem in praise of Saadi the Sufi poet at a time when Saadi and other Sufis were being discovered in the West. Apparently Emerson saw in Saadi a kindred spirit. Thoreau was quite unabashed in his praise of the Bhagavad Gita. The mysticism of Thoreau is for many, more inspiring than the philosophically penetrating writings of Emerson. Also, Thoreau was built of the renunciate mold far more than Emerson was. His sojourns in the wild are well-known by many because he wrote prolifically.

Many have wondered why Transcendentalism did not influence more people than it did. The distractions and conflicts of the 20th century have played no small role in making the movement a shadow of its former self. Instead one has noticed a greater pull towards Eastern paths among spiritual seekers.

Theosophy spawned other movements, as well as a renewed interest in the Philosophies and Mysticism of other cultures, not to mention a great expectation that a World Teacher would appear and save the world. And these additional movements gained momentum with or without the blessings of the Masters. For example, the somewhat more radical movements, such as Aleister Crowley's and the Agni Yoga Society of Nicholas Roerich also took root.

When Blavatsky and Olcott opened a significant Theosophical campus in Madras, India, in a way it also gave some Indians ideas... Ideas of experimenting if ancient Indian spirituality would now be better accepted in the West. In turn Transcendentalism's and Theosophy's comments regarding Indian spirituality led to a growing interest in it in the West, and in 1893, Swami Vivekananda was invited to speak at the World Parliament of Religions that was held in Chicago. Leaders from all religions attended this Conference, the like of which had never been held before.

Even though things took a different turn from what the Theosophists expected, looking at things from a global perspective, J. Krishnamurti went on to influence as many people as he would have if he had remained a Theosophist... and as for the Masters, they are eternal, and when the time is right, they will once again be active among us...in fact there are signs they are already being so. Besides, the two Sai Babas and other teachers have really opened up the heavens for those of us who are sensitive enough to respond appropriately.

Ramakrishna Paramahamsa and Swami Vivekananda have played no small role in 20th century spirituality even though Ramakrishna left His body in 1886. The Gospel of Ramakrishna is a work that has captured the imagination of many. Aldous Huxley was one of the many well-known admirers of Ramakrishna who embodied the phrase "God-intoxicated saint" perhaps better than anyone in recent history.

His protégé, Swami Vivekananda, too has received praise beyond most teachers of the 20th century, though he has also received some criticism... His remarkable life resulted in many changes in the way the Ramakrishna Mission progressed. The teachers of the mission were energized with a zeal rarely seen outside of their community. They went all over the world preaching the teachings of the two Masters and established the Vedanta Society (or its equivalent, *Ramakrishna Mission*) in many countries. Swami Vivekananda liked to draw parallels between the Imitation of Christ by Kempis and the Bhagavad Gita.

We now move into the 20th Century: Shirdi Sai Baba continued His mission until 1918. And soon Sathya Sai Baba (who took over the baton so wonderfully from Shirdi Sai Baba) began His mission. He is today considered the Avatar of the Age by over 25 million devotees all over the world. His aura was once observed by a Kirlian photographer Dr. Frank Baranowski who made two noteworthy comments about it: First of all Baranowski said the aura was pink in color, which the good doctor insisted was extremely rare because it was a sign of selfless love, and also the aura itself was incredibly huge.

Sri Aurobindo was a great 20th century teacher and saintly man from Bengal, who wrote at great length about the immense spiritual potential of man. So much so that he envisioned a new race of humans who were so transformed spiritually as to be the basis of a new earth. A well-known work of his is entitled *Integral Yoga*. As we have seen, Integral work of any kind has greatly increased in the Age of Dattatreya. In 1926, the year Sathya Sai Baba was born, Aurobindo declared, *Divinity has descended on the Earth.*

Ramana Maharishi (the great seer and propagator of "*Who am I*") who at a very young age had an enlightenment experience after which he left home to move near the Arunachala Hill in South India, one of the holy spots for the Dravidian Shaivites and considered the Southern Kailash, or another home of Lord Shiva.

After years of solitude he began attracting the curious who ended up staying on to become his students and devotees. This great sage's teachings soon reached the West thanks to visitations by Paramahamsa Yogananda and the spiritual writer Paul

Brunton. After 1930, visitors began to visit his ashram from all over the world. He left us in 1950.

Kahlil Gibran, the great mystic from Lebanon, who wrote the legendary book *The Prophet*, and who migrated to the US, and passed on in 1931. Few spiritual books have sold more copies than The Prophet. Gibran was influenced by Theosophy, Sufism and the Abrahamic religions. He wrote: *I love you when you prostrate yourself in your mosque, and kneel in your church and pray in your synagogue. You and I are sons of one faith—the Spirit.*

Jiddu Krishnamurti (the once upon a time darling of the Theosophists) whose life was made famous by the triple biography written about him by Mary Lutyens. Later, an Indian admirer, Pupul Jayakar, also weighed in. J.K. attracted huge crowds wherever he spoke and regularly visited Europe, the US, and India. His direct style of addressing large audiences appealed to many. He was much less extroverted during one-on-one meetings though and in fact rarely encouraged them. But Krishnamurti and Osho Rajneesh, the apparent rivals, who seemed to swap devotees all over the world have certainly made the 20th century more colorful...

The Krishna Consciousness Movements like ISKCON (founded by Srila Prabhupada) and Jagadguru Kripalu Yog, which has my friend Swami Mukundananda as a prominent member. ISKCON has certainly attracted notice (not all of it benign) but has come to be seen as somewhat extreme by the lay population.

Who would have thought when a 70 year old man boarded an innocuous looking ship bound for the United States, it would be a great beginning? So much so that CNN has called Srila Prabhupada one of the most "wildly successful" people of all time. It is quite interesting noting the influence Prabhupada had even on very young people, who were young enough to be his grand-children...But this movement (which Prabhupada insisted took place entirely at Krishna's behest) has become a legend.

The amount of literature this organization has managed to spread in the world is quite significant indeed.

Mother Teresa, who probably needs no introduction. Winner of the Nobel Prize and one of the most "hands-on saints" the world has seen. She has since Ascended. This was announced by Mother Mary in a channeling session just two days after Mother Teresa left Her body...

Time to acknowledge Padre Pio, who bore the stigmata of Christ and performed what could only be termed miracles, as well as Edith Stein who died at the hands of the Nazis and was a great mystic.

The intrepid teacher Meher Baba, the great Anandmayi Ma of Bengal and her deep compassion, Nisargadatta Maharaj the spiritual lion, the maverick Osho Rajneesh who established a spiritual township in the United States, and the Hugging Saint, Amrit-anandmayi Ma all deserve more than a mention. However, the sheer number of enlightened souls in the last 100 years however has forced this writer to be a little parsimonious at times.

Swami Muktananda the propagator of Siddha Yoga in the East and West was recognized as a true Master during his tenure on earth. His guru Bhagavan Nityananda gave him a solid grounding in Kashmir Shaivism, after which Muktananda never looked back...

The Self-Realization Fellowship: Even though the Self-Realization Fellowship has a somewhat limited presence in the United States, the same can hardly be said of Yogananda's book: Autobiography of a Yogi, which has become a legendary work. This organization in some ways has introduced a new Monasticism to the west which is based on the immense legacy of Avatar Babaji and His illustrious followers such as Lahiri Mahasaya, Yukteswar, and Paramahamsa Yogananda. We have seen them before in the chapter on Avatar Babaji, whose presence is still felt. Enlightenment Magazine once featured an article on Avatar Babaji's more contemporary chelas and devotees, some of whom claimed direct contact with the Master.

The Neo-Buddhists

I speak here of Paul Carus (author of The Gospel of Buddha) and also the Beat Poets especially Jack Kerouac the "American Bodhisattva". Let me not forget Paul Reps (author of the delightful "Zen Flesh Zen Bones"), and the redoubtable Alan Watts who was blessed with a certain spiritual charisma...all of whom gave the waning religion of Buddhism such a boost that their effects will be felt for a long time.

Add to this the Tibetans, the Sri Lankans, and DT Suzuki of Japan who helped to bring Zen to the West and Christmas Humphreys who also contributed his mite and we had a true Buddhist renaissance in the world, especially the West. Whether this is something that is intimately connected with the Buddha taking over the Lordship of Sanat Kumara when the latter decided to return to Venus is unclear but quite likely... The energy of the Buddha has received a spurt in the world and the Buddha is in many parts of the world a household word, even if the details of His doctrine are not. Reports of channeling the Buddha also have increased. Krishnamurti insisted the Buddha would visit him sometimes...

Many of us have heard of Meher Baba, the great Zoroastrian Saint, who spent decades in silence. He would sometimes convey through writing that He would come out of silence in the near future but it never happened... Meanwhile, through His writings He established a worldwide presence. He insisted that He had several (angel) agents working for Him in various parts of the world. He was quite forthright in declaring He had descended to save...in other words He was an Avatar who had descended with purpose. However, His influence hasn't really endured, and that is at least in part because this is the Age of Dattatreya, and the sheer Presence of Datta Avatars is the predominant factor in the world...

Meher Baba however has made contributions in that He could communicate in a way that both Easterners and Westerners could relate to. Many were the devotees of this charismatic teacher who once said, "To end all starvation of body, mind, and heart once and for all is the birthright of every human being."

His teacher for many years was Upasni Maharaj and He greatly appreciated the work of Shirdi Sai Baba and Tajuddin Baba.

The 20th century also saw a revival of an over 1000-year-old spiritual faith, Kashmir Shaivism. This happened through two streams, that of Pandit Lakshmanjoo who lived in Kashmir in the 20th century and drew the curiosity of people like Paul Reps and Indira Gandhi, and also through the Siddha Yoga movement which began in Maharashtra and which included Swami Muktananda and His guru Bhagavan Nityananda.

The latter's teachings, apparently often delivered in trance states over a period of some years, were compiled into a book called the Chidakasha Gita. The word Chidakasha translates as "The Sky of Consciousness". This Gita is a beautiful synthesis of Shaivism and Vedanta. But here too, this master mentions the value of Bhakti (or Devotion) when he says: *Without Bhakti there can be no Mukti*. In other words, no liberation without devotion to a Master. Truly the face of Nirvana has changed during the spiritual history of Planet Earth. One can see the Chidakasha Gita is also an Integral work.

Muktananda often said that the turning point in his life was when he received a direct "Shaktipat", or intense energy transmission, when he looked directly into his guru's eyes. The energy he received was so tremendous according to Muktananda that soon after he manifested powers he had not manifested before...He considered Nityananda to be an enlightened Master who taught that the original religion as taught by Lord Shiva to humanity was the one he followed. Nityananda says in the Chidakasha Gita: "All is Shiva. Justice and its opposite are both Shiva." And, "Shiva is the Omkar and the Omkar is the elite of all. Shiva cannot be attained by the mind."

There was a tendency in this school to equate Shiva with Purusha and to think of Prakriti (or Shakti) as maya. And so the saying by Nityananda, "In Shiva is Shakti, in Shakti there is no Shiva". Muktananda opened many meditation centers and ashrams all over the world.

Swami Shivananda of the Himalayas was a great soul who lived for many years in Rishikesh at the foot of the Himalayas, a unique "ashram town" that has a great number of temples and ashrams all in the vicinity of the Ganges river that flows through this town, lending it a spiritual charm not to be easily found in other parts of the world. He was known for living his message and performing acts of public service almost every day of His life. He was a spiritual magnet, attracting not only great teachers but also Avatar Sai Baba to Rishikesh.

The Arcane School of the Ascended Tibetan Master Djwhal Kul who taught us through His messenger Alice Bailey, has its headquarters and also an esoteric/occult library in New York City. Alice Bailey began her spiritual life at the Theosophical Society but later branched off on her own. She would later write copiously about the teachings and messages she received from the Ascended Master DK.

The Hermetic Order of the Golden Dawn was another organization that was undoubtedly influenced by the Theosophical Movement (though it also drew inspiration from the Freemasons and Hermeticism) in that it sought to better understand the world of the occult and the paranormal and to promote spiritual growth. At one time it drew several well-known personalities such as the poet W. B. Yeats, and it later influenced spiritual movements such as Thelema (which has been described as the resurrection of the Ancient Egyptian religion). Thelema also seeks to bring together elements from the Hermetic Kabbalah, Tantra, and Yoga. In that sense, it is to be regarded as an attempt to integrate various mystical traditions...

The founder of Thelema, Aleister Crowley, has become a controversial figure. He claimed to have done most of his writing under the inspiration of a guardian angel called Aiwass. And he did write prolifically. Thelema is in some ways a mini-religion, having a holy book of its own, as well as a deity who happens to be the Egyptian goddess Nuit.

The Agni Yoga Society was yet another esoteric society based on Ascended Master teachings. It was founded by Nicholas Roerich and his wife Helena just after the First World War. It acknowledges the Hierarchy of Masters that serve this earth. In particular the Ascended Master El Morya's teachings were put down by Roerich in a delightful work: *Leaves of Morya's Garden*. The Agni Yoga Society attempts to integrate Eastern and Western spiritual systems and thought. Is the word Integral starting to show a pattern here? As mentioned before, this is a feature of the Age of Datta.

Maharishi Mahesh Yogi who founded the TM movement and who built a Vedic City in Iowa and started Meditation Centers and Universities in various places does deserve a mention here. Advanced meditation practitioners have been known to levitate. While this master is not known for his teachings, he has indeed done much to further the development of schools and universities.

Swami Rama of the Himalayas who built a great ashram in Pennsylvania and brought Yoga in a big way to the West did end up attracting several devotees. He was one of the early yogis to be studied by Western scientists and he famously once made his heart skip a beat while being fully monitored with instruments such as ECG. This teacher also ventured into Tantra and has given discourses on the Sri Vidya Tantra and Kundalini Yoga.

Da Love Ananda (also known as Adi Da Samraj) the teacher of the Dawn Horse Communion which later became known as Adidam. Da Love was a maverick teacher who left his body in 2008. He was a "progressive guru" in the vein of Osho and Chogyam Trungpa and was also surrounded by controversy like the afore-mentioned teachers. But to his credit it must be said that someone like Ken Wilber had many positive things to say about Adi Da, while also acknowledging the dubious happenings in the Adi Da community. Adi Da insisted that he was a Supremely Blessed One, who was born with a "spiritual spoon in his mouth" and also very experienced even in this life, having been through a variety of teachers and paths, including Shaivism, Vedanta, and Scientology.

In the early 1970s he claimed, "I experienced the Bright at the Vedanta Society Temple in Los Angeles." This was his way of saying he had been through an enlightenment experience. He taught for many years after that, but never had a significant following. He even claimed a sort of Avatar-hood, but not many finally accepted him as a full-fledged Avatar even if they felt he was a significant teacher. He is yet another example of a teacher falling by the wayside, unaware of all the Avataric Activity of the Omnipresent Sai Babas that is already going on. Later he went through several breakdowns because he felt all his work had been quite futile...In the meantime he drew a lot of negative attention from the media. To his credit, he did propagate a Bhakti Yoga even if he made himself the center of it. In this he ignored the ancient Deities and that again was his undoing.

In this Age of Kali, it is said several dubious teachers will appear and be a burden, while still showing glimpses of great spiritual insights and wisdom. In other words Purusha will be corrupted by a wayward Mind, with Mind indulging in blatant Impersonation...Unfortunately, for new spiritual seekers, it can all end up being very confusing...It is simple and direct teachings that are destined to endure rather than complex teachings presented garishly.

Lightworkers, Channelers, Mediums galore have appeared in recent times. Among them one finds spiritually motivated practitioners, who are mostly very open to the Spiritual Universe, often channeling beings of various faiths and persuasions. I'm reminded of the show titled An Hour with an Angel, wherein wonderfully inspiring advanced beings have been channeled. While there may be a few bad eggs in that basket, this writer for one doesn't believe in throwing out the whole basket...

Quantum Healing, as practiced by Connie Shaw & Braco: A form of healing that happens through eye contact with a blessed medium. This is similar to Shaktipat as practiced by Hindu Masters as well as Avatars. Connie Shaw is a blessed soul who has support from the Ascended Masters, with the result that they actively participate in the process. Many mysterious and miraculous events have occurred during the gazing sessions and this writer has experienced some of them. Connie Shaw holds gazing sessions with audiences around the world.

I have skipped a few luminaries, such as Gurdjieff the Russian mystic and L. Ron Hubbard of Scientology. In this no slight is intended. Gurdjieff was a teacher who drew a lot of attention from lovers of esotericism and especially Western esotericism. In some ways he was one of the early pioneers of what came to later be known as the Consciousness Movement or the Human Potential Movement...He insisted that humans had almost infinite potential. He described humans as living mostly in a state of "waking sleep". He left his body in 1949.

The Scientology Movement has shown some resilience down to this day... Ron Hubbard's ideas, while being progressive and having a distinct color of their own, do show signs of being inspired by various faiths and paths. His approach was decidedly psycho-spiritual and he was greatly concerned with liberating humans from the clutches of the reactive mind. At one time he even claimed he was Maitreya. However, like some others mentioned in this chapter, he and his community became very controversial indeed. He had to spend many years in hiding. He left his body in 1986.

Chapter Thirty-One

From Vedanta with Love

Like the waves in the ocean, the worlds arise, live and dissolve in the Supreme, who is the substance and cause of everything---*Adi Shankara*

In the old traditions, it is said that Vedanta is the crowning glory of Hinduism, and the Ultimate Goal of life. There is scarcely anything beyond that...Non-duality is the ultimate state of oneness with the Universe. Why should a human aspire for anything else? For, are not the gods limited in their own ways...This conviction has inspired non-theistic religions and even esoteric paths.

Enter the two most recent Avatars...Shirdi Sai Baba and Sathya Sai Baba. The sheer magic of these Avatars and the countless anecdotes of their Living Presence on earth can fill a library.

No, they teach us: This Universe needs Love and heightened involvement (yes, even on other planes if necessary), and not some glorious state of self-sufficiency, followed by a solitary existence in some corner of a remote plane... This Universe also needs heightened spiritual awareness *as well as faith*. And above all, a devotee needs to be patient and surrender to the Divine, and there needs to be an ever present willingness to serve. In short...*It is all about Radiation and not spiritual introversion.*

And that's one of the reasons They have descended. Sai Baba said: Love is My Form. The physical bodies of the Avatars undergo changes but the Divine Spirit in their bodies remains the same. It is omnipresent, eternal, and changeless. The Lord is the only constant friend, relative, guide, and protector.

"Love All Serve All" may sound like a simplistic exhortation to some, but it has inspired millions worldwide. Isaac Tigrett, one of Sai Baba's apostles, adopted the slogan for his Hard Rock

Cafes all over the world. Sai Baba was once asked what the meaning of His Avataric Descent was and He simply said, "I am the servitor of humanity." His life was His message and now He would like our lives to be His message.

The triumvirate of Avatars (Shirdi Sai, Sathya Sai, and Prema Sai) will span more than two centuries. However, it would not be accurate to see them as following one another in that order. Rather they are *parallel phenomena*. Shirdi Sai Baba is continuing to make His presence felt and so is Sathya Sai Baba. And they both will continue to bless us during the life of Prema Sai Baba who is going to declare His Avatar-hood and Mission within the next two decades. It is the first time in the spiritual history of the earth that three super-Avatars will be present together, even if two of them will be in their subtle form...

This *integration* of Love, Service, Awareness, Receptivity to the Life Spiritual (i.e., being a Student of Life) and Devotion to *all* Divine Figures even while accepting a Guru, is the acme of spiritual evolution. Such an integration will bring about purity and detachment in due course. As Sai Baba said, "It is all Reflection, Reaction, and Resound." The day is not far off He said, when Heaven and Earth will come together like never before, and gods, angels, and humans will walk side by side on this earth.

Speaking of service, in a very revealing book by Berniece Mead titled *Letters from "J"*, which are communications received by Berniece from her son Jay who is in a coma but able to communicate with her (through a medium), from the mental plane (the plane of Mind), we hear some intriguing revelations. Among them: Service activities are needed even in other planes such as the plane that people go to when they leave their bodies. .. Sometimes souls that become suddenly disembodied due to a traumatic end such as an accident or act of Nature are sufficiently traumatized as to need immediate help from the souls already inhabiting that plane. According to Jay, he has been assigned the task of administering to such needy souls...

Also, notes Jay, "they keep seeing Sai Baba all the time". Berniece met with Sai Baba in the late 90s and discussed her son with Him. Baba said: Jay is now mostly a mind with minimal bodily functions. Baba went on to say: *Mind is everything, mind is everywhere, and mind is all that Jay has...*

Mind as we have seen before, is the mist that results when Purusha (Spirit) collides with Prakriti (Matter) and more specifically, when Purusha collides with the grey matter of living creatures....this mist then spreads everywhere. The collective Unconscious (or the Species-Specific Unconscious) that leads to the 100th Monkey Effect, is also part of the Mind. Mind thinks it originated from the physical and so it is wedded to the physical or in other words, wedded to Prakriti.

What is preventing us from evolving, or attaining liberation? In this Age of over stimulation, the mind has become distracted and dependent on many props... Baba has said that the modern mind has become weak mostly because of imitation. The amount of imitation in the present age is so prodigious as to go unnoticed....All the lifestyle choices we can make, all the activity choices we can make, and so on.....they almost all connote some level of imitation. The world is made up of mostly consumers, not creators....almost everything we consume has a mental or imitative component to it...

Baba says we need to talk with our Minds more...in friendly but firm language. We need to make the mind more conscious of itself...and we need to constantly remind and cajole the mind into accepting that it came from Silence, not Matter...We need to speak to our minds both in small and specific contexts that we encounter in daily life as well as in large and Divine contexts that we get from our Gurus or Teachers. This is one of the reasons the Guru becomes important...the vast majority of us are incapable of mobilizing ourselves, let alone saving ourselves...And of course the irony of it all is (as Baba has said): *Joy is your birthright and peace is your innermost nature.*

Sai Baba gave a stirring Shiva Darshan to a group of devotees about 5 decades ago. He ascended a hill and then took on the appearance of a sun-like object. He began radiating so much heat that His devotees below exclaimed that it was becoming unbearable. Baba then said, "Is that so?" Now He began to radiate cold like an icy wind. This went on for a few minutes. At the end of it all Baba came back down and escorted the devotees as they staggered shell-shocked back to the ashram. The above incident has been written about by more than one devotee.

The Crowning Glory of Dattatreya Avatars

In terms of Sacrifice, Love, Sheer Power, and Graciousness, one is hard-pressed to find another being analogous to Lord Sathya Sai Baba. His Omnipresence, His Love, and His Benevolence have taken the world by storm.

Lord Sathya Sai has been described as a descent of Shiva and Shakti but this is now generally accepted as only one facet of this Avatar. While it would be presumptuous of me to try and explain Him completely, the closest I can come is with this naive equation:

Dattatreya + Shakti + Sympathetic Resonance of all demigods = Sathya Sai Baba

While He is an appearance of Lord Dattatreya and Shakti (or the Goddess Principle), He packs the energy of all gods, since all gods are ultimately servitors of Lord Vishnu and Lord Shiva...

Baba has said many a time: Do not try and figure me out...And yet, the temptation is irresistible, especially for devotees who have been in contact with Him for a long time.

Angels have been found flying above the ashram of Sathya Sai Baba. He revealed to some of His devotees, "My agents are everywhere." Baba has also said, "One day, gods, angels, and humans will walk side by side on this earth." The brotherhood of man recognizing the fatherhood of God will go a long way in bringing this about more speedily says Baba.

The Integration of Head and Heart is evident in the type of meditation that Baba taught His devotees. It has been called Jyoti meditation or Light meditation. Here, a flame is visualized to be between the eyebrows (or the sight of the 3rd eye). But after a couple of minutes the flame is visualized to descend to the heart area and the meditation continues... Baba has said, "The end of knowledge is love."

To get a better understanding of this Avatar, the teachings of Sathya Sai Baba are the biggest piece of the puzzle. Anyone who reads the following books by Sathya Sai Baba would feel very close to this Avatar. Here is a partial list of books written by Sathya Sai:

Prasnottara Vahini

Jnana Vahini

Dhyana Vahini

Bhagavatha Vahini

Dharma Vahini

Prema Vahini.

Prasanthi Vahini

The books are given in the approximate order in which they should be read. These books leave no spiritual stone unturned... More involved seekers have long ago realized that the teachings of this Avatar that are to be considered more important than His materializations, His powers or His charismatic presence, overwhelming and exhilarating though these may be. Getting to know the teachings, the life, and the sacrifices of Avatars is far more important... Too many people have formed judgments from afar...and as I've said before, from a distance every Avatar will appear murky. It is only when one comes close that one begins to understand the weight of the Avatar.

Everything is shown up by being exposed to the Light, and whatever is exposed to the Light itself becomes the Light--St. Paul

Well what about our karma one may ask. If we learn to give more than take, that is more than half the battle. In other words, sacrifice is built into the equation. No permanent salvation is possible without service and sacrifices. The lives of the Avatars are examples of that. They all sacrificed for humanity.

One may still ask: Does taking care of karma alone get us salvation? One may argue that perhaps we only get a temporary respite because of good karma or merits earned. And here is where an Avatar's parenting is invaluable. An Avatar can accelerate your karma….which of course implies that one should be willing to face trials and rough weather when one comes under the tutelage of an Avatar...and an Avatar by His sheer grace can also provide permanent salvation.

Real evolution is not meant to be a bed of roses. Rather it's a path fraught with plight and peril. Over millennia, and over several lifetimes, we are buffeted at times and pampered at times...An Avatar appears great to the great and as a man to men. He appears a spirit to the spiritual and an intellectual to the intelligent and even a charlatan to the street smart.

All Avatars have an X-Factor within them. They are never completely understood. They each have their own format. Their ability to communicate with others at various levels and through various means is prodigious. They also have the power to literally offer a quantum of themselves as a permanent gift to their devotees. An Avatar can plant a seed within hundreds and thousands of individuals. And this is no ordinary seed...it is a nucleus of great power and permanence. And in some ways, this is the ultimate sacrifice of the Avatar.

Their teachings grow within us, especially if we approach them directly and refuse to accept intermediaries between us and the Avatar. Contemplation and meditation come naturally to us when we have received the grace of an Avatar.

But is the commitment that we have towards an Avatar guaranteed to sustain itself in a future life? No, there is in fact a strong likelihood that we may go off on another track in our next life...The good news however is: the Avatar will never forget you. Even if you have strayed away for several lives and are now finally knocking on His door...

If you have come this far in this book, you have probably been a devotee of Deities and/or Avatars in at least one of your previous lives. They are therefore just a heartbeat away from you. Perhaps you have already contacted at least one Cosmic Being in this life, or at least come under His umbrella...

Lord Narayana appeared in my dream one night. In this life, I had given emphasis to other Cosmic Beings. He came and stayed only for a few seconds...a brilliant light shining behind Him and presenting Him in silhouette. But those few seconds were enough. My soul cried out, "Narayana! Narayana!". In a few seconds an old and primordial relationship was rekindled and I was in touch with my Bliss Body. Unfortunately, I wasn't merged with that Bliss Body. Instead I was observing it from a short distance... It is this distance that needs to disappear, and that's what life is mostly about. Love, teach the Avatars, is the way. Bliss is after all in the heart, not the intellect...

I would like to sum up the contents of this book before I move on to a brief chapter entitled "A Futurology of Spirit". I wish to point out that humanity has been blessed with Great Avatars and Great Teachers. We would do well to pay attention to them.

The Five Great Avatars are: Dattatreya, Krishna, Jesus Christ, Shirdi Sai Baba, and Sathya Sai Baba. They are the absolute super heroes of humanity.

The Five Great Teachers of humanity are: The Buddha, Lao Tzu, Avatar Babaji, Adi Shankara, and Saint Germain. One could refer to them as the "second tier" of Avatars. These Cosmic Chelas have also made significant contributions to humanity.

Instead of looking at all these teachers as independent of each other and quite apart from each other, the Age of Integration has arrived. We would do well to expose ourselves to their teachings and understand that all sincere teachings ultimately come from One Source. There is only One Teacher.

Of course there have been other significant Avatars and teachers too, and here is only a partial listing: Rama, Sage Vasishtha, Hermes Trismegistus, Mahavira, Bodhidharma, Gorakhnath, Kabir, Guru Nanak, Ramakrishna, Ascended Masters El Morya and Kuthumi, and Sri Aurobindo.

Mankind owes a debt of gratitude to all these celestial beings named above.

Before I begin the last chapter, I wish to echo the words of Kahlil Gibran: *Half of what I say may be meaningless, but I say it so that the other half may reach you...*

I wrote this book also to make spiritual acquaintances. My research (much of it serendipitous in nature) has introduced me to many a fascinating soul...

Chapter Thirty-Two

A Futurology of Spirit

Our descendants will sooner or later reach, as a race, the condition of cosmic consciousness, just as long ago, our ancestors passed from simple consciousness into self-consciousness---***Richard Maurice Bucke***

We've looked at the spiritual past, beginning from most ancient times, and now one may feel: Why stop with the present? What does the future bode for us…What could, or will, happen in the near and distant future? How is the spiritual evolution of mankind unfolding?

There are quiet revolutions going on. One of them is the Human Potential Movement. I'm reminded of the Esalen Institute on the Pacific Coast in Big Sur. The idea of a vast reserve of human potential lying untapped is something that intuitively appeals to many. There is little doubt that progress will be made in this area even if things are going somewhat slowly.

Another is the Consciousness Movement. There has been a noticeable increase in the number of debates on Consciousness. A search on the Internet and on YouTube will reveal that. There are many branches of this movement…there are many benevolent interest groups trying to raise human consciousness regarding the finite resources of this earth and its fragility…

But more in keeping with the nature of this book, there are periodic spiritual experiences that people are having (which according to the most recent Avatar are very important), and there has been an increase in them worldwide. However, things are by no means easy for the spiritual seeker and aspirer…Over a period of time however, humanity will begin to appreciate these experiences and we will better be able to integrate them into our lives which in turn will be increasingly seen as finite and fleeting.

We will also in significant numbers begin to see the limitations of science while continuing to have a positive relationship with science. I'm reminded of the Functional Medicine movement in the US where many traditionally trained doctors (MDs) are beginning to go the Holistic Route, and integrating natural and revitalizing Processes and Supplements with their existing knowledge.

The million dollar question remains however: Will humanity move towards a strong integrated effort of mindfulness, devotion to Great Teachings (Avatarism?), selfless service, and becoming both cognitively and emotionally closer to Godhead. Dattatreya's teachings combine both the transcendental and evolutionary principles of Shaivism and the sanctity and devotional optimism of Vaishnavism. Dattatreya empowers us to handle adversities and also not take for granted our good times…Jesus Christ's teachings also combine the transcendental with the devotional and so do Lord Krishna's…

And how should we place progressive social reforms, whether it is Occupy Wall Street, or the Arab Spring…In this writer's view at least, these are only relatively minor manifestations. The greater manifestations are happening *internally* through virtually unpublicized spiritual experiences of devotees worldwide and through the Transformative Power of Avatars. And the two Sai Babas in particular are active all over the world. They have appeared spontaneously in various parts of the world, and have made positive consequences occur. Sometimes these positive consequences can be felt and noticed only by an individual or a small group however. This has the effect of sculpting those individuals while also keeping the positive change away from public knowledge and censure…

There is also activity from governing deities such as Vishnu and Shiva (as evidenced by sightings and the work of Lightworkers in the West)…And yes, the Ascended Masters continue to work among us. However, the confusion regarding Maitreya appears destined to continue, despite the efforts of Benjamin Crème and others. Perhaps predictably, many people throughout our history have claimed to be Maitreya, a figure made legendary by the predictive words of the Buddha who said Maitreya would follow in His footsteps. However, if by Maitreya the Buddha meant the "next great Ascended Master" that Maitreya may well have come down long ago....And if Benjamin Crème's Maitreya is indeed *the* Lord Maitreya, we have another example of an Ascended Master taking a back seat out of His respect for the Avataric Descent of Lord Sathya Sai Baba, who is a Dattatreya Avatar. <u>Interestingly, this Maitreya referred to Himself as a Planetary Avatar and referred to Sathya Sai Baba as a Cosmic Avatar.</u>

Mother Mary is also active and will continue to be active among Her admirers and devotees. She has appeared in various parts of the world. Jesus Christ will continue to work with humanity of course and often in partnership with the Sai Babas as revealed by Sathya Sai Baba.

One feature about the Dattatreya Avatars is that their consorts also were (if tangentially) involved with that Avatar. And so, these Goddess Entities, consorts of Brahma, Vishnu, and Shiva, are now also making their presence felt. The Goddess Shakti will play an important role in the next Avatar, Prema Sai Baba. The Age of Dattatreya is conducive to the activities of female consorts of Deities and also to the female of the human species...The spiritual growth of women in particular is destined to receive a boost over the next 100 years.

Though the West is not known for significant adoration of the Goddess Principle, Goddess worship on a significant scale is happening especially during certain festivals amongst Hindus all over the world. This writer and his wife have more than a few times visited a house in Burbank, California, where every evening during a nine-day festival (the Navaratri festival) Goddesses were manifesting. They were appearing through a medium who has had astounding experiences with them, but has also paid a karmic price for it, contracting cancer ten times as well as other crippling ailments, while always recovering miraculously...Another case in point is Shree Lall, who manifests Shirdi Baba at her home in South San Francisco...She too has been diagnosed with cancer more than once and always recovered. What these individuals are experiencing, the world seems to also be experiencing with the advent of enormous spiritual energy to the planet in the form of Avatars and Masters.

With the grand arrival of Prema Sai Baba, who it is said, will manifest the Goddess Principle of Shakti (the consort of Shiva) to a large extent, we can expect Goddess worship and adoration to increase substantially in the world in the next 100 years. Some goddesses are being channeled for their ancient wisdom. The spiritual past is coming alive once again…and this is another reason books such as this are being written. Modernity has had its say, and now it's perhaps time to look at applying our spiritual heritage to the problems of the present...

Regardless of chronological considerations, the Age of Aquarius hasn't quite begun yet. However it is only a matter of time…This world is diverse enough that it will take time for world peace to slowly settle in. And much cleansing may be needed first. For example we have the ISIS movement which is, needless to say, destined to fail.

One FAQ about modern spirituality is: "Why is it that so many gurus in the 20th century came from India?" Let us not get too carried away with such a perception however. There are also a lot of unenlightened practices and modes in India. The majority of Indians are quite ignorant about their own religion and spirituality…However the depth and gravity of Hinduism (easily the oldest religion in the world) does manage to bring forth in every generation an enlightened few, who are then able to transmit what they have received not just to their countrymen but also to the rest of the world…

While India has paid a heavy price during the last ten centuries in terms of foreign domination, we have seen that there always has been the Presence of a few enlightened souls. Sometimes they are able to make their presence felt in the public eye, but often they live secluded lives in the mountains or retreats. Hinduism however, is making a resurgence and will continue to do so…the knowledge and appreciation of Hinduism will increase worldwide during the next Avatar, Prema Sai Baba, who will become active within the next two decades.

What about the various schools of spirituality, or integral thinking, or humanism in the social sciences, or indeed "enlightenment seeking"? While there are many encouraging signs we need to keep in mind that Mankind will always display great diversity, and there will always be "old" and "new" souls on the planet…There will be beings who have lived scores of lives as well as beings that have lived only a few and even beings who are in their first human body…One of the reasons for that is humans are the worst predators on the earth, putting to death thousands of living creatures every day, for food, etc. The law of karma then kicks in, and these beings move up the evolutionary ladder…

The spiritual front-liners on the one hand will experience great insights, wisdom, and happiness courtesy of Divine beings that will walk the earth in increasing numbers. The spiritually sensitive stand to gain much…while the insensitive will feel the weight of life and would do well to steel themselves into a life of awareness and an ever willingness to serve. For service destroys negative karma.

And what of the work of Light-workers all over the world, who are consciously reaching out to Spirit Quantums? There are many channels today, albeit not all of the same credibility. Great Spiritual Quantums will always reach out to humanity from above through these channels or mediums, and seek to reassure humanity that we are not alone...

Will the tide slowly turn, and the world become more spiritually oriented? The good news is: All the potentialities are there. The not-so-good news is: We have a lot of work to do, and a lot of openness to muster up, as well as a lot of transformation to undergo. And it can be downright disappointing at times…There are a lot of people today who feel they just "can't change". However taken in the larger context of future lives on earth and the slow inevitable evolution that must take place, it is almost axiomatic that change indeed will come one day. Even a tiny spark lit by an enlightened being can manifest itself in some future life. Sai Baba was once found to be talking high philosophy regarding the human soul to some uneducated village folk in India. When asked why He had chosen to do this, Baba replied, "They may not grasp what I am saying now, but some lifetimes from now, this spark that I have lit in them will flower."

Evolution however, is never without its twists and turns, for even as we are evolving, the cognitive space between human beings is increasing. It is as if we are all diverging from a Centre (Source) we are all individually connected to but ignorant of... Today, there are so many lifestyle options, forms of knowledge, interests, skills, and aptitudes in the world...And the growth of alternative world views and "isms" of course makes it all even more complicated...but let us note an important point: The One is not in a hurry. Ever. What is far more important is the robustness and purity of the spiritual advancement. If this needs thousands of years of mindfulness, knowledge gathering and devotional practices, so be it. But the sincere, the patient, and the devoted will obtain salvation according to the most recent Avatar.

As spiritual aspirants, our spiritual antennas need to be always unfurled and never coiled up in introversion...in other words, our spiritual curiosity needs both receptivity and space to flower...and various gurus hopefully operate in that vein. More work is of course needed in this area.

Instead of being dazzled by technology, can we see its limitations... And use technology instead to satisfy our inner curiosity and spiritual hunger...and to share spiritual insights, experiences, prayers, mantras, and hymns. This is in fact happening already: spirituality and technology are indeed coming together on the Internet.

Other efforts have been made and will continue to bring science and religion together...such as the Science and Non-Duality Conferences and the Science and Religion conferences. This is the very nature of the Age of Integration (the Age of Datta). The Internet in a sense is allowing us to intelligently investigate almost anything, including spirituality, by making all of human knowledge and experience accessible to almost everyone. It is truly an important (if distracting) platform that is bringing people together on an unprecedented scale. This, needless to say, will continue to happen and create a world that is less specialized and more inclusive. Humans will no longer take too much pride in achieving much in a narrow field, but instead seek to examine the interconnections of everything. And we will begin to increasingly see that everything is connected.

We need to recognize that capitalism is a divisive force in the world of today, but so are almost all systems and organized religions…Instead of being complacent about the state of Mother Earth or merely mildly concerned, we need to embrace Oneness and shared responsibility.

The human ego has been described as "the only true calamity" and "a terrorist". What can soften the ego but a sense of wonder, awe, and a realization of our smallness in the Universe said one. What can soften the ego more than realizing we are God and all One, said another. Take your pick, but yes, we do have our egos to contend with. Not just the individual ego, but various collective egos, for after all, we are members of various groups, be it family, community, linguistic group, country and so on. Is it possible for the power of spiritual growth and increasing awareness to go beyond these group identifications. The answer appears to be a resounding yes…one of the benefits of Kali Yuga is that it is becoming increasingly clear to many people that every individual is essentially alone on this earth…This same message was echoed by Sai Baba who said, "Humans are connected to God rather than one another." Any connection between two humans is through God and not a direct connection. This is hardly any cause for despair, but rather another reason atheists deserve our pity and compassion.

We need to be receptive to the spiritual experiences of our neighbors, instead of dismissing them as "mere anecdotes"…If you hear of a Ganesha statue, or any other statue for that matter, drinking milk, let us go there ourselves and see what's happening, instead of hearing some desperate rationalist insist on the media that it is all just "capillary action." One of my sisters once told me, "I held a cup of milk under Ganesha's face and the milk disappeared *very quickly*." The speed with which it happened convinced her that this was no capillary action…

A permanently open and inquiring mind regarding such anecdotes will go a long way, and that includes an investigative nature that decides to take steps sooner rather than later. The not-so-palatable truth is that some of us are indeed born with a spiritual edge over the average person. That's just a fact of life. And it is of course a function of previous lives. There are indeed such variables as Past Spiritual Experience and Spiritual Sensitivity.

Having said that, it has also become all too common for spiritually evolved individuals to fall from their noble stature, all because of over-stimulation in the physical world of the senses.

We ignore the anecdotes surrounding Avatars to our spiritual peril. For most of us are in "karmic trouble". Sai Baba has made statements regarding the need to keep in mind the downward spiral that is sometimes caused by the deadly combination of karma and negativity. As I've said before, no one can assist a person as much as an Avatar can. No one is standing on as high a mountain as an Avatar is, and no one has more love and compassion for humanity, and especially for students on the path.

The Avatars of Dattatreya are Integral Avatars, and are assisted by a galaxy of archangels and other agents. They also are very familiar with modern diversity and various ways of living and thinking for after all, they reside within our hearts too. Their teachings, beginning with the teachings of Lord Datta himself, are progressive, all-encompassing, and truly open. They are able to galvanize large sections of people purely by Soul Attraction. During a grand birthday celebration in a stadium at Sai Baba's ashram in South India, with thousands of people present, He said: *Most of the people here today were present at Lord Rama's wedding function.* This kind of soul magnetism only an Avatar can achieve. And there were people from all over the world in that audience. Talk of Oneness.

When more and more people come under His influence, a critical mass is reached and the avatar is truly captured by humanity for a very long time. His love for humanity keeps Him with us. The Avatars of Dattatreya are extremely potent and compassionate, and offer a lot of hope for the spiritually hungry and the world-weary. These Avatars are not here to be mere witnesses, but rather to sensitize us to other dimensions of Life, and to make us better students of Life. They have the power and the graciousness to deliver us. And their prolonged presence will sooner or later bear fruit.

The numbers of the world-weary will grow in the future, and the sweet complement of that is, the number of beings gaining liberation will also increase. Theism and Gnosis, which appear to be on the wane, will rise once again, even if there are some faltering starts… Yes, even among people who have been living in somewhat closed environments. More recently, even devotees from countries like Arabia have started coming to Puttaparthi in South India to the ashram of Sai Baba. They sing bhajans (spiritual hymns) and praise the Lord.

And Sathya Sai Baba, who displayed such Love, Power, Sacrifice, and Active Omnipresence, and who left His physical body in 2011, will soon merge into His next Avatar, Prema Sai Baba, who will bring the light of love into this world. He will be the third of the triumvirate of Avatars that began with Shirdi Sai Baba, and continued with Sathya Sai. All three of them will work together… This book could not have happened without Sai. He has inspired me in His inimitable way, silently…

Throughout His physical presence among us He repeated some core messages. In order to attain liberation the individual must do his or her best to:

1. Perform continuous service.
2. Realize there is no greater adversary than the human ego. The ego far exceeds the environment in its negative effect on us.
3. Realize that nothing is more important than one's inner transformation. The Avatar has come down mostly for

this. Chanting the names of God is a good step towards this (*"Call Me by any name and I will respond"*).
4. Accept the continuous uninterrupted Presence of Universal Spirit, the Supreme Consciousness, who is beyond time and space and is the Witness of all. The Inner and Outer Guru are One.
5. Spend time in good company, and maintain a positive outlook. Let happiness rule. Love God and fear sin (not God). i.e., "If you wish to fear something, fear the law of karma..."

Through the combined powers of Lord Vishnu and Lord Shiva (i.e., Lord Dattatreya or Guru Datta), this world will see a revival of Spirit doctrines. For this earth belongs to Their Lordships...They have cared for and saved this world repeatedly by nurturing their devoted chelas or students, making cameo appearances, taking care of dangerous elements, or descending through Avatars. Ganesha and Subramanya (Sanat Kumara) are part of the family of Lord Shiva as also is Goddess Durga. The Goddess Principle will also descend more into this world. The next Avatar, Prema Sai Baba, will manifest the Goddess Principle. The great example of selfless service that the consorts of Lord Vishnu and Lord Shiva have demonstrated will inspire both men and women.

Lord Sathya Sai's prophecy, "A day will come when men, angels, and gods will walk side by side on this earth." is already showing signs of beginning to happen, with both Shirdi Sai and Sathya Sai appearing at the same place and sometimes being accompanied by Parvati. Recently an appearance of all three occurred just outside Bangalore India.

And what of the present chaos, corruption, competition, and craving for the fruits of the environment? Surely, man's fundamental nature cannot change so easily? What of the inherent psychological limitations of individuals...let alone the machinations of society?

The key to the above appears to be this: Conceivably, the number of people with spiritual experiences will grow so much, that the whole world of spirit will be seen as far more significant than mind and matter, and that in turn will slowly reduce the vice-like hold our minds and the material world will have upon us. Growing numbers of people are already seeing this....In the 20th century, great beings like Yogananda Paramahamsa and Sri Aurobindo introduced us to the presence of highly evolved spiritual beings on earth. After all there are 7 billion people on earth and there is a lot of diversity, i.e., many levels of Experience on earth...While on this point, this writer is making a rather pointed prediction: The twin concepts of reincarnation and karma will become more accepted in many parts of the world in the not-too distant future.

Yes, there will always be some people in society who display all the limitations that human beings are known for, but their influence on the rest of us will diminish...there won't be the same grinding intensity of reactions, reflections and resound that we see in the world today, leading to the poor psychological conditioning of most of humanity, that has led to the world of power struggles, capitalistic greed, coupled with cynicism and violence. Instead there will be a loosening of the hold that vested interests have over the rest of us, not so much in material terms, but more in psychological and spiritual terms.

Speaking of psychology, there has been an increasing interest in the inner workings of the mind in the last century. Psychology is still a nascent science, and it is still going through a "trial and error" phase...however, efforts at the inner psycho-synthesis of the individual as propounded by the likes of Roberto Assagioli are commendable. The Integration of the inner world is of course as important as the outer, if it can indeed be brought about. Some people call it the integration of Thought, Word, and Deed. While on the subject of Psychology there are already indications that Freudian Psychology and Behaviorism (a la BF Skinner) will give way to more humanistic schools.

In the Golden Age, science's limitations will be exposed, as spiritual and metaphysical experiences become much more common. Scientists will be seen for what they are: Specialists who have knowledge of a focused kind, rather than of a holistic kind... And connections between fields of knowledge will become seen as being more important than the fields themselves...The future is not only going to be technological, scientific, social, or political. The future is also going to be spiritual...

All the non-theistic schools of thought will be seen as being incomplete and also as limiting forms of knowledge. Instead, people will embrace in growing numbers the notion of Divine Will and Purpose. Not just Physical Yoga, but more spiritual forms such as Kriya Yoga will grow in importance. Mass meditation will also be seen as worthy and doable. Spiritual assertions and affirmations will also increase. Adi Shankara set off the modern era of transcendental affirmations when He declared, "Shivoham, Shivoham" and "Aham Brahmasmi" (*I am Shiva* and *I am Universal Spirit*)

Lord Sathya Sai Baba repeatedly said, "Why fear when I am here." Our views of worldly trials and tribulations will increasingly take on a different color: *If God is always with me and witnessing everything, is it still suffering?* Or is it that my limited mind is trying to convince me that I am suffering. We are after all, neither our bodies nor our minds...The mind (through the limited limbic brain) is too wedded to the body, which is obviously limited in its scope.

So can we really trust ourselves? Or instead should we turn to Godhead and see ourselves as limbs or outposts of the One? And in that case, should we not try and live in a larger field than the finite most of us are currently in...Our efforts will gradually turn in that direction. But first, we have to fill ourselves with Gratitude to the Avatars. And awe.

READING LIST
(in no particular order)

Richard Smoley	*The Dice Game of Shiva--- How Consciousness Creates the Universe*
Herbert Puryear	*Why Jesus Taught Reincarnation*
Cindy Riggs	*Vishnu Speaks: Messages of Enlightenment from the Ancient Deity*
Gene Matlock	*Yishvara 2000: The Hindu Ancestor of Judaism Speaks to This Millennium*
Antonio Rigopoulos	*Dattatreya: The Immortal Guru, Yogin, and Avatara*
Swami A. Saraswati	*The Uddhava Gita: The Final Teaching of Krishna*
Antonio Rigopoulos	*Life & Teachings of Sai Baba of Shirdi*
Rashmi Khilnani	*Shiva Speaks*
Swami S. Giri	*Kriya Sutras of Babaji*
C. Isherwood	*Shankara's Crest Jewel of Discrimination*
Nicholas Roerich	*Leaves of Morya's Garden*
Alice Bailey	*Light of the Soul*
Amit Goswami	*The Self-Aware Universe--- How Consciousness Creates*
Jaideva Singh	*Shiva Sutras: The Yoga of Supreme Identity*
Stephen Knapp	*The Secret Teachings of the Vedas*
David Frawley	*Tantric Yoga & the Wisdom Goddesses*
Paramahamsa Yogananda	*The Yoga of Jesus*
Sheldrake and Fox	*The Physics of Angels*

APPENDIX 1

The Root Races according to Theosophy

The Aryan races...now varying from dark brown, almost black...down to the whitest creamy color, are yet all of one and the same stock -- the Fifth Root-Race---***Helena Blavatsky.***

1st Root Race: Ethereal Beings from outer space were the first *Intelligent* Life on Earth and comprised both Good and Evil Beings, i.e., we had both Benevolent and Power-Hungry Beings. These Beings were led to Earth by beings that had already evolved on other planets both in our solar system and beyond...

2nd Root Race: Beings born from the interaction of ethereal beings and primitive humans and therefore Half Ethereal and Half Human. This race is now extinct...

3rd Root Race: Began in an old landmass called Lemuria. Lemurians were giants who were mostly Blacks, inhabited a huge continent extending from Africa to Australia. Many parts of the old Lemuria are now under the Indian Ocean. People who are clearly Negroid in origin are still found in islands of the Indian Ocean such as the Andamans... Giant skeletons have been unearthed in various parts of the world. Recent underwater excavations in the Indian Ocean and Arabian Sea have revealed cities that are more than 25,000 years old...

4th Root Race: These were the Atlanteans who inhabited the continent of Atlantis which was located in the Atlantic Ocean considered to be largely submerged... Much New Age literature has dealt with Atlantis and how some people have experienced flashbacks to their previous life or lives in Atlantis. Atlantis became popular after being written about by Plato who claimed Atlantis met its end after a major cataclysm around 9000 BC.

5th Root Race: They are the so-called present day Aryans who actually embrace people of many skin-tones...Millennia of interactions with other races have made the "Aryans" a "loose-boundary" race. The same blood flows in all.

APPENDIX 2

The Five Sheaths

Access to the Vedas is the greatest privilege this century may claim over all previous centuries.---**Julius Robert Oppenheimer.**

The sense of morality (stemming from the voice of conscience) and personal responsibility that most people spontaneously display comes neither from the ego-mind nor does it come from our intellectual side. Rather it comes from the Higher Realms of the individual...In the discussion of Koshas below it is important to know that they are all highly intertwined and so a human is a "continuum rather than a bunch of separate entities".

The Divine soul is "encased" in a sheath of Higher Consciousness almost as if to protect it... And one of the Divine attributes of the Higher Consciousness is our Conscience. The rare faculty of Divine Bliss is an integral part of all our souls. Another Divine attribute is intuition, sometimes accompanied by extra-sensory perception. This sheath in turn is encased by a cloak of intellect, which then is encased by the senses and the emotions, then by the limbic brain (the primitive part of the brain, and the cause of much distress to the sincere seeker), and finally by the body...which in turn is made up of various grades of matter and by that I mean less gross and more gross matter...for example the organs are imbued with more consciousness than the flesh and the flesh with more consciousness than say the waste products of the body...

The above model has been adapted from the Principle of 5 Sheaths that emerged from the Vedanta philosophy of the Hindu texts known as the Upanishads, which are the later scriptures of the Hindus. More specifically, the Principle is given in the Taittiriya Upanishad...The Upanishads are said to have been written down by very spiritually evolved sages of ancient India. According to this Upanishad, the innermost sheath of a human is the Bliss Sheath, and moving outward we then have the Higher

Consciousness Sheath, followed by the Mind-Stuff Sheath, then the Energy Sheath, and finally the Gross Sheath or body, created by the imbibing of food. The concept of Sheaths is important because in most situations, only the "innermost sensitivities of the innermost sheaths" are reincarnated...However the exact mechanism of reincarnation is known only to the Divine Powers and humans can only surmise.

Especially when a person becomes more spiritually- oriented and also increasingly devoted to the Higher Life and/or to a great Teacher, something else happens...by the Grace of the Divine, the core of the individual becomes a living ground for spiritual beings or God Quantums to dwell in... Thus it is said, God lives in the heart.

Universal Spirit is always caressing us through our koshas and chakras, especially the upper chakras. Both *descent* and *evolution* are present in each individual's journey. We are all avatars and we are all also evolving in an "upward spiral" sense, though this evolution can take many thousands of years and even result in a downward spiral for some of us, because of the influence of karma, inertia (or resistance to change) and/or moral decay...

Almost needless to say, for many of us, our ego-minds and the lower chakras predominate and make us insensitive to the presence and influence of Spirit. Some human beings however, begin to respond to this influence. If all goes well, and the individual begins to accumulate good karma over lifetimes, and also evolves through experiences or chelahood or simply divine presence and grace, this transformation becomes increasingly more pronounced and finally the individual is ripe for enlightenment, even while on earth. He or she then becomes a *Jivanmukta*, one who attains liberation even while occupying a physical body.

Karma and Mind/Ego can either interact with each other positively and result in an upward spiral, or relate with each other negatively and create a downward spiral...Unfortunately for some, Karma and Mind can also interact to produce undesirable physical deformities, such as those found even in newborn babies...As we know, so many children suffer from inexplicable congenital disorders. Even more unfortunate is the tendency of attributing such congenital defects to an angry and unforgiving God.

Positive action and altruism often make us feel good don't they. They exert a positive influence on the upper chakras of the body and can even alter the brain waves in the body...And of course service unto others is quite simply, good karma. People are known to come out of depression and other mental conditions after doing service...Sai Baba has said: "The nature of man is to perform service, but this basic nature has been covered up by other considerations and distractions." Love of God and of humanity is even stronger at creating positive results...love is after all the strongest force in the Universe.

2½ letter word - Love
Love All SERVE ALL

Made in the USA
Charleston, SC
09 January 2017